Indian Philosophy - A Counter Perspective

Indian Philosophy

A Counter Perspective

Daya Krishna

DELHI
OXFORD UNIVERSITY PRESS
CALCUTTA CHENNAI MUMBAI

Oxford University Press, Great Clarendon Street, Oxford OX2 6DP

Oxford New York
Athens Auckland Bangkok Calcutta
Cape Town Chennai Dar es Salaam Delhi
Florence Hong Kong Istanbul Karachi
Kuala Lumpur Madrid Melbourne Mexico City
Mumbai Nairobi Paris Singapore
Taipei Tokyo Toronto

and associates in
Berlin Ibadan

First published 1991
Oxford India Paperbacks 1996
Second impression 1997

ISBN 0 19 563837 9

Printed at Rekha Printers Pvt. Ltd., New Delhi 110020
and published by Manzar Khan, Oxford University Press
YMCA Library Building, Jai Singh Road, New Delhi 110001

To The Memory Of

THE LATE PT. BADRINATH SHUKLA

The Outstanding Representative Of
The Ancient Philosophical Tradition
Who Made Us All Realize
How Rich And Alive It Still Is In This Country

Preface

The articles in this book, though written over a long period of time, show a common concern with respect to the past philosophical traditions of India. And this is, how to rescue those traditions from the long and varied spiritual quest of India with which they have become associated and entangled due to the diverse exigencies of history from the late eighteenth century to the first half of the twentieth century. The interests of western Indological studies combined with the search for a spiritual self-identity in the face of overwhelming western superiority in all fields of knowledge seemed to have led to the creation of a certain picture of India's philosophical past which has become fixed in the minds of successive generations of students and teachers, both in India and abroad, through innumerable text-books which render it almost impossible to question the picture or build a different one. To break the picture, its outlines and patterns and foci, have been the first concern of these articles.

The second task which perhaps is even more important, is to take seriously India's philosophical past and relate it to the active philosophical concerns of the contemporary philosophical situations in India and abroad. Somehow, the context of contemporary intellectual life in India, even in the field of philosophy, has no relationship with India's intellectual traditions of the past, but rather with the way these disciplines have developed in the west and the way they are developing there at present. Western thought in all fields of knowledge is rooted in its own past. And, this is as it should be. But the story is not the same with other non-western cultures of the world; for them the living intellectual past is also that of the west, and not that of their own past traditions, even if they were fortunate enough to have one. The past intellectual traditions of these cultures have become a matter of historical curiosity; they have little relationship with the alive intellectual concerns of today. The problem, therefore, is how to break this attitude and re-establish a living continuity with India's philosophical past to make it relevant to the intellectual concerns of the present.

The third concern is to take a close look at the classical texts of the Indian philosophical traditions with unblinkered eyes. So much seems to be taken for granted even by well known scholars writing on Indian philosophy; yet the moment one starts looking even casually at the evidence, one is amazed how little ground there is for many of these assertions. Questions that leap to one's mind which appear obvious from looking at even a single page of the text seem not to have been asked, or if asked, seem to have been evaded so cleverly, as if they had not really been felt to be questions or issues at all. The articles on the *Vedas*, the *Upaniṣads* and the *Nyāya-sūtras* are examples of this. Yet, what is perhaps still more amazing is the fact that the evidence amassed in these articles has failed to make the slightest dent in the assertions of those who have had the occasion to know a little closely of their contents. This would not have mattered if the arguments had been controverted, the evidence questioned or the counter-evidence produced. But, by and large, nothing of this kind has happened. Occasionally, there have been some responses, even attempts at rebuttal, but generally of the most perfunctory kind. In a recent seminar devoted to a discussion of my thought, five papers were presented on what I have written on Indian philosophy. But, except for the paper by Prof. J. N. Mohanty, no one even tried to come to grips with the central conclusions of my papers or the arguments and the evidence presented therein. Karl H. Potter is the only exception, but his response to my detailed critique of the reply he made earlier is so tangential that one begins to wonder if any serious discussion can be held about issues in Indian philosophy with scholars in the field.

The response of the traditional pandits has been no different, though as many of them do not know English, they can hardly be blamed for not doing so. But even when a shorter version of the article entitled 'The Vedic Corpus: Some Questions' was presented in Sanskrit to a gathering of the most outstanding *Mīmāṁsā* scholars at Tirupati, not a single person said anything. Some of the most eminent *Nyāya* pandits failed to see any problems posed by the text of the *Nyāyasūtroddhāra* or by the fact that some of the *sūtras* have not only variant readings, but contradictory ones in different versions of the text as given by different authorities. And I am still to find a person, traditional or modern, who has felt any shock at the fact that a portion of the

Aitareya Āraṇyaka, which proclaims itself to be an *Upaniṣad*, is not included in the text which calls itself the *Aitareya Upaniṣad*.

Perhaps the reason for all this is two-fold. One, the articles were written in a piece-meal fashion at long intervals and hence could not make that cumulative and concentrated impact which presumably they should have had. Second, the failure in making any relevant response might lie in the fact that a scholar may not know what to do with the arguments or the evidence marshalled in the articles. Even scholars are so accustomed to see things in a certain way, so habituated to entertain a certain picture of India's philosophical past that unless it can be replaced by a *different* picture, mere questioning of that which prevails is bound to be ignored.

The first reason will no longer operate with the availability of most of these articles at one place in this collection. Their ready availability and their mutual interrelatedness should provide a cumulative impact which may prove to be more challenging. At least, I am sure, the need for a relevant reply would be felt by most readers of these articles. I only hope that they translate this need into an *actual* reply so that I may know where I have been mistaken and, if necessary, revise my position. As for the second, I do hope that I will be able to present before interested readers a counter sketch, if not a full picture, of the way I conceive the traditions of philosophizing in India to be. Till then, the reader has to be satisfied with the demolition of the currently accepted picture. In case he agrees with the argument and the evidence he hopefully may try to build his or her own new picture in its place. It would be exciting to see these new pictures, as and when completed. But before that can be done, one has to loosen the stranglehold of the picture that holds us all in its grip. These articles should help in that direction.

DAYA KRISHNA

Acknowledgements

I am grateful to the editors/publishers of the following Journals for permission to reprint the articles first published in them.

'Three Myths about Indian Philosophy', *Diogenes* (July–September, 1966); 'Three Conceptions of Indian Philosophy', *Philosophy East and West* (Jan. 1965.); 'Indian Philosophy and Mokṣa: Revisiting an Old Controversy', *Journal of Indian Council of Philosophical Research* (Vol. II, No. 1., Autumn 1984); 'The Vedic Corpus: Some Questions', *Journal of Indian Council of Philosophical Research* (Vol. III, No. 1, Autumn 1985); 'The Upaniṣads: What are They?', *Journal of Indian Council of Philosophical Research* (Vol. I, No. 1, Autumn, 1983); 'The Text of the *Nyāya-Sūtras–Some Problems', Journal of Indian Council of Philosophical Research* (Vol. VII, No. 2, Jan.–April, 1990); 'Is Īśwara Kṛṣṇa's *Sāṁkhya-Kārikā* really *Sāṁkhyan*?', *Philosophy East and West* (July, 1968), '*Adhyāsa*–A Non-Advaitic Beginning in Śaṁkara Vedānta', *Philosophy East and West* (July, 1969); *Vedānta*–Does it really mean Anything?', *Conspectus*; '*Yajña* and the Doctrine of *Karma*–A contradiction in Indian Thought about Action', *Journal of Indian Council of Philosophical Research* (Vol. VI, No. 2, Jan.–April 1989); 'The Myth of the *Puruṣārthas*' *Journal of Indian Council of Philosophical Research* (Vol. IV, No. 1, Autumn 1986).

Contents

Part I

CHAPTER ONE

Three Myths about Indian Philosophy*

I

Indian philosophy, like Indian culture, seems peculiarly prone to arouse either violent antipathy or fervent enthusiasm. Rarely does it engender an attitude which tries to present and assess it coolly and calmly, without positive or negative emotion. Nothing perhaps stands more in the way of such an attitude than the universally accepted ideas which I wish to explore in this essay. These three ideas are treated as indubitable facts about Indian philosophy. They seem so self-evident to enthusiasts and detractors alike, that to question them is to question the very concept of Indian philosophy as it has been traditionally conceived and presented by almost every writer on the subject. Yet, it seems to me that the time has come to question the traditional picture itself, to raise doubts about the indubitable, to investigate the sacrosanct and the self-evident. Myths have always masqueraded as facts and many a time the emperor's nudity has only been discovered by a child's disingenuity.

The self-evident claims about Indian philosophy are legion. First and foremost is the claim to spirituality. Who does not know that Indian philosophy is spiritual? Who has not been told that this is what specifically distinguishes it from western philosophy, and makes it something unique and apart from all the other philosophical traditions of the world? The claim, of course, is never put to the test. In fact, it seems so self-evident as to require no argument or evidence on its behalf. Nobody, neither the serious nor the casual student of the subject, deems it worth questioning. Yet, the moment we begin to doubt the claim

*This article is dedicated to Dr. B. N. Consul and his staff without whose help and skill it might never have been completed. Dr. Consul holds the Chair of Ophthalmology at the Medical College, University of Rajasthan, Jaipur, India.

and examine it for what it is worth, we find it spurious and mythical, to say the least.

After all, what exactly is meant by describing a whole philosophical tradition as 'spiritual'. The term, in the ontological context, means that the nature of ultimate reality is held to be the same or similar to that of mind or spirit. Its distinctive feature lies in the assertion of the primacy of consciousness as opposed to the inertness associated with and displayed by objects that are purely material in their nature. Spirit is opposed to matter and the spiritualist metaphysics implies that spirit alone is real and what appears as matter is only an appearance, something illusory, something unreal. The qualifying terms 'alone' and 'only' are of the utmost importance, for without them the view held cannot be characterized as 'spiritual' in the ontological sense of the term.

Viewed in this perspective, Indian philosophy can hardly be characterized as spiritual in character. It certainly is true that most of the schools of Indian philosophy do recognize the ultimate reality of spirit in some form or other. But so do they also recognize the ultimate reality of matter in some form or other. The Jainas, the Vaiśeṣikas and the Sāṁkhyans recognize it so openly that it can hardly be missed by even the most starry-eyed student of the subject. The Cārvākas need not be mentioned in this connection, as they are regarded as 'unmentionable' for this very reason by everybody except Debiprasad Chattopadhyaya and Walter Ruben who turn the tables, and regard all others as the 'untouchables' of Indian philosophy. The Naiyāyikas are usually supposed to accept the Vaiśeṣika metaphysics, but it is seldom noted that they go a step further in the Cārvāka direction. Unlike the Cārvākas, they certainly believe in the ontological reality of soul but they then deny to it the essential characteristic of consciousness which alone, according to everybody else, differentiates it from matter. Consciousness, according to the Naiyāyikas, is not an inalienable quality of the soul but rather, as the Cārvākas say, a quality which arises in it when a collection of circumstances accidentally comes to pass. In a radical sense, then, the Naiyāyika thinker comes closer to the classic position of materialism as propounded in the history of thought. He, of course, believes in the ontological reality of God also, but that is another story.

There remain the Buddhists, the Mīmāṁsakas, the Vedāntins and the followers of the so-called Yoga school of philosophy. Among these, the Mīmāṁsakas subscribe to the metaphysical reality of all the substances which the Nyāya-Vaiśeṣika thinkers hold to be real, while adding a few of their own. Anyone who contends for the ultimate reality of earth, water, fire and air among other things, can hardly be considered to believe in the reality of spirit *alone*. As for the Buddhists, their fundamental denial is of substantiality, whether it be that of spirit or of matter. In fact, two of the traditional schools of Buddhism assert the reality of the external world while denying its substantiality. It is only the Yogācāras who explicitly contend for the ideality or mentality of whatsoever exists. The Mādhyamikas, like the Advaita Vedāntists of a later date, accept phenomenal reality and deny the ultimate reality of anything that can ever possibly be asserted.

Vedānta, of course, is not only Śaṁkara-Vedānta. It is merely a name to suggest that the philosopher who chose to call himself or his thought by that name consciously assumed the added responsibility of showing that that is exactly what the Upaniṣads really meant. Any doctrine, therefore, can call itself Vedānta, provided it is prepared to sustain that it alone expresses the true and authentic meaning of the Upaniṣads. There are frank dualists such as Madhva who regard matter or *prakṛti* as an eternal, independent principle in its own right, who call themselves Vedāntins. There is Rāmānuja, who believes in the ultimate distinction in the nature of matter from God, but denies its independence in the sense of its not being subordinate to Him. And, then, there is the great Śaṁkara who believes that the assertion of anything is in itself the surest sign of its ultimate unreality. For him, the individual soul and God are as unreal as *prakṛti* or matter.

Matter, thus, is not unreal for Vedānta either. It is clearly asserted to be ultimately real by the two major schools, those of Rāmānuja and of Madhva. For the only remaining major school, that of Śaṁkara, it is as real as anything else. As for Yoga, it is perhaps counted among the traditional schools of Indian philosophy only as a matter of courtesy. There seems little reason to do so, as it is entirely a system of practice, and no one contends that it has any distinctive philosophical views of its own except the Sāṁkhya view of the independent reality of *prakrti*. It thus constitutes no exception to the almost universal acceptance of the ontic reality of matter among the various schools of Indian philosophy.

Ontologically, then, the characterization of Indian philosophy as 'spiritual' is completely erroneous. The only other context in which it may be regarded as 'spiritual' is that of morals or ethics. Here, it is certainly true that Indian thought has held spiritual salvation to be the highest goal of individual effort. But this, it should be remembered, is a generalized feature of traditional Indian culture as a whole. Philosophy, as it were, only accepts this goal which culture in general had set for the individual. It articulates, accentuates, defines and redefines the goal in a clearer and more conscious manner.

Even here, it would be interesting to point out that it was not until later that *mokṣa* as a distinctive separate goal was accepted in Indian thought. As is well known, the early formulations of the goals of human seeking limited them to three in number. These were *dharma, artha* and *kāma* which may roughly be described as the realms of law, rule or the prescribed, on the one hand (*dharma*), and those of the things desired (*kāma*) and the instrumentalities for their realization (*artha*), on the other. The introduction of a fourth goal was not so much the result of philosophical speculation, as of the emergence into prominence of certain trends which were already present in the religious atmosphere of India. The so-called *Śramaṇa* tradition of Sāṁkhya, Bauddha and the Jains, is the root source of the ideal of *mokṣa* in the orthodox Vedic traditions of India.[1] These traditions, at the time of their origins, were primarily religious, and their importance lay rather in the spiritual exploration of man, than in philosophical speculation. However, in the course of their evolution, they produced philosophical thinkers who articulated and argued for the theoretic and conceptual position supposed to be relevant to the specific differential insights of the original religious founders of their traditions.

The ideal of *mokṣa* was, thus, a later incorporation from the non-Vedic religious and spiritual traditions of India. In this process, it was given a more positive content than it had in the relatively more negative traditions of Buddhism, Jainism and Sāṁkhya. The philosophers, now as then, defined and redefined, pointed out the difficulties of the concept and tried to meet these difficulties. But in the initial discovery of the concept they were not the initiators or innovators, but only followers who worked and reworked what they had taken over, or what had been handed down to them.

It may equally be remembered in this connection that there are few philosophers in any of the great historic traditions whose views on the ends of human life are not idealistic in some sense or other. The only distinctive feature of the Indian philosophers in this context seems to lie in their emphasis on the spiritual as against the moral, and the creation of a dichotomy or division between the two. The addition of *mokṣa* as the fourth and final end of human seeking and striving was not a fulfilment of the original three, but ultimately their denial or negation.

Many later thinkers have striven to bridge the gulf between morality and spirituality, but the original dualism has persisted unchanged. The baffling paradox of a country which is felt by almost every foreigner to be, at one and the same time, the most spiritual and the most immoral, can perhaps be rendered intelligible only in this way.

II

Indian philosophy, however, is not uniquely and distinctively characterized in terms of 'spirituality' alone. There are other characterizations which are almost as universally current and which, on examination, are found to be as mythical as the one regarding spirituality. The other such characterization is in terms of 'authority'. Almost invariably, each writer on Indian philosophy begins his account by drawing a distinction between the 'orthodox' and 'unorthodox' schools of Indian philosophy. This distinction is drawn in terms of their acceptance or non-acceptance of the authority of the Vedas.

This is a commonplace fact about Indian philosophy, one which is repeated with such assurance of its self-evident nature, that no possible doubt could be entertained about it. But what exactly is meant by the acceptance of the Vedas as an authoritative basis for one's philosophical system? As far as I can see, the only legitimate meaning of such a claim in the philosophical context would be to maintain that the Vedas contain the ultimate philosophical truth, and that the test of the truth of a philosophical position is whether or not it is in accordance with what is written in the Vedas.

If this really was the case, then the differences between the so-called 'orthodox' schools of Indian philosophy would arise from their varying interpretations of what the Vedas really meant. But, is this really so? Is it true to say that Sāṁkhya or Yoga or Nyāya or Vaiśeṣika differ regarding the exact meaning which is to be put on the Vedic texts? Are they, so to speak, schools of interpretation which clash over what the Vedas really mean? This obviously is not the case. The classical texts of the various schools are not, even in form, a commentary upon the Vedic texts. The two schools which seem to be an obvious exception are Mīmāṁsā and Vedānta. The former specifically upholds the authority of the Vedas and the latter ostensibly champions a genuine interpretation of the Upaniṣads, which are supposed to be a part of the Vedas. The various schools of Vedānta may be said, with some justification, to be schools of interpretation, in the technical sense of the term. But even if they may legitimately be so designated, it would not do to interpret the differences between Mīmāṁsā and Vedānta in the same way. They appear rather to differ as to what is to be regarded as really constituting the Vedas.

What is to constitute the Vedas, then, seems to be the crucial question which has to be first answered if one is to have a meaningful discussion over their authority in regard to Indian philosophy in particular, and to Indian culture in general. The authoritative Vedas themselves were originally thought to be only three in number. Later, the authority of a fourth Veda began to be accepted. In any case, the Vedas, it should be remembered, were always plural in number. Moreover, their authority was not equally or securely established even during the times of their composition. Further, on the most conservative estimate, it took them at least a thousand years to assume their present form. During this time at least, their authority was never such as to preclude the possibility of making further additions to them. This obviously does not speak very much for their authority in those times. Even among those who have upheld their authority, there has always been a difference of opinion regarding the portion of the Vedas which was to be regarded as authoritative, and regarding which subject matter, and for what purpose.

The latter, it has not always been noted, is almost as important as the former. The Mīmāṁsā, for example, does not only deny the Upaniṣads the privilege of being counted among the corpus of Vedic authority, but also contends that any utterance which is not a pure injunction, that is, either a command or a prohibition, is not to be considered as Veda. This, it should be emphasized, is a revolutionary position whose implications for the issue of Vedic authority for philosophy in India have hardly noted. The Vedas, according to this view, have no philosophic content whatsoever. Being pure injunctions, they have nothing to do with epistemological or metaphysical speculations, or even with ethical reflection. A command or a prohibition, however moral, is not a reflection on the nature and problem of morals which ethics undoubtedly is. The Mīmāṁsaka's own philosophy, thus, is not a Vedic philosophy at all, since according to him, the Vedas do not contain any philosophy, whether of their own or of any other kind. Vedic philosophy, strictly speaking, is a contradiction-in-terms and is thus the purest type of non-being that we can imagine.

The Vedāntins, for their part, certainly recognize the authority of the Upaniṣads, but not of the Upaniṣads alone. They also recognize the authority of the Gītā and the *Brahma-Sūtra*, which are definitely not regarded as a part of the Vedas by anybody. Equally, they give scant recognition to the authority of the non-Upaniṣadic portion of the Vedas. Their attitude to Vedic authority is quite casual, almost pickwickian in manner. Śaṁkara, for example, in his commentary on the *Brahma-Sūtras*, explicitly implies that they are not to be taken seriously when they deal with empirical matters of fact.[2] They are deemed authoritative only when they deal with transcendental matters. Thus, for Vedānta as well as for Mīmāṁsā, the term Veda is restricted not only to certain portions of the classical Vedic literature, but also to some of their contents or subject matter. The Vedas, in this way, enjoy only a very circumscribed authority, even for Mīmāṁsā and Vedānta, the only schools which seem to take them seriously.

The notion of 'Vedic' authority, then, is a myth. It certainly cannot be held to be the dividing line between the schools as has been stated by almost every text book on the subject. Yet, it may be contended that the issue of authority in Indian philosophy is far broader than the question of the authority of the Vedas. Even if it be conceded that the Vedas hold little authority for most schools of Indian philosophy, is it not true that something else fulfills that function? Do not the *Sūtras* hold the same position, and does not the time-honoured way of writing philosophy in the form of commentaries on the traditional texts prove this? And is not *śabda* or testimony regarded as an independent *pramāṇa*, that is, both a criterion and a source of valid knowledge?

These two contentions seem so obviously convincing as to finally clinch the question of authority in Indian philosophy. But is it really so? Would not a closer look reveal something entirely different? Why should philosophers, of all people, be taken in by appearances without critically examining them? After all, does not one of the so-called 'orthodox' schools of Indian philosophy, that is, the Vaiśeṣika not accept *śabda* or testimony as an independent source of valid knowledge? Why should these things be glossed over as if they were of no importance whatsoever? As for the authority of the *Sūtras*, one may legitimately ask what is the authority of the *Nyāya-Sūtras* after Gaṅgeśa?

This, we should realize, is not just a rhetorical question asked to save a desperate situation. Rather, it should be seen as a plea for looking at the facts from a different angle. After Gaṅgeśa, Nyāya does not merely take a new turn, which was recognized as such by his contemporaries and the thinkers who came after him, but enters on a path of continuous development which leads later to such giants as Viśvanātha, Gadādhara and Raghunātha Śiromaṇi. Such a continuous development and its proliferation into other schools provides decisive evidence against the view which gives to the *Sūtras* an unquestionable authority for the whole school itself. Authority goes on changing and as soon as some new thinker appears on the scene, the mantle of authority falls on him, and his ideas become the point of departure for further thought.

This, it should be remembered, is not the case for Nyāya alone. The situation is not very different for Vedānta, Mīmāṁsā, Vaiśeṣika, or Sāṁkhya. Yoga, as we have said earlier, is hardly a school of philosophy, and thus need not be considered in this connection. It may, for example, be reasonably asked what is the authority of the *Brahma-Sūtras* after Śaṁkara for Advaitic Vedāntins? The numerous Advaita thinkers after Śaṁkara take their point of departure from him, and not from the *Brahma-Sūtras*. Is this not true for such outstanding post-Śaṁkarite figures as Padmapāda, Sureśvara, Prakāśātman, Citsukha, Prakāśānanda, Vācaspati Miśra and Madhusūdana Sarasvatī? Even the famous *Brahmasiddhi* of Maṇḍana Miśra is an independent work and not a commentary on the *Brahma-Sūtras*. There is, in fact, hardly any significant Advaitic commentary directly on the *Brahma-Sūtras* after Śaṁkara. They were just not seriously taken into account and if, in the present century, Radhakrishnan has chosen to write a commentary once again, it is due to the desire to follow in the steps of the great ācāryas than due to any real belief in their overriding authority for his own philosophical thought.

It is, of course, true that Rāmānuja, Madhva and Nimbārka wrote their independent commentaries on the *Brahma-Sūtras* after Śaṁkara. But they did this simply because they wanted to deviate fundamentally from the Advaitic interpretation of the *Brahma-Sūtras*. The great subsequent thinkers of these schools cared little for the *Brahma-Sūtras*. There is no difference in this respect between the post-Śaṁkarite thinkers of the Advaitic school, and, the post-Rāmānuja, the post-Madhva and the post-Nimbārka thinkers. Thus, even where a great thinker tries to buttress his new thought by an appeal to the traditional texts, his immediate successors take him as the point of departure, and not the text from which he presumably derived his ideas. The same may be said about Mīmāṁsā, the other great school which ostensibly argues a great deal in favour of the authority of the traditional texts. The *Sūtras* of Jaimini hold little interest or authority after Prabhākara and Kumārila. It is they who are discussed, argued, assented to or differed with. Sāṁkhya and Vaiśeṣika have no major independent lines of outstanding thinkers around them. The first has hardly any original *Sūtras* which could even reasonably be construed as providing the authoritative text for the system. Īśvarkṛṣṇa's *Sāṁkhya-Kārikā* is the oldest known text of the system. But, as everybody recognizes, the system is much older than this text, and Īśvarkṛṣṇa can hardly be said to enjoy any exceptional authority, except as a clue to some of the main tenets which the thinkers belonging to this school generally held. As for the

Vaiśeṣika, it is Praśastapāda who provides us with a real perspective on Vaiśeṣika thought. Subsequent Vaiśeṣika thinkers generally start from Praśastapāda's work. *Sūtras* themselves, it should be remembered, are only summaries of previous thought. They are, thus, simultaneously the end of a line of thought, as well as the point of departure for a fresh philosophical enterprise. It is only thus that they make sense, and not as the final arbiters of what may legitimately be thought by a philosopher in India. The latter manner of presenting them is usual, but it is so totally false that one wonders how it ever came to be propagated and accepted.

The Buddhists and the Jainas have no sacred philosophical texts, except the *Abhidharma*, which may be regarded as vested with the type of authority that the Vedas and the *Sūtras* are supposed to enjoy in the so-called 'orthodox' tradition of Indian philosophy. There are important thinkers and important books but none is vested with a divine or superhuman authority. This is as it should be, and my contention is that it is the same with the so-called classical schools of Hindu philosophy.

III

The myths of spirituality and of authority are not the only myths about Indian philosophy. There is a third one which is even more subtle. This is the myth of the schools without which no book on Indian philosophy has yet been written. The myths of spirituality and authority are stated on the opening pages and then conveniently forgotten. The schools, however, are in a different category. They are the very stuff, out of which, and around which the whole story of Indian philosophy has been woven. Indian philosophy is divided first into 'orthodox' and the 'unorthodox' schools, and then these are subdivided into Buddhism, Jainism and Cārvāka on the one hand, and into Nyāya. Vaiśeṣika, Sāṁkhya, Yoga, Mīmāṁsā and Vedānta on the other. This is the common classification that one finds. The only attempt at a different classification is that of Karl H. Potter in his *Presuppositions of India's Philosophies*. But Potter has only tried to diversify the picture a little, and not to question its very foundations.

The classification into schools is time-honoured and accepted even by the classical thinkers themselves. Why, then, should we attempt to question it? But it is equally obvious that the veil of authority and the veil of spirituality were also woven and accepted by the classical thinkers. So there is nothing distinctively different in this respect which may be said to apply to the problem of 'school's alone.

The concept of 'school' is closely connected to the concept of 'authority' in Indian philosophy. If the authority of the Vedas or the Upaniṣads or the *Sūtras* is final, then what is presumed to be propounded in them as philosophy is final also. Thus, there arises the notion of a closed school of thought, final and finished, once and for all. This may seem fantastic, but most presentations of the various schools of Indian philosophy are so non-historical in nature that they believe the title *History of Indian Philosophy* under which they are usually presented. History is always the story of change, development, differentiation and innovation. How can there be any real history if some primordial authority is posited at the very beginning of thought? If, therefore, we deny the 'authoritative' character of Indian philosophy then, in an important sense, we deny the concept of 'schools' also. There is no such thing as final, frozen positions which the term 'school', in the context of Indian philosophy, usually connote. If 'schools' change, develop, differentiate and divide, then they are never closed, finished or final with respect to what they are trying to say. There could, then, be no fixed body of Nyāya, Vaiśeṣika, Sāṁkhya, Mīmāṁsā, Vedānta, Buddhist, Jain or Cārvāka positions except in a minimal sense. These would, on the other hand, rather be styles of thought which are developed by successive thinkers, and not fully exemplified by any. Nor would these styles be treated as exhausted by any group or groups of thinkers belonging to any particular historical epoch.

The difference between a 'school' and a 'style' of thought is not merely a verbal one, as many may think. The question centres on the issue of how one is to conceive these so-called schools of Indian philosophy. Are they something like the various schools that one meets with in western philosophy? Are they something of the same kind as, say, 'empiricism', 'realism', or 'idealism'? If so, there is no problem, for while each of these has a recognizable identity of its own, it has had, and is still capable of continuous development in new and varied directions. No single thinker or group of thinkers could ever exhaust what is signified by any of these schools of western philosophy. The case of Indian philosophical schools would then be similar.

However, the traditional presentation of the schools of Indian philosophy is hardly ever along these lines. They are treated as something finished and final. No distinction, therefore, is ever drawn between the thought of an individual thinker and the thought of a school. A school is, in an important sense, an abstraction. It is a logical construction springing out of the writings of a number of thinkers who share a certain similarity of outlook in tackling similar problems. On the other hand, it is also some sort of an ideal governing the direction of thought as well as a Platonic Idea, more or less exemplified in one thinker rather than another. In more modern terms, it may also be conceived as a morphological form which both governs the evolution of species and is intuited from a continuous and varied observation of them. These different ways of understanding the concept of 'school' should be treated not as exclusive alternatives, but rather as complementary to one another.

Basically, this is the reality of the 'schools' of Indian philosophy. Yet it is never presented as such. Śaṁkhya, for example, is identified too much with Īśvarakṛṣṇa's work, or Vedānta with the work of Śaṁkara. But this is due to a confusion between the thought of an individual thinker and the style of thought which he exemplifies and to which he contributes in some manner. All that Śaṁkara has written is not strictly Advaita Vedānta. Nor is all that Īśvarakṛṣṇa has written, Sāṁkhya. Unless this is realized, writings on Indian philosophy will continuously do injustice either to the complexity of thought of the individual thinker concerned, or to the uniqueness of the style of thought they are writing about. If such an injustice is to be avoided, then the history of Indian philosophy will either have to be the history of individual thinkers in relation to one another, or the history of styles of thought as they have grown over a period of time. In this it will be no different from the history of western or any other philosophy which can be, and has been, written in either of the two ways.

IV

Indian philosophy, therefore, is neither exclusively spiritual nor bound by unquestionable, infallible authority, nor constricted and congealed in the frozen moulds of the so-called 'schools' which are supposed to constitute the essence of Indian philosophy by those who have written on the subject. These are just myths, and unless they are seen and recognized to be such, any new or fresh look at Indian philosophy would be impossible. The dead, mummified picture of Indian philosophy will come alive only when it is seen to be a living stream of thinkers who have grappled with difficult problems that are, philosophically, as alive today as they were in the ancient past. Indian philosophy will become contemporarily relevant only when it is conceived as philosophy proper.[3] Otherwise, it will remain merely a subject of antiquarian interest and research, which is what all the writers on Indian philosophy have made it out to be. It is time that this false picture is removed, and that the living concerns of ancient thought are brought to life once more. The destruction of these three myths will be a substantial step in this direction.[4]

NOTES AND REFERENCES

1. See G. C. Pande, *Studies in the Origins of Buddhism* (Allahabad: Allahabad University, India).
2. 'A conflict of statements (in Vedānta-passages) regarding the world would not even matter greatly, since the creation of the world and similar topics are not at all what the scripture wishes to teach . . . the passages about the creation and the like form only subordinate members of passages treating of *Brahman*.' *A Source Book in Indian Philosophy*, (eds.) Radhakrishnan and Moore (Princeton: Princeton University Press, 1957), p. 516.
3. See my article 'Three Conceptions of Indian Philosophy' in this book. It has been asked what I mean by 'Philosophy proper.' The only thing I wish to make clear in this context is that the Indian philosophical tradition is 'philosophical' in the same sense as the western philosophical tradition is supposed to be.
4. I have been greatly helped in this paper by discussions with Dr. G. C. Pande, the outstanding scholar on Indian philosophy and culture, at present Tagore Professor of Indian culture at the University of Rajasthan, Jaipur, India. I am also thankful to Dr. S. K. Gupta of the Sanskrit Department in the University for bringing to my attention the different meanings of the term 'Veda' in the tradition of clasical Indian thought.

CHAPTER TWO

Three Conceptions of Indian Philosophy

Indian philosophy has been an antiquarian's interest, a study of something dead and gone, a preserve of the Indologist, something relevant only to the student of ancient India, its thought and its culture. It hardly forms a part of the philosophical climate of today—not even in the sense in which Plato and Aristotle form a part—not even in India, where at least, it may legitimately be expected to be so. The fault for all this lies squarely on the shoulders of all those who have written on the subject and tried to create an impression that Indian philosophy is not philosophy proper, but something else—something they regard as more profound, but certainly not the sort of thing which goes under that name today. If such is really the case, then philosophers, whether Indian or western, are surely justified in ignoring it since its propounders have already proclaimed its irrelevance for their purposes.

Indian philosophy, on the very first page of any book dealing with the subject, is proclaimed to be something dealing with the final and ultimate liberation of the spirit, or what is technically known as *mokṣa*. This, it should be remembered, is not, in the opinion of these writers, just one among the many things it deals with. It is, in their opinion, the focal concern around which the whole of Indian philosophy is woven, and in the light of which alone it achieves its distinctive sense in contrast to other philosophical traditions. Furthermore, this view contends that it is only in this perspective that Indian philosophy makes any sense at all.

This is a view of Indian philosophy which is widely shared by experts and laymen alike. It is treated as axiomatic by almost all who write on the subject. It seems to require no proof for its establishment. *Prima facie*, it should strike us as a great problem to be solved, as to how all the varied problems which Indian philosophy has dealt with in its long past are concerned with or related to the single issue of spiritual liberation which is supposed, by common consent, to be its central concern. However, it does not seem to strike anybody as a problem at all. Each writer, after making this claim on the first page or in the first chapter, goes merrily along, forgetting about it, and writes of other matters, as if the claim had not been made at all. In fact, the writer may even go on to claim parallelisms in the thought of Indian thinkers with that of their western counterparts, conveniently forgetting that he has to explain the parallelism in view of his contention that Indian philosophy is radically different from the western in that the former is intrinsically and essentially concerned with spiritual liberation, while the latter is not. Obviously, if western philosophy is not concerned with spiritual liberation and yet raises the same problems as does Indian philosophy, there is something wrong either with the contentions that western philosophy is not so concerned, or the claim that Indian philosophy is so concerned, or that Indian philosophy is concerned only with this and with nothing else at all.

It, is of course not quite true to say that there is not a single writer who has been struck by the problem of finding the relation between the various speculative concerns of Indian philosophy and *mokṣa*, or spiritual liberation, with which it is supposed to be really concerned. Karl H. Potter in his book *Presuppositions of India's Philosophies* is concerned with this very issue. In fact, he is perhaps the first person who has tried to take seriously the claim of Indian philosophy to be concerned with *mokṣa*. The central question behind Potter's enquiry seems to be "how to reconcile the apparent conceptual and theoretic concerns of Indian philosophy with its presumed and proclaimed real concern." He has not exactly framed it this way, but that is perhaps the best way to describe what he has tried to do. There is, in fact, a chapter entitled "*How Speculative Philosophy Comes in*," as if this were the real question which any writer on Indian philosophy must first attempt to deal with. He has to justify the whole speculative enterprise of Indian philosophy, as it seems to be in conflict with or, at least, to be irrelevant to its presumed primary and sole concern with *mokṣa*.

The necessity of speculative philosophy in the Indian tradition arises, according to Potter, because of the necessity of meeting the doubts that may assail the seeker after *mokṣa*. The doubts, of course, have to be intellectual in character, since, presumably, philosophical thinking can hardly remove doubts of any other kind. Potter writes: "It is the business of speculative philosophy in India to combat skepticism and fatalism of both the universal and the guarded variety."[1] This appears to limit Indian philosophy to combating only skepticism and fatalism, and that too, if and only if, they interfere with the pursuit of *mokṣa*. The latter conditional clause is not explicitly stated by Potter, but it is implied throughout his discussion, and I am sure he will take no exception to my formulating it in this way. He concedes, of course, that "there were, according to tradition, both skeptics and fatalists in ancient India."[2] However, presumably he would deny them the title of Indian philosophers, since, otherwise, his own way of showing how speculative philosophy comes in would be shown to be inadequate to that extent.

Philosophy in India, then, is supposed to arise, according to this conception, in the attempt to meet the intellectual difficulties that may obstruct a person from pursuing the path to *mokṣa*. As the presumed difficulties are essentially intellectual in character, they may be removed only by reflection and by argumentation that is strictly intellectual in nature also. This would reconcile the apparent incongruity between the actual concerns of Indian philosophy which are speculative and conceptual in character, and its supposedly real concern with *mokṣa*, spiritual liberation, which is essentially non-intellectual and non-conceptual in nature. Potter has confined himself to considering skepticism and fatalism as the only two intellectual obstructions on the path to *mokṣa*, but this limitation is neither necessary nor desirable for the consideration of the truth or validity of this conception concerning Indian philosophy. In fact, any intellectual difficulty that could possibly obstruct a person from embarking upon the path to *mokṣa*, or from pursuing the goal when once one has embarked upon it, could, in this view, give rise to philosophy. There seems, therefore, no necessity to confine these difficulties to those of certain specific types only.

Unfortunately, this conception of Indian philosophy rests on assumptions which, when articulated, would appear to be highly questionable, to say the least. First, it should be noted that such a conception of Indian philosophy does not necessarily make it integrally related to *mokṣa*. It is contingent on the condition that intellectual difficulties arise in the mind of a person with respect to *mokṣa*, and that these difficulties are of such an overpowering nature as to make it impossible for him to pursue the ideal or realize it or even start on its quest until they are removed. Obviously, it would be best if the difficulties were not to arise at all. From the viewpoint of *mokṣa*, it is just a waste of time. Nothing is really gained through philosophy except the removal of that which, in the first place, should not have been allowed to arisc at all. Intellectual difficulties, in this view, are certain illnesses which hinder a man from pursuing what he really ought to pursue, and philosophy is the presumed proper therapeutic discipline which helps in their removal and cure.

The affinity of such a view with certain contemporary views about philosophy in general will be obvious to anyone who is even slightly acquainted with the contemporary scene in the realm of philosophic thought. Potter might be surprised at such a coincidence, but basically, any view of philosophy that is suspicious of its claim to autonomous validity would end in one of the numerous varieties of the view mentioned above. The contemporary varieties, of course, do not confine themselves to *mokṣa*. In fact, they do not know of any such thing, though the contemporary existential thinker might possibly formulate his attitude toward traditional philosophy in those terms. The irrelevance or meaninglessness of philosophy as a cognitive enterprise and its obstructive and therapeutic roles with respect to genuine cognition, on the one hand, and authentic living, on the other, are issues that require examination in their own right. This, however, is not the place to undertake such an enterprise, since it is not central to what we are concerned with in this essay. This much, however, may be said, that all the reasons which one might regard as validly holding against the generalized view would, with equal validity, hold against the specific view which limits it to the context of *mokṣa* alone.

Philosophy, in this conception, may shed its contingency if it were held that intellectual difficulties on the path to *mokṣa* arise inevitably and necessarily because of the rational nature of man, and that their removal, thus, is a necessary precondition for anyone's starting or continuing on the path itself. This, obviously, would make philosophy in India central to the whole enterprise of spiritual liberation, though still in a negative way. Yet, even if this is granted, such a conception would still suffer from presuppositions that seem extremely questionable. First, it seems to be implicitly assumed in this view that intellectual difficulties of a purely rational and cognitive kind can stand in the way of the practical pursuit of ends which are non-cognitive, non-intellectual, and non-rational in nature. This, obviously, is incorrect. No one has been deterred from walking because there have been insuperable intellectual difficulties with respect to the nature of motion, not even Zeno, who is supposed to be the first philosopher to have been continuously assailed by them. And this, as everybody knows, is equally true of all other philosophical difficulties, whether they be about time, space, self, matter, plurality, change, or anything else.

There are no differences in this respect between east and west. This apparently is not what Potter wishes to say in the matter. The doctrine of the unreality of the world has not stood in the way of the Indian philosopher's effective dealing with his contemporaries, either in the world of thought or of living. In fact, contrary to what one would be led to suppose if one accepted Potter's theory, the leading Indian philosophers were not the sort of persons whose pursuit of *mokṣa*, or even its attainment, was visibly hindered by their intellectual difficulties. On the contrary, the leaders among them have always been thought to be persons who had already attained *mokṣa*. It would be almost blasphemy to think that a Śaṁkara or a Rāmānuja had not attained spiritual liberation and that their philosophical thinking was concerned with removing the intellectual doubts which were hindering them from pursuing the path to *mokṣa*. It should be remembered in this context, that most of these philosophers wrote their philosophical works *after* they are alleged to have attained *mokṣa*. If Potter's view were correct, they would have had no reason to engage in such an activity, except, perhaps, for removing the intellectual doubts that were standing in the way of their disciples' pursuit of the same goal, or of that of other persons who hesitated to become their disciples and thus pursue the path due to the same difficulties.

However, deeper than the presupposition that purely intellectual difficulties can stand in the way of the practical pursuit of a goal lies another presupposition which, perhaps, is even more questionable than the first. It is the presupposition that purely intellectual or conceptual difficulties can be resolved or dissolved once and for all, so that there is no trouble on the path to practical action, at least from them, thereafter. Unfortunately, as everyone knows, this just does not happen to be the case. Intellectual difficulties seem to possess an enormous fecundity of their own, so that each, even in the process of its own death and dissolution, gives rise to innumerable others equally clamouring for their solution. And even that which seemed to have been decently buried and given over to the elements to do their natural work of dissolution and destruction, rises again like some mythological Titan to trouble man and call him to battle once more.

The point, obviously, is that, if philosophy is conceived as the removal of those intellectual difficulties which emanate from the nature of pure intellect itself, and yet obstruct man on the path of relevant action, then its task would be perennially self-defeating, since those types of difficulties would arise anew from the ever present fountainhead of intellect itself. Man would, then, never be able to act at all, for unless the chain of problems were finally to snap and the possibility of their ever arising again be effectively and demonstrably removed, he would always be at the mercy of the intellectual difficulty that had just arisen or which was lurking just around the corner.

It may be contended, of course, that such a situation is not peculiar to philosophy alone. After all, even the fight against physical disease is perennial and self-defeating in the same sense. The cure of a disease does not ensure that one will not suffer from the same disease again, or that the cure itself will not give rise to some other disease in the future; ultimately, as everybody knows, all cures are only provisional attempts to stave off the certain and final victory of disease, which is death. The parallel would be clearer if we remember that the physician may himself catch the disease, and that an ailing physician may try to cure another who is diseased or even himself, and that they may disagree about the exact nature of the disease from which they themselves or somebody else might be suffering.

The analogy, though interesting, fails, however, in an essential respect. The purely intellectual difficulties which are being treated as analogous to physical disease in this attempt to meet our objection are themselves, so to speak, the result of philosophers' activities in the realm of thought. The sort of difficulties which philosophers try to solve are themselves philosophical in nature, that is, the result of a thinking which is philosophical in character. The philosopher does not merely try to heal the disease, once it has arisen. It is also a fact that the disease would not have arisen but for the philosophers' own activity. Philosophy, it should be remembered, is simultaneously a name for the disease and the attempt at its cure. Each philosopher, of course, regards all the others as diseased and infected and reserves to himself the sole therapeutic function *par excellence*. The strict parallel would hold, then, only if the physical doctors were themselves the creators of the disease and its healers also.

The two basic, though unacknowledged, presuppositions behind Potter's conception of Indian philosophy, when thus articulated, seem to render it completely untenable. As the presuppositions are equally shared by the disease-cum-therapeutic view of philosophy so widely propagated today, their clear and complete untenability would affect the very foundations of that view also. Modern philosophers who argue for this view have yet to show that purely intellectual difficulties can stand in the way of the pursuit of practical ends, and that there is some method or means by which they can be resolved or dissolved completely and finally, once and for all. All the discoveries of modern psychology and the whole history of contemporary philosophizing, even among the thinkers who ostensibly and self-consciously subscribe to such a view, stand against the possibility of their showing these presuppositions to be reasonably true.[3]

However, Potter's is not the only attempt that tries to show in an intelligible way how Indian philosophy is related to *mokṣa* There is at least one other conception which tries to do the same thing, though in a manner so oblique and implicit that it is doubtful that anyone would even be aware of it, without its being pointed out to him in as direct and explicit a manner as possible. This view lies embedded in the writings of K. C. Bhattacharyya on Indian philosophy,[4] and I have referred to it in my review article published in 1960 in *The Visva Bharati Quarterly*.[5] This is our second conception of Indian philosophy. But even before articulating and examining the conception in detail, it should be obvious that the question as to whether the alleged view is actually implied or presupposed by what Bhattacharyya has written on the subject, is essentially irrelevant for our purposes. The conception has been suggested by the writings of Bhattacharyya, and, as far as I know, no one else has even remotely suggested such a conception in his writings on the subject. In any case, the textual-historical question as to whether Bhattacharyya actually held or implied such a view is different from the question as to whether it accounts intelligibly for the alleged relationship between Indian philosophy and *mokṣa*. The second question alone concerns us here, and therefore no attempt will be made to answer the first. Also, let us assume that the first question has been satisfactorily answered, and, thus, call the conception to be described and examined Bhattacharyya's conception of Indian philosophy.

According to this concept, Indian philosophy is the essential theoretic counterpart to that which, when practically realized or verified, is called *sādhanā* (practice) or *yoga*. It is philosophical reflection alone which leads to the awareness and envisagement of certain possibilities which are then actualized or realized by a practical process of *sādhanā* or *yoga*. The point, basically, is that without the so-called philosophical reflection man would not become aware of *mokṣa* as the only innermost reality of his being, without realizing which he would always remain essentially ignorant and incomplete. *Mokṣa* is certainly non-conceptual, but only a conceptual reflection can make us aware of it as the ultimate and inmost possibility and reality of our being. In the language of Bhattacharyya, it is philosophic reflection alone which makes us aware of certain possibilities which demand to be actualized, even though the process of actualization itself is not philosophical in nature. Philosophy, thus, is an essential and inalienable preliminary to spiritual liberation, for without it we could not even be aware of the idea of spiritual liberation itself.

Indian philosophy, in this conception, is integrally related to *mokṣa*. In fact, it is far more integrally related than in Potter's conception, since the very awareness of *mokṣa* is contingent here on some sort of philosophical reflection. Furthermore, the relation here is not only integral but also positive in character. Without philosophical reflection, it is contended, man would not have become aware of those possibilities, or rather, realities of his own being, whose realization alone gives one *mokṣa*. Philosophy, then, in this view, would be analogous to a theoretical discipline whose conceptually discovered realities are verified by a process of practical application which is traditionally known in India as *sādhanā*. Philosophical and spiritual disciplines would thus be intimately and integrally related to each other, each interacting with and affecting the other.

There can be yet another analogy deriving from the Bhattacharyya model for understanding the relation of Indian philosophy to spiritual liberation. This would be on the pattern of the arts or morality, where something is theoretically apprehended either by imagination or intuition or even by ratiocination, and then sought to be embodied or actualized in concrete reality. Philosophical reflection, in this interpretation, would lead man to have awareness of his deepest valuational potentialities, which would then have to be actualized, embodied, and given concrete shape by the process of spiritual discipline, traditionally known as *sādhanā*.

Bhattacharyya never wrote explicitly on the subject, and thus all these varying interpretations lie half-hidden in the way he has approached the various schools of Indian philosophy in his essays. There is, therefore, all the more reason to distinguish between the alternative suggestive interpretations deriving from and clustering around the central nucleus of what may be called the Bhattacharyya model. The essential, basic point of the nucleus common to all the interpretations is the notion that philosophic reflection provides the awareness of something whose truth or reality is then established by a process which is the reverse of the theoretic, and which basically is both practical and experiential through and through. The alternatives basically concern the nature of what is apprehended through philosophic reflection and the exact nature of the relationship between that which is theoretically apprehended, and that which is realized or actualized through the practical-cum-experiential process of *sādhanā*.

Philosophic reflection may be taken as leading to the theoretic awareness of certain ontic realities whose actual verification is achieved through a process of spiritual *sādhanā*. Or, philosophic reflection may be taken as leading to the awareness of the unreality of the world, as revealed through sense and reason due to certain purely theoretic considerations which then lead to the search for 'the real reality' through processes which are essentially non-sensory and non-rational in nature. Or, philosophic reflection may be taken to lead to the awareness of complete and absolute freedom as both the natural and the ideal condition of one's being which is then attempted to be realized through any and every process that appears to have the promise to lead to it. Or, philosophic reflection may be taken as leading to the awareness of certain ultimate ideal valuational possibilities of one's own being which then are attempted to be embodied, actualized, and concretized through any process that seems to lead to them.

All these conceptions of philosophy closely relate it to practice, and thus sustain the usual view concerning Indian philosophy that it is integrally and possitively related to spiritual practice. But, basically, it is only the third view, that is, the one concerned with complete and absolute freedom, that relates it specifically to *mokṣa*. The other three interpretations of the Bhattacharyya model can be so construed as to mean the same thing as the explicit interpretation in terms of *mokṣa* alone. But this is not necessary. The first conceives of philosophy on the model of theoretical science, with spiritual practice as an essential verificatory part without which it would lapse into pure imagination. The second conceives of philosophy as essentially negative in character. Its task is merely to show the unreality of all that which, without its critical reflection, would be accepted as real by everybody. The fourth view conceives of philosophy as creative imagination with respect, not to objective being as does art in general, but to that being which is through and through subjective in its essential nature and character.

However, even though the differences among the four interpretations are substantial and merit independent consideration on their own, they do not affect the general considerations which seem to weigh decidedly against the acceptance of Bhattacharyya's conception of Indian philosophy as adequate or valid. First, if this conception were really correct, then Indian philosophy would have had a short career indeed. The possibilities opened up once by philosophic reflection are for all time available to human awareness, and one does not even have to go through the process of philosophic reflection again to become aware of them. Once the possibility of *mokṣa*, for example, has been grasped by the philosophic intellect, there is nothing more for it to do except to lapse into quietude. The only task that remains for each individual is to realize it in his or her own life. Philosophy cannot help in this process, and, in fact, once awareness has permeated and been accepted by the culture, it ceases to have any function at all.

It could hardly be denied that both of these things were achieved very early in Indian culture and that philosophical reflection continued to flourish until almost the time when India entered the modern age. The idea of *mokṣa* as the highest ideal for man was accepted in India as early as the time of the Upaniṣads and the Buddha. Philosophic reflection, on the other hand, is supposed to have continued creatively until almost as late as the seventeenth or eighteenth century of the Christian era. How to reconcile these two basic facts of Indian philosophic history is the main hurdle for Bhattacharyya's conception of Indian philosophy. Philosophers certainly could not have gone on apprehending the same possibility and articulating it for ever. Philosophic reflection, based on the Bhattacharyya conception, becomes as redundant and superfluous as it is on the conception of Karl H. Potter. The only difference between the two is that, in the former conception, it is at least indispensable and necessary in the beginning, while, in the latter, it never has that status at any time in its career.

In a certain sense, the Indian spiritual tradition confirms, as does every other tradition, the essential irrelevance of philosophy to the pursuit of liberation (*moksa*). Thus, even if it were true that the possibility of *mokṣa* was apprehended by an act of philosophic reflection, as in the Upaniṣads, it soon came to be realized that, if one were to be seriously concerned with the realization of the possibility, indulgence in further philosophic reflection would only be a hindrance rather than a help in the matter. Potter's conception of Indian philosophy may be urged to come in at just this point and make the philosophical activity go forward. Nothing is gained by apprehending once again the possibility one has already apprehended. But doubts may certainly arise about that possibility, and philosophic reflection may come in for the removal of those doubts. Unfortunately for this happy marriage of the views of Battacharyya and Potter, the Indian spiritual tradition quickly realized that these doubts were unending and multifarious and that, if one got into the process of intellectually tackling them, one would never get on the path to *mokṣa*. Instead of the intellectual removal of doubts, therefore, what was inculcated was faith, which was essentially non-intellectual and non-rational in nature. In spite of this supersession and rejection by the genuine *mokṣa*-seeking spiritual tradition of India, Indian philosophy continued to flourish and grow. This is the basic fact which both Bhattacharyya and Potter have to account for in their theories, and which they are unable to do. As a matter of fact, this is a challenge to everybody who tries significantly to link Indian philosophy with *mokṣa*; and, as there is hardly anyone who does not do so, it is a matter of real surprise that nobody has even seen the necessity for meeting the challenge and for squaring the theory with the fact.

The one possible way of saving the Bhattacharyya view of Indian philosophy against the objection raised here is to conceive of the possibilities apprehended through philosophic reflection as essentially inexhaustible and infinite in their very nature. Even if the possibility apprehended is confined to one ideal type, such as *mokṣa*, it may be contended that its theoretic comprehension is never complete. There are innumerable shades to be apprehended, articulated, and explored in their infinite variety. Or, the interaction between the theoretic apprehension and the experiential realization may be conceived, on the pattern of science, as unending and infinite in nature. It is extremely unlikely that the experiential realization would confirm the theoretically apprehended possibility in every detail. Equally, it would be extremely surprising if the significant difference in experiential realization were not to be theoretically articulated and reflected upon. This would give rise to a continuous dialectic analogous to that which is prevalent in almost all other areas of human seeking and experience. After all, there seems little reason for *mokṣa* alone of all human ideals to be conceived in purely static terms. It, too, may be thought of, like truth or beauty or goodness, as an ideal vaguely apprehended, but never completely realized.

However fascinating such an interpretation of the Bhattacharyya view may appear, it is open to at least two basic objections which render it untenable. First, the Indian tradition, both spiritual and philosophical, stands decidedly against the dynamic interpretation of *mokṣa*. It is not conceived as an ideal which is ever approached but never reached. It is rather an ideal—perhaps the only ideal—which is claimed not only to be completely realizable in principle, but to have already been completely realized, as a matter of fact, in the lives of many persons in the past and the present. The Indian would lose faith in *mokṣa* if he were to find that it is not completely realizable in this or any other life granted to him in infinite time. In fact, *mokṣa* is, for an Indian, the final and complete liberation from time, which alone is the basis of that perpetual dynamism and discovery which we are trying to read into the concept.

On the other hand, even if it be accepted that, as a matter of fact, the concept of *mokṣa* has been diversely explored and articulated in the course of the development of the Indian spiritual tradition, it would be difficult to show that it has been progressive or evolutionary in character. Its development is similar to that of the arts, than to that of cognitive sciences. The latter discovery or creation with respect to the concept does not necessarily supersede the former, or even include it as a relevant component of itself. Rather, the new stands alongside the old, and both claim equal and sometimes even exclusive validity. There is thus little continuing interplay between the theoretic articulation and the actual experiencing which the scientific analogue to the Bhattacharyya model seems to suggest.

Even more important than this seems to be the difficulty of actually correlating the supposedly varying concepts of *mokṣa* with the different schools of Indian philosophy. What, for example, are the Vaiśeṣika, Nyāya or the Mīmāṁsā concepts of *mokṣa*? Unless one is prepared to argue that there are specific concepts which are integrally related to the particular philosophical positions of these schools, there seems little point in arguing that Indian philosophy is essentially and inalienably concerned with *mokṣa*. Neither Potter nor Bhattacharyya nor anybody else has ever tried to show, or perhaps even felt the necessity of showing, such a relationship, and yet they are convinced that there is such a relationship. The uncritical naiveté of writers on Indian philosophy could not have gone further.

The basic trouble about the view that Indian philosophy is concerned with *mokṣa* is how to make intelligible its multifarious other concerns in terms of this supposedly central perspective, which alone is presumed to give it meaning. Unfortunately, there seems to be no way to do this, for the concerns of philosophical speculation in India seem to be almost the same as those in other traditions or countries. This fact is attested to by every writer who tries to draw parallelisms between Indian and western philosophy, and their number happens to be by no means small. There seem to be a host of problems in Indian philosophy which do not appear to have any direct or indirect relation, even in the remotest way, to *mokṣa*.

This brings us to the third conception of Indian philosophy. It thinks of Indian philosophy as philosophy proper and not as something radically different from what goes under that name in the western tradition. It denies that Indian philosophy has anything to do with *mokṣa* and asserts that the alleged association is due to a complete misunderstanding of the actual situation, facilitated by the uncritical acceptance of the claim as handed down by writer after writer on the subject. This view has not been formulated or argued for by anybody. Yet, it seems to be the view which meets all the difficulties which militate so fatally against the generally accepted view. It certainly has difficulties of its own; yet they do not seem so formidable as not to be overcome by a closer examination of the matter.

The only major difficulty which such a conception has to account for is the explicit claim made by all the schools of Indian philosophy that their philosophy is concerned with, and would lead to *mokṣa*. If all the *sūtrakāras* (authors of the *sūtras*), for example, write in the very beginning of their work that it leads to *mokṣa*, then *prima facie*, the case is overwhelming that, at least in their view, philosophy is concerned with and justified by its concern with *mokṣa*. This obviously is the reason why every writer on Indian philosophy has accepted and repeated the claim, for the classical writers themselves and almost every basic sourcebook on the subject makes it on the very first page, and seriously too.

Yet, though the facts are obvious, it is surprising that for millennia none should have asked himself the simple question as to how the author of the *Vaiśeṣika-sūtra* can be taken seriously when he asks us to believe that the knowledge of his various categories such as *dravya* (substance), *guṇa* (quality), *karma* (activity), *sāmānya* (generic qualities), etc., would lead to *mokṣa*.[6] Or, for that matter, when the author of the *Nyāya-sutra* tells us that a knowledge of the various *pramāṇas* (means of knowledge) and the logical fallacies would lead us to the same goal.[7] Or how, for example, the controversies between the various schools of Buddhism are supposed to lead to *nirvāṇa*.

The situation would appear even more intriguing if we were to remind ourselves that hardly anyone, even in those times, would have agreed that these things could ever lead to *mokṣa*. Except for the *sūtrakāra's* (author of the *sūtras*) own saying, it is difficult to believe that anyone could seriously believe that he or anyone else could achieve *mokṣa* through a knowledge of the types of *padārthas* (objects of experience) to be found in the world, or through a knowledge of the *pramāṇas* (means of valid knowledge), or the *hetvābhāsas* (logical fallacies) which are relevant in the field of reasoning and argumentation. It is not as if we alone are questioning the relevance of these things to *mokṣa*. It is the tradition itself which decisively rejected these claims almost at the very time when they were being put forward. It is inconceivable that anyone genuinely desirous of seeking *mokṣa* ever attempted the Nyāya or the Vaiśeṣika way. The relevant question then is, why this claim was made in the first place, and why it has continued to be made, when everyone knew that it was not relevant at all.

The answer is not as difficult as it may seem. The first clue in this connection may be provided by asking if it is philosophy alone which makes this claim in India. Surprisingly, this just does not happen to be the case. There is hardly any pursuit or study or discipline which does not make the same claim. Whether it be painting, poetry, music or dance, each is supposed to lead to *mokṣa*.[8] Such is also the claim with respect to the sciences of sex, economics, medicine, grammar and politics.[9] This claim, therefore, is a generalized feature of every systematic study in India, rather than a particular, specific character of a clearly differentiated and demarcated area within the total whole. Philosophy, then, is not unique in making the claim to be the purveyor of *mokṣa* in India. Nor, for that very reason, can that be considered its specific essence in any relevant sense of the term. Like *Brahman* or Being, it may be the essence of everything, but certainly it does not and cannot distinguish or differentiate the one from the other. If painting, for example, claims to lead to *mokṣa* as much as philosophy does, then, obviously, the distinction between the two cannot be drawn in terms of *mokṣa* at all.

But why is the claim made at all? Why is it that everything in India must claim to lead to *mokṣa*, even when *prima facie* it is concerned with something entirely different? The answer most probably lies in the fact that *mokṣa* was accepted as the highest value and the ultimate goal of life by the whole of Indian culture, and, thus, anything, to be respectable and draw attention to itself, had to be related to *mokṣa* in some way or other. If it could not be so related, it would lose in appeal and would have a lesser place in culture. However, nobody wanted to lose this charismatic appeal and make only modest claims for his own discipline, especially when the competitors were making the tallest claims for their own paths and pursuits. Like the gods of the Vedic pantheon, each study or discipline claimed to be the highest and the noblest, and the only one that led to the final and supreme knowledge.

The claim, however, deceived none except the historians of Indian philosophy and culture. It was allowed to hide the real divergence of pursuits and interests, and the modern historian of Indian philosophy was the first to be taken in by it. Surely, the Indian philosopher who had such surpassing love of hair-splitting argument and real fondness for intellectual debate could hardly ever be deceived by the ritual reiteration of the *mantraṁ* of *mokṣa* on the first page of his book.

Does philosophy, then have nothing to do with *mokṣa* in India? There are many philosophers and many schools of philosophy in India that have literally nothing to do with *mokṣa*. The Nyāya, the Vaiśeṣika, and the Mīmāṁsā are predominant in this group. Then, there are others which are concerned with *mokṣa*, but only in certain portions of their work. They are never exclusively concerned with *mokṣa* and *mokṣa* alone, as many writers try to imply. Nor are they predominantly concerned with it. And what is more important still, the nature of their concern is primarily philosophical. It has been conveniently forgotten that *mokṣa*, like almost every other thing, may give rise to philosophical issues, and it would have been really surprising if, in a culture which gave such supremacy to *mokṣa*, philosophers would not have reflected on it or discovered the most perplexing problems with respect to it. But these are basically philosophical problems, and reflection on them is essentially philosophical in nature. There is nothing in them which differentiates them, in essence, from the philosophical problems which arise from other realms of human experience. Many of the problems in post-Śaṁkarite Vedānta are, for example, of this nature.

Mokṣa, then, is not the exclusive concern of Indian philosophy. Nor is it its predominant concern either. Many of the thinkers and many of the schools are not concerned with it even marginally. Many others are concerned with it only in a peripheral manner. There are very few for whom it is a major concern, and even they are concerned with it only in a philosophical manner. The propagandistic statements by classical writers in the course of their works, along with the failure to note that *mokṣa* may give rise to genuinely philosophical problems as much as anything else, have created the myth that Indian philosophy is intrinsically and inalienably concerned with spiritual liberation, and not with what may be called proper philosophical problems. It is time that the myth is dispelled, and Indian philosophy is treated seriously as philosophy proper.

NOTES AND REFERENCES

1. Karl H. Potter, *Presuppositions of India's Philosophies* (Englewood Cliffs. N. J.: Prentice-Hall, 1963), p. 30.
2. *Ibid.*, p. 50.
3. For a related discussion on this issue, see Krishna, Daya, 'Some Considerations on Morris Lazerowitz's "The Structure of Metaphysics," ' *Mind*, 1958, LXVII, No. 266. pp. 236–43.
4. K. C. Bhattacharyya, *Studies in Philosophy*, Gopinath Bhattacharyya, (ed.), (Calcutta: Progressive Publishers, 1956), Vol. I.
5. 'K. C. Bhattacharyya on Indian Philosophy', *The Visva Bharati Quarterly*, 1960, XXVI, No. 2, pp. 137–49.
6. See appendix.
7. See appendix.
8. See appendix.
9. See appendix.

APPENDIX*

1. Salvation is attained by the true knowledge of the common and distinctive features of the categories of substance, quality, motion, universals, ultimate distinctions, and inherence. This true knowledge itself proceeds from distinctive merit or virtue.

Vaiśeṣika-sūtra, 1.1.4

2. Salvation is attained by the true knowledge of the means of right cognition, the objects of such cognition, doubt, purpose, instance, conclusion, discussion, debate, sophistry, fallacy, quibbling, faulty reasoning, and losing (a debate).

Nyāya-sūtra, 1.1.1

3. For the science of polity has been regarded as the support of all, maintains social order, underlies virtue, wealth, and pleasure, and confers salvation.

Śukra-nīti, 1.1.3

4. This (grammar) is the first step in the stairway of attainment. It is the straight royal road for seekers of emancipation.

Vākyapadīya, Brahma-kāṇḍa 16.

5. Who are able to praise the greatness of music? It is the unique means of virtue, wealth, pleasure, and emancipation.

Saṅgīta-ratnākara, Padārthasaṁgrahprakaraṇa, śloka 30.

6. This worldly as well as otherworldly good is to be found here (in medicine).

Suśruta-saṁhitā, sūtra ą.1.

7. In this insubstantial world of phenomena, substance belongs only to the happiness of feminine company of which the ecstasy has been held comparable to the supreme bliss of the highest self.+

Anaṅga-raṅga, 1.1.5

* Some quotations relevant to the contention referred to by footnotes 6, 7, 8 and 9. I am indebted for many of these quotations to Dr. G. C. Pande, the outstanding scholar on ancient India, and Shri J. N. Asopa, both of the University of Rajasthan, Jaipur, India.

+ Here, of course, sex is not regarded as a means to *mokṣa*, but as its equivalent. This supports our contention that in traditional Indian culture everything had to be related to *mokṣa* in order to get real respectability and attention. I have chosen to

8. According to an early treatise, "painting is the best of all arts' and is 'conducive to *dharna* (right conduct) and emancipation (the goal of living)".†

---

quote from a straight book on sex rather than from works on *Tantra* from which even stronger statements could be quoted.

† Quoted in W. G. Archer, *Indian Miniatures*, from *Vishṇudharmottara*, Stella Kramerisch, trans. (Calcutta: University of Calcutta, 1928).

CHAPTER THREE

Indian Philosophy and *Mokṣa*: Revisiting an old Controversy

Almost two decades ago I had published two articles[1] questioning the integral relationship between Indian philosophy and *mokṣa*, on the one hand, and the exclusive characterization of Indian philosophy as spiritual, on the other.

Few scholars in the field of Indian Philosophy have taken any serious note of either of the contentions or of the arguments offered on their behalf in the articles concerned. Prof. Karl H. Potter is one of the few exceptions, as he has not only devoted a substantial portion of his paper entitled "Indian Philosophy's Alleged Religious Orientation"[2] presented in the conference on the same subject held at Brockport, U.S.A. in 1972 but also referred to it again in his *Encyclopedia of Indian Philosophies*, Vol. ii. As the issue may be deemed to be of fundamental import for the very articulation of Indian philosophy, it may not be amiss to try to discuss and clarify the points in the debate once again.

The issue, in a sense, derives its vital power from what one conceives of philosophy to be and from one's desire to find in the Indian tradition that which one thinks ought to be there. There is even a deeper cleavage in the debate between those who, for some reason or other, feel negatively or positively toward anything that is designated as 'spiritual' or 'religious'. Deeper than this, perhaps, is the division amongst those who are hostile or antipathic to tradition, and those who have not only an admiration or nostalgia for the past, but also feel that without a living relationship with their own intellectual culture they cannot be themselves or grow and contribute to the global cognitive concerns of today.

Yet, whatever the divisions and the motivations amongst the participants in the debate, some ground rules will have to be accepted if the dispute claims to be cognitive and thus, at least in principle, settlable in character. The following ground rules are offered in the hope that they would provide at least a tentative beginning in the formulation of what may be called a meaningful discussion on the subject.

The first and foremost precondition of a serious cognitive debate may be taken to be the acceptance of a common criterion or a set of criteria for the admission of a text or a thinker or a tradition as philosophical in character. Even if this is not accepted on Wittgensteinian grounds, one may be expected at least to subscribe to the negative contention that in case one uses any criterion whatsoever to designate a text, a thinker or a tradition as philosophical, then one would have to admit all other texts, thinkers or traditions as philosophical if they display the same characteristic or characteristics. In case one wants to deny even this on some such ground as 'everything is what it is, and not another thing', then not only would one opt out of the cognitive debate but also deprive himself of the possibility of even the first characterization, as there was nothing in it intrinsically to confine it to just that object alone unless it happened to be a definite description, or a rigid designator in Kripke's sense of the term.

If this is accepted even provisionally, and if it is also accepted that the term 'philosophy' arises from within the western tradition, deriving in the main from Greek thinking on the subject, then it is obvious that whatever will display these characteristics would have to be understood not only as philosophy, but as philosophy bearing the same characteristics which philosophy in the western tradition is supposed to have. The terms 'spirituality' and 'religion' should share the same constraints, and if someone complains that this is to surreptitiously underwrite the western concept as the only concept of philosophy and treat it as paradigmatic and thus impose it on other traditions, we would only say that it will be better in such a situation if some other terms are used to avoid confusion.

Further, in a discussion of this sort, one may be legitimately expected to use the same characterization on the basis of the same criteria, irrespective of the fact whether one is talking about one philosophical tradition or another. In the light of this, we may formulate the questions whose answers we are seeking in the following manner:

1. Is Indian philosophy 'spiritual' in a sense in which western philosophy cannot be characterized as such?
2. Is the concept of *mokṣa* distinctive of Indian philosophy in the sense that no analogous concept is to be found in the western philosophical tradition?
3. Even if such an analogous concept can be found in the western philosophical tradition, is it a fact that it (i.e., *mokṣa*) occupies such a central pivotal place in the Indian philosophical tradition that the latter cannot make sense or even be possibly understood without reference to it?

The characterization of Indian philosophy as 'spiritual', and the contention that it is integrally related to *mokṣa* in the sense that it cannot be intelligibly understood without reference to it are usually taken to be identical by most writers on Indian philosophy. Yet the two contentions, though closely related, are not identical. In fact, one may hold the one without holding the other, as the two may vary independently of each other. The former contention is generally supposed to entail the later, but only if the term 'spiritual' is understood in a very specific sense of the word. *Mokṣa* is a concept which may be said to belong to practical philosophy or to what Kant called 'practical reason'. It designates a goal to be pursued, an ideal to be actualized, and as such it will have to be related, evaluated and understood in relation to other values, goals or ideals which have also been prescribed for man's realization. True, there is a feature of *mokṣa* as an ideal which does not belong to most other ideals, particularly those that pertain to something outside the self. *Mokṣa* is supposed to be the realization of the true nature of the self itself even if it be the case, as in Buddhism, that there is no true nature either of the self or of anything else.[3] But if it is the *true* or *real* nature of the self, or no-nature as in Buddhism, then how can it ever be lost? This is the point of dispute between those who have argued for the *nitya-siddha* nature of the self as against those who have argued for the *sādhana-siddha* nature of the self. Also, in Śaṁkara-Vedānta *mokṣa* cannot be relegated to the practical sphere as it cannot, in principle, be the result of *karma* or action.

Yet, whatever the difficulties in assimilating *mokṣa* to the practical sphere, it should be remembered that the difficulties are *theoretical* in character, and that it would be even more odd to treat it as belonging to the cognitive part of the philosophical enterprise in India. The problem of *mokṣa* arises because what is ontologically required to be the case is not existentially such —a situation which is radically different from others where what 'ought to be' does not happen to be so as a 'matter of fact'. Normally, the 'ought' when it obtains with respect to any objective situation whatsoever is not treated as ontologically real, even though in the Platonic framework the difference between the 'idea' and the 'ideal' vanishes, and everything is supposed to be judged for its reality in relation to the idea which it more or less embodies in itself. Yet, even in the Platonic context, one may assume some difference between those sense objects with respect to which one cannot do anything towards the lessening of the discrepancy between them and their idea, and those where such is not the case. Even amongst the latter, one may assume a radical difference between such an awareness with respect to one's own self and every other thing in the world which may possibly be brought nearer to its idea through effort on one's part.

The paradox with respect to one's own self lies in the awareness that though ontologically one is what one ought to be—and it cannot be otherwise—one does not feel it to be so. Kant faces this dilemma in the dichotomy between the Holy Will which ought to *be* and the Moral Will which is determined by the sense of Duty, and where the Holy Will is actually supposed to be in its ontological reality. Yet, if the sense of Duty arises from the contrary pull of desires and inclinations, and if the latter are the necessary material for the will to exercise its function upon, then how can the idea of the Holy Will be tenable in principle? The alleged unity between the theoretical and the practical reason in Kant raises a similar problem, though in a different context. For Kant there is a deep dichotomy between knowledge and action, and the transcendental presuppositions, which each one of them has, are radically different from each other. Also, for Kant, the ontological freedom which action presupposes is *only* in the context of moral action which is the same as the doing of an action from the sense of duty, which itself makes sense only because of the existence of desires and inclinations on the part of the person concerned. On the other hand, the freedom which the Indian talks about is not so much the freedom involved in moral action as that of enjoying a state of being or rather of just being or being as such. *Mokṣa*, therefore, in the perspective of Indian philosophy, is more talked about in the context of knowledge of what truth is, and knowledge in this case being of the self ensures or rather coincides with its own reality, that is, the real nature of the self.

Mokṣa then is not *dharma*, that is, it does not belong to the domain of moral action even though the latter may prepare the ground for the true knowledge of the self to arise and thus, in a sense, to also bring it into being. The central problem for the Indian philosophical reflection, therefore, has been that of error and not of evil as has been the case in the western tradition. And, depending on the way one conceives the true nature of the self to be, one also conceives of what the realization of *mokṣa* would consist of. But the acceptance of such an ideal would not necessarily make Indian philosophy spiritual, just as the acceptance of any other ideal, even with respect to the self, would not make any philosophy spiritual or non-spiritual.

A philosophy is usually characterized as 'spiritual' or 'non-spiritual' because of the way it conceives of the nature of 'reality' and not because of the manner in which it conceives of the ultimate or highest ideal for man. It is its answer to the question about the reality of matter that determines whether a philosophy is to be considered as 'spiritual' or not, and not its answer to the question about the supreme end which human beings ought to pursue.

Thus a philosophy would not be entitled to be called 'spiritual' if it posits as the highest or ultimate goal for man the freeing of himself or itself from the bondage of matter, or the involvement in the embodied state and all the attendant problems that it involves. Rather, it would be worthy of that characterization if, and only if, it denies the reality of matter, and argues for the ultimate reality of only consciousness, or that which is more akin or analogous to consciousness in our experience than to what we call matter. Judged in this perspective, the 'theistic-atheistic controversy' regarding the predominant characterization of the Indian philosophical tradition in terms of one or the other is irrelevant to the issue of its characterization as 'spiritual' or otherwise. Potter is right in pointing out that one's view about the predominance of 'theism' or 'atheism' in India would depend upon the date one chooses for the characterization. If, for example, one chooses the second century A.D., one would discover that 'the major systems extant at that time—Sāṁkhya, Mīmāṁsā, Nyāya and Vaiśeṣika, Jainism, the several schools of Buddhism, and Cārvāka—are none of them theistic'. But 'if one slices instead at, say, the fourteenth century A.D. one finds that Nyāya-Vaiśeṣika has become pronouncedly theistic, that Buddhism and Cārvāka have disappeared, and that several varieties of theistic Vedānta have come to prominence'.[4] Yet, however true, this cannot help Potter in establishing the 'spiritual' character of the Indian philosophical tradition. In order to do that, he should have tried to show that there was an increasing denial of the independent reality of matter on the part of a large number of philosophers in India. But this would have been difficult to establish as, except for Vijñānavāda Buddhism hardly any school of Indian philosophy has denied the independent reality of matter in the ontological sense. Most Indian philosophers have been pluralists in their ontology, and those who have opted for an uncompromising monism, like the Advaita Vedāntins, have also generally opted for the position that the ultimate reality cannot be described with any differentiating characterizations, even though it may be pragmatically more convenient and intellectually more adequate to understand it at the phenomenal level as more analogous to the nature of consciousness that we know of, than in terms of that which is experienced by us as its opposite, that is, matter. From the strictly Advaitic point of view, the characterization of ultimate reality as 'that which is material' is as incorrect as 'that which is conscious, or that which has the nature of consciousness'.

The issue would perhaps be clarified a little more if we raise it in the context of the western philosophical tradition. Would the acceptance of God by a philosopher in his system make us characterize his philosophy as 'spiritual' in nature? In case Potter's answer to this question were to be in the affirmative, he would be hard put to find a philosopher in the entire history of the western philosophical tradition who has not accepted God in some form or other. There are, of course, a few exceptions and their names are known to everybody, but if one were to count heads on this score there is little doubt that the Indian philosophical tradition would be found to be far less 'spiritual' than the western in this respect. In fact, if one were to make comparative study of the role that God plays in the two philosophical traditions, one would find that this role in the Indian intellectual traditions in the field of philosophy is far more marginal than in their western counterparts.

Yet, even though most persons in the field of comparative philosophy have known these facts, few have raised these questions with respect to the western philosophical tradition. In fact, it is strange to find that issues and questions which have been so persistently raised with respect to the Indian philosophical tradition have never been so raised with respect to the philosophical tradition in the west. 'Is western philosophy essentially spiritual?' or 'is it essentially concerned with man's liberation?' are questions which have never bothered the students or historians of western philosophy. This is not the occasion to go into the historical reasons which were responsible for the obsessive concern with these issues in the context of Indian philosophy. But it would be strange if we do not note the complete blindness of scholars who have taken part in the debate towards the existence of those very features in the western philosophical tradition on the basis of which they distinctively characterize the Indian philosophical tradition one way or another.[5]

At the ontological level, then, the characterization of any philosophical tradition as distinctively 'spiritual' would lie not in its acceptance or denial of God or of its acceptance of the independent reality of 'consciousness' but in its denial of the independent reality of what is usually understood by the term 'matter' in common parlance. Judged on this basis, it would be difficult for Potter or for anybody else to characterize Indian philosophy as 'spiritual' at any period in its more than two milennia long history of growth and development.

But philosophy, as everyone knows, is not just asserting an ontological or epistemological proposition, but rather giving reasons for it *and* countering possible objections that may be raised against it. This is what philosophical activity consists in—argument and counter-argument, *pakṣa* and *pratipakṣa*—and this is what philosophers in India did all the time. The very format of philosophical writing demanded that one present the counter-position, the *pūrva-pakṣa* first and, only after refuting it, establish one's position. Many of the positions are now known only through the statement of these counter-positions as the texts in which they had been argued have been lost. Also, the greater the philosopher, the more powerful his statement of the *pūrva-pakṣa*, the ideal always being that even the proponent of the counter-position could not have presented it better. Potter knows this, as does everyone else. And yet he alleges that "it is not clear to what extent Daya is offering persuasive definitions in the language of factual claims."[6] According to him, "the crux of the problem Daya raises is: should we use the word 'philosophy' in some appropriate way *drawn from contemporary western* practices or should we redefine it to fit a concept employed within Indian philosophy itself?"[7] (italics mine). But there is no need to go to contemporary or even older western sources to find what philosophy is when the Indian tradition itself spells it out so explicitly. Each *śāstra* or field of knowledge has to have its *uddeśa*, *lakṣaṇa* and *parīkṣā*; and *parīkṣā* presupposes *vimarśa* or *saṁśaya*, that is, doubt. Doubt or *saṁśaya* arises because there is *vipratipatti*, i.e., two opposite positions seem to be supported by equally weighty arguments. It is true that "the word 'philosophy' is not a Sanskrit word"[8], but there is no reason to suppose there is no Sanskrit analogue to it in the Indian tradition. Surely, the term *āvīkṣikī* comes as close to it as one may want it to be. Also, one should not forget that the traditional Greek meaning of the term 'philosophy' related it more to wisdom than to what it has gradually come to mean in its usage in the western tradition.

Potter tries to take help from the theory of *puruṣārthas* to support his contention that philosophy in India is centrally and inalienably related to *mokṣa*. He writes: 'There *is* in India a traditional distinction among fields of knowledge, according to which treatises devoted to such fields may be divided according as they fall into *arthaśāstra*, *kāmaśāstra*, *dharmaśāstra* or *mokṣaśāstra*'.[9] He goes on to argue that

> the logic of the four aims of life is such that one who transcends the first two by coming to view life in terms of *dharma* does not thereby leave behind the points of view (subject-matter, methodology) of the first two but rather combines them into a new and more adequate overview of life. The same thing, in turn, is said to happen when one advances towards *mokṣa* or liberation. Since in this way the point of view of liberation not only constitutes the highest value and the ultimate

goal, but also represents the most adequate understanding of anything worth understanding, it is evident why treatises on all sorts of subjects were introduced in such a fashion as to suggest that the work would present its subject under the aspect of liberation.[10]

It is surprising to find a scholar as eminent as Potter succumbing to the rhetoric of *puruṣārthas* and not be able to see through it. First, how are the so-called *arthaśāstras* and *kāmaśāstras* related to *artha* and *kāma* of the Indian tradition? The former relate to the science of politics and the latter to the science of sex. *Artha* and *kāma* as *puruṣārthas*, on the other hand, are not supposed to be confined just to these. Where then are those *śāstras* which are concerned with these as *puruṣārthas*, unless every treatise which is not concerned with *dharma* or *mokṣa* is treated as being concerned with either *artha* or *kāma* by definition? Further, as is well known, only three *puruṣārthas* were accepted in the beginning and the fourth *puruṣārtha*, that is, *mokṣa* came to be added only later under the influence of the *śramaṇa* tradition.[11] Also, there was always a tension between *dharma* and *mokṣa*, as the latter denied all significant relationship with others, a relationship without which *dharma* would cease to have any function or meaning. The heart of *dharma* was obligation to others, while *mokṣa* was always treated as the transcendence of all obligations whatsoever. The realm of *dharma* was the realm of *dvandva* (duality), while the realm of *mokṣa* was *dvandvātīta* (beyond all duality).

This is not the occasion to go into a detailed exegesis of the *puruṣārthas* and their interrelationship, but it should be obvious that while there may be some justification for integrating *dharma* with *artha* and *kāma* and suggesting that 'a new and more adequate overview of life' is reached with it, there is little justification for doing the same with *mokṣa*. The term 'liberation' as a translation of *mokṣa* is systematically misleading as it suggests the essentially this-world-centred western secular ethos of the term. *Mokṣa*, in most Indian systems, is either a *denial* or a *transcendence* of the world. It is linked with the fourth *āśrama*, that is, *sannyāsa* in which one is supposed to be *ritually* dead to the obligations of society, i.e., the world. Hence it would not be correct to say, as Potter does, that it is only in the perspective of *mokṣa* that 'the most adequate understanding of anything worth understanding' can occur. What is understood is that nothing else was worth understanding, and that one was under a basic illusion when one thought they were worth understanding. In fact, the pursuit of *mokṣa* as a *puruṣārtha* or even its awareness as such makes one realize the hollowness and fruitlessness of the enterprise of understanding.[12] *Jñāna* certainly has always been regarded as one of the paths to *mokṣa*, but then *jñāna* is not knowledge in the usual sense of the word. Rather, it is a denial of the possibility of that knowledge, and its relegation to the realm of ignorance or *avidyā* as it is founded on the distinction between self and object and the acceptance of *bheda* or difference as real. It may be urged that this is to accept the *advaitic* position as paradigmatic for the understanding of the notion of *jñāna* in the Indian tradition. But even when the ontological position is held differently, as in other schools of Indian philosophy, the situation in respect to secular knowledge is no different. In the state of *kaivalya* in Sāṁkhya, for example, it is difficult to see how after the de-identification with *buddhi*, any knowledge can remain there at all. The whole enterprise of knowledge even in Sāṁkhya occurs within the ambit of, and is made possible by, the identification of *puruṣa* with *prakṛti* which is the root cause of both ignorance and bondage in this system. Similarly in Nyāya-Vaiśeṣika, the soul in the state of *mokṣa* is not supposed to be conscious at all, and thus the question of its providing 'a new and more adequate overview' to what had been known earlier cannot even arise. As for the Buddhists, everything is *vikalpa*, a conceptual construction whose constructional character comes to be known in *nirvāṇa* and hence given up. Or rather it falls of itself when the nature of truth comes to be known; for 'giving up' would imply an act of will or choice which is perhaps not possible at this stage. The Jainas, of course, ascribe omniscience to their realized souls, but it seems difficult to settle whether this means adding *syāt* to all knowledge, or leaving it behind, as it was a sign of finitude and ignorance.

Thus, Potter's attempt to see a continuity between the *puruṣārthas* and their final fulfilment in *mokṣa*, however interesting and laudable in itself, is hardly sustained by the way *mokṣa* is conceived of in most systems of Indian philosophy. One would have to radically reinterpret the notion of *mokṣa* to make it perform the function which Potter wants it to do in his way of looking at the whole thing.

Similar is the problem with his attempt to see philosophy as "a moment in every inquiry, rather than a distinct kind of inquiry" itself.[13] Now, if philosophy is to be a moment in every inquiry, one should know what philosophy is and what role that philosophical moment plays in different enquiries. Unfortunately, it does not seem that Potter is clear about the issues involved in his formulation. He writes, for example: ". . .the interrelated totality of the various sciences should ultimately issue in a systematic account reflecting the various discoveries of specific sciences conditioned and synthesized through philosophical criticism."[14] But this is to assume that the specific science should have completed their task before the philosophical activity can perform its function—an assumption that would render philosophical activity impossible as it is difficult to understand how the various sciences could have completed their task at any point in historical time. There is not, and cannot be, a fixed list of sciences as Potter assumes. New sciences continuously come into being and disturb whatever 'interrelated totality' might have been achieved. But the deeper problem is with this 'interrelated totality' itself and the so-called 'philosophical criticism' through which it is 'synthesized'. Why should 'philosophical criticism' be considered necessary for achieving this 'interrelated totality' of the discoveries of the various sciences? Why cannot science itself perform this function? And what is this moment of 'philosophical criticism' over and above the critical function which all scientists exercise with respect to each other's work? If 'there is no special method of philosophy distinct from the method or methods utilized in the several kinds of enquiry', and if one should view 'the various sciences as specialized facets of the general pursuit of philosophy', as Potter contends, then why use the term 'philosophy' at all, for it has nothing distinctive to convey from that which is already conveyed by 'science'? Further, if this is what Potter wanted to say, then it was misleading of him to talk of philosophy being 'a moment in every inquiry'; for it is not just a *moment* in every inquiry but rather the whole of the inquiry itself. To see philosophy as identical with the whole cognitive enterprise of man is to do justice neither to philosophy, nor to the cognitive enterprise, or even to illumine anything in this regard. But Potter seems dissatisfied even with this limited identification, and wants to go beyond it and identify philosophy with all other enterprises of man as well.

That there are non-cognitive quests seems to be accepted by Potter, at least by implication. Whether these are to be considered as philosophical or not remains unclear in his formulation. Are they to be regarded as 'philosophical' because there is an essential intellectual moment in them or because 'philosophy' itself need not be essentially cognitive or intellectual in character? The distinction is important, as the quest for liberation, i.e., *mokṣa*, seems to be regarded as philosophical on both grounds. He writes: "thus the quest for liberation involves an intellectual component, though doubtless it is not exhausted in intellectual inquiry."[15] And that "if the quest for liberation involves intellectual as well as non-intellectual moments, and if liberation represents among other things an ideal state of cognitive attainment towards which all branches of inquiry ultimately aim, then the contrast between what he [Daya] thinks of as philosophy and what he takes to be the non-rational pursuit of liberation collapses."[16] Now, an 'intellectual moment' cannot make a non-cognitive quest cognitive. And what are the 'other things' which liberation also is supposed to represent? And does *mokṣa* represent 'an ideal state of cognitive attainment' in the usual sense which is attached to the word 'cognitive'?

These questions have to be posed and answered in as clear and straightforward a manner as possible, for Potter's formulation seems to thrive on systematic ambiguities in the terms that he chooses to employ. When he writes that 'the search for liberation is a search for an ultimate understanding of the truth', the reader forgets that the use of the terms 'understanding' and 'truth' have little in common with the way they are used not only in common parlance, but also in a scientific context. In most schools of Indian philosophy, the state of *mokṣa* is conceived of in such a way that either there is no object left to be known, or if any object is allowed at all, no relationship with it of any kind, whether cognitive or otherwise, is permitted. In Advaita Vedānta , the very awareness of something as an object is a sign that one is still in ignorance and that *mokṣa* has not been achieved. In Sāmkhya, though the ontological reality of *prakṛti* is accepted, *puruṣa* in its state of *kaivalya* cannot be aware of it as it is dissociated from *buddhi* which alone permits *viveka*, that is, distinction between *prakṛti* and *puruṣa* .[17] As for Nyāya-Vaiśeṣika, the soul is supposed to be unconscious in its state of liberation, and hence the question of knowledge cannot even arise in that state. In *nirvāṇa*, according to the Buddhists, the flame is extinguished and what remains can hardly be regarded either as knowledge, or its fulfilment in the usual sense of these words. Jainism, of course, has the notion of a *sarvajña*, the all-knowing person, in the state of liberation and this may be said to fulfil Potter's understanding of what *mokṣa* means in the Indian tradition. But one swallow does not a summer make, and it would be strange if the Jain position in this regard is taken as representing the dominant Indian tradition in this respect.

These facts are well known and it is difficult to believe that Potter is unaware of them. In fact, the way he himself articulates the so-called 'intellectual moment' in the pursuit of *mokṣa* should make clear not only its accidental and adventitious character, but also that it cannot survive in any significant sense in the state of *mokṣa* when achieved. According to him, "this intellectual component can in the case of Indian philosophy be best understood as the effort to remove doubts and fears which, deriving from sceptical and fatalistic views, threaten to render a person incapable of undertaking the quest."[18] But what if one has no such doubts and fears? Would one still need philosophy for undertaking the quest? On all ordinary understanding of the sentence just quoted, the answer would be a definitive 'No'. In fact, it is not even clear how Potter would characterize the so-called sceptical and fatalistic views which generate doubts and fears which 'render a person incapable of undertaking the quest.' Would he regard them as a part of philosophy or not? Or, in his view, there can be no sceptical or fatalistic philosophies, but only those which are the opposite of these and arise only in the context of their refutation. Furthermore, would he distinguish between 'doubts and fears' which arise from 'sceptical and fatalistic views' and those which have no relation to them? And if so, would he hold that it is only the former sort of 'doubts and fears' which 'render a person incapable of undertaking the quest' for *mokṣa*? And should not one distinguish between 'doubts' and 'fears' in this connection? The notion of 'doubt' generated by *purely* intellectual considerations is well known to philosophers, but one can hardly say the same thing about 'fear'. The deeper problem, however, concerns the issue whether 'doubts and fears' raised by purely intellectual considerations can ever render a person incapable of undertaking a quest of any kind whatsoever. I had raised this issue in my earlier discussion of Potter's position, but for reasons best known to him he has chosen to remain silent on the subject. The evidence from the history of philosophy on this point is at least *prima facie* against Potter's contention. Not a single paradox from Zeno to Russell or later has ever stood in the way of man's quest, whether cognitive or practical. Also, there is a gratuitous assumption in Potter's thought that sceptical and fatalistic views cannot find new arguments to sustain themselves against their opponents. The history of philosophy in India and elsewhere shows the untenability of such an assumption. In fact, sceptical and fatalistic positions seem as perennial in philosophy as those that are supposed to be their opposites. The relation of theoretical positions to non-theoretical quests is not easy to determine, but it would be gratuitous to assume, as Potter does, that the latter need always be obstructed by the former. In fact, Potter's own formulation seems to confine the presumed relationship between 'the sceptical and fatalistic views' and the inability to undertake 'the quest' for *mokṣa* to Indian philosophy only. But it is not quite clear why the 'doubts and fears', 'deriving from sceptical and fatalistic views', should render only an Indian 'incapable of undertaking the quest'. In case the relationship holds, all men should suffer from it and not Indians alone. It would not do to say that as the Indians alone were concerned with *mokṣa* the restriction is confined to the Indian case only; for presumably the difficulties created by sceptical and fatalistic views affect all quests equally, and not just the quest for *mokṣa*. But if such were to be the case, it would apply to all philosophers, whether Indian or not, and thus be a characteristic of philosophy in general, and not just of Indian philosophy in particular.

Furthermore, there is the diversity of schools in Indian philosophy; and if each one of them is supposed to be integrally related to *mokṣa*, then either *mokṣa* itself would have to be conceived in a pluralistic manner or only *one* of them (no matter which) would be truly related to *mokṣa*, and the rest only spuriously. The Mīmāṁsā, for example, does not even ritually proclaim itself as concerned with *mokṣa*. Yet Potter does not see any difficulty in the situation; and though he quotes my statement that 'many schools of philosophy have literally nothing to do with *mokṣa*. Nyāya, Vaiśeṣika, and Mīmāṁsā would predominantly come within this group', he chooses to discuss only the first two and not the third.[19] The discussion even with respect to the first two is carried on in a manner that leaves much to be desired. Potter writes:

> The first part of Daya's argument must be met by showing what the path to liberation is according to Nyāya-Vaiśeṣika, and how theoretical speculation gets involved in the life of the freedom seeker. . . As for the charge that belief in *mokṣa* is a matter of lip service without sincere conviction, I think it will become apparent from the nature of the arguments used by Naiyāyikas . . . that liberation is always on their mind even if not uppermost in the question of the moment.[20]

Potter's discussion of the issue does not take into account the fact that there are serious doubts about the text of the *Nyāya-sūtras* in its present form. The most detailed discussion regarding this problem may be found in the *Introduction* by Debiprasad Chattopadhyaya to the volume on Nyāya published in the series 'Indian Philosophy in Its Sources.'[21] It is, of course, true that Potter could not have taken this into account as the second volume of the *Encyclopedia* was published long before the volume in which the *Introduction* by Debiprasad Chattopadhyaya appears. But it is inconceivable that the material to which Debiprasad Chattopadhyaya refers in his *Introduction* could have been unknown to Potter. In fact, Potter refers to H. P. Sastri's article 'An Examination of the *Nyāya-Sūtras*', which opens with the statement that "anyone who carefully reads the *Nyāya-Sūtras* will perceive that they are not the work of one man, of one age, of the professors of one science, or even of the professors of one system of religion."[22] But he has referred to the article as containing 'comments of interest concerning the author of the *Nyāya-Sūtras*' and not in connection with the author's remarkable contention regarding the contents of the *Sūtras* themselves.[23] This is surprising since the author does not accept the second *sūtra* on which Potter relies for his argument for the integral relation between Nyāya and *mokṣa*, as against my contention to the contrary. He writes: "What is not clear from Kaṇāda's account is how knowledge is related to this process (of liberation).

Gautama's *Nyāya-Sūtras* makes this more explicit. In his second *sūtra* he presents a fivefold chain of causal conditions leading to bondage."[24] But as H. P. Sastri pointed out: "The second *sūtra* contains topics which are not enumerated in the first . . ." and that "the only reasonable explanation of this double enumeration seems to be that some later writer has interpolated the second *sūtra* with a view to add philosophical sections to the work."[25]

There can be little doubt that the second *sūtra* is not just a repetition of the first but that it adds a totally different dimension to the so-called purpose of the *Nyāya-Sūtras*. The first *sūtra* lists the *distinctive* concern of the Nyāya which is supposed to deal with argument or reasoning. The second deals with what may be regarded as common to most of the philosophical and non-philosophical traditions in India after the Vedic times. Potter himself notes the similarity of the 'fivefold chain of causal conditions leading to bondage' mentioned in the second *sūtra* with the 'twelvefold chain of Buddhism' without seeing the devastating implications of what he is saying. He writes: "This is reminiscent of the twelvefold chain of Buddhism (*pratītyasamutpāda*) which leads from ignorance (*avidyā*) to rebirth and misery in a somewhat more complicated series."[26]

But if this is the *central philosophical issue*, what happens to the radical differences between the Nyāya and the Buddhist positions, and the great debate between the successive giants of the two schools, a debate which lasted for more than half a millennium and which has been so ably documented by D. N. Shastri in his *Critique of Indian Realism*?[27] Surely, the debate was not about the fact whether the so-called causal chain leading to bondage was five-fold or twelve-fold, or even about the nature of liberation and the means by which it could be attained. This is important, for anyone who seriously wishes to argue that Indian philosophy is integrally related to *mokṣa*, has to show that the differences between the so-called schools of Indian philosophy centre around their differing conceptions of *mokṣa*, or the way in which it can be realized, or regarding issues deriving from these. But, as far as I know, nothing of the kind has been attempted, let alone shown by anyone, including Potter. In fact, Potter accepts that the generalized method which all philosophical systems accept for the attainment of *mokṣa* is what in the Indian tradition has come to be known as Yoga. But if this is the situation, how can *differences* between philosophical schools be accounted for on this basis? Ultimately, it is the differences, or rather the arguments for the differences that define the separate identity of a school or system from others. One of the cardinal principles of philosophical exegesis in this connection is to try to interpret the texts in such a way as to preserve the differences in philosophical positions rather than blur them. The tension between the actual text and the ideal type philosophical position would, of course, always be there. But then the way out would be to distinguish between the actual philosophical position attributable to a thinker on the basis of an extant text and the alternative positions that could possibly be held logically on the issue concerned.[28]

Potter has tried to suggest that, at least in the case of Nyāya, a distinctive method for attaining *mokṣa* could perhaps be found. As he writes: "This true knowledge, Gautama explains, is to be achieved by the classical methods of concentration, meditation, and yoga, but he significantly adds that one may get it by discussion with others."[29] And he adds: "It is this latter means that the Nyāya system is especially concerned to expedite . . ."[30] The reference here obviously is to *sūtra* 47 of the 4th *adhyāya, āhṇika* 2 which prescribes *saha-saṁvādaḥ*, i.e., discussion for purposes of gaining *jñāna*, i.e., knowledge. Now, even if the term *jñāna* is taken to mean *mokṣa*, as some of the traditional commentators did, it is difficult to be clear about the relation between 'concentration, meditation, and yoga' mentioned in the forty-sixth *sūtra* and the discussion with learned people mentioned in the forty-seventh *sūtra*. Normally, the latter is needed only until the former processes of *sādhanā* have been firmly established, for they alone, when perfected, will lead to *samādhi*, i.e., *mokṣa*; in no case can the latter by itself lead to *mokṣa*. The sequence of the *sūtras*, on the other hand, leads one to think that the practice of yoga, etc., is only a preliminary exercise to *sahasaṁvādaḥ*, i.e., discussion with others without which the ultimate good cannot be realized. But 'discussion with others' may at best lead to *niḥśreyasa* as promised in the first *sūtra* and not to *apavarga* which is mentioned in the second *sūtra*. In fact, the attainment of the latter, i.e., *apavarga* would make *sahasaṁvādaḥ* impossible as in *sūtra* 45 it is clearly stated that in the state of liberation the body does not exist, and presumably there can be no discussion without the body. Rather the presence of the latter, i.e., 'discussion with others' may be taken as a sure sign that *apavarga* or liberation has not been achieved.

Potter's statement also gives the impression that, according to the Nyāya, 'discussion with others' is an alternative means to 'classical methods of concentration, meditation, and yoga', and that this is its distinctive contribution to the methodology of liberation in Indian philosophy. But it would be difficult for even a Naiyāyika to accept this interpretation, as 'discussion with others' may lead to clarity regarding what is to be realized, but not to the realization itself. Not only is it not a sufficient condition, but it may not even be regarded as a necessary condition, as few in the Indian tradition have maintained that without 'discussion with others' one could not realize *mokṣa*. In a sense 'discussion with others' will have a uniform role to play in all systems, as it is hoped by each system that 'discussion with others' would lead both to the acceptance of what is regarded as true by the system, and to clarity regarding the goal that it holds to be desirable above everything else. The fact that such a situation has never obtained does not trouble Potter any more than it did any of the Indian philosophers in the past, for the simple reason that as philosophers they were interested more in argumentation than in *mokṣa*. To the extent that they were interested in *mokṣa* as a *puruṣārtha*, they practiced the usual time-honoured yogic practices along with all the other non-yogic ones which had been handed down by tradition, and through the practice of which one hoped to reach whatever was designated as *mokṣa*. In fact, it would be difficult to correlate the difference in the practical pursuit of *mokṣa* on the part of a philosopher, in case he pursued any such thing at all, and the philosophical positions he held and the arguments he gave for holding them. The two had little to do with each other and formed almost autonomous realms where each could be pursued independently of the other.

There is another problem with respect to the use of two different terms—*niḥśreyasa* and *apavarga* in *sūtras* 1.1.1 and 1.1.2 of the *Nyāya-Sūtras*. Normally, both are taken by most translators to mean the same thing, i.e., *mokṣa*. But as D. P. Chattopadhyaya has argued, the two need not mean the same thing.[31] As he writes, there is 'the long drawn habit of the Indian thinkers to conceive "the highest good" in terms of "liberation" itself. *But the habit is unfounded* (italics mine).'[32] And Mrinalkanti Gangopadhyaya goes even further when he writes:

> And therein lies the most obvious objection against the explanation of Vātsyāyana—that he has taken the two words *niḥśreyasa* and *apavarga*—to be synonymous which is not a fact. The word *niḥśreyasa*—dissolved, as *niścitam śreyaḥ*—literally means 'definitely beneficial'; it does not necessarily stand for an extraordinary (*alaukika*) state like liberation only . . . In fact, as has been pointed out by the commentators, there are two kinds of *niḥśreyasa*—*dṛṣṭa* or ordinary, such as the obtainment of a garland and *adṛṣṭa* or extraordinary, such as the attainment of *svarga*. Thus, the word *niḥśreyasa* is wider in meaning than the word *apavarga*, the state of liberation being merely one of the kinds of *niḥśreyasa*.[33]

Gangopadhyaya goes on to argue further that 'in the first *sūtra* Gautam most probably is concerned with *dṛṣṭa niḥśreyasa* only and has got little to do with *adṛṣṭa niḥśreyasa*'.[34]

There is, of course, the added problem that the *Vaiśeṣika-Sūtras* in 1.1.2 talks also of *niḥśreyasa* in connection with a *dharma*, which is supposed to be the declared topic of the *sūtras*, as mentioned in *sūtra* 1.1.1. Of course, the second *sūtra* also talks of *abhyudaya* and seeks to define *dharma* mentioned in the first *sūtra* by the fact that it leads to the attainment of *abhyudaya* and *niḥśreyasa*. This is a very strange definition, as it is a definition not in terms of the distinguishing properties of the notion concerned, but in terms of the *consequences* it has for the person who pursues *dharma*. This is not the place to discuss the *Vaiśeṣika-Sūtras* in detail, but it may be pointed out that the definition of *abhyudaya*, which was immediately required by the second *sūtra*, is not given till 6.2.1., and even that hardly provides a definition of *abhyudaya*, as it is a purely negative definition in that it identifies *abhyudaya* with any and every *prayojana* that does not happen to be *dṛṣṭa*. *The sūtra* 10.20 again gives almost the same definition of *abhyudaya*. Besides the fact that it suffers from the same defects as the earlier definition, there is the added problem that it occurs almost at the end of the *Vaiśeṣika-Sūtras*, and thus seems to give it an importance over and above *niḥśreyasa*, giving an appearance of making it the central concern of the *sūtras*, which goes against the whole spirit of the traditional way in which they have been interpreted. Moreover, the definition of *niḥśreyasa* given in the fourth *sūtra* suffers from various difficulties.[35] First, the definition is once again given in terms of causes of which it is supposed to be the consequence. It is *tattvajñāna* that is supposed to result in *niḥśreyasa*. But that is an empty formula which would be accepted by everybody. The differences would arise concerning how the blanks are to be filled in; what is to count as *tattvajñāna*, and what as *niḥśreyasa*. Unless independent criteria are provided for both and their invariable concomitance established, the phrase *tattvajñānātn niḥśreyasam* would have little meaning. There is, of course, the added problem whether the two are *identical* as is presumably held in Advaita Vedānta or whether, as the *sūtra* seems to indicate, the latter is a *consequence* of the former. Further, there is the question as to how the word *jñāna* is to be understood in these contexts. At least in the context of the subsequent *sūtras* there can be little doubt that as far as the *Vaiśeṣika-Sūtras* are concerned, the term *jñāna* is not to be understood on the pattern of what it is supposed to mean in Advaita Vedānta. It is clearly stated in the *sūtra* that the *tattavajñāna* which the *Vaiśeṣika-Sūtras* are speaking of and which is supposed to lead to *niḥśreyasa* is the knowledge of *sādharmya* (similarity or resemblance) and *vaidharmya* (difference) between *padārthas* which themselves are extensionally defined as *dravya, guṇa, karma, sāmānya, viśeṣa*, and *samavāya*. Each of these is later, as is well known, defined extensionally also.

Besides the extensional and the causal characteristics of the definitions offered by the *Vaiśeṣika-Sūtras*, there is another peculiarity which seems to have escaped as much notice as the former by writers on the subject. The fourth *sūtra*, which purports to give the definition of *niḥśreyasa* which is supposed to tell at least partially about *dharma* as is clearly enunciated in *sūtra* 1.1.2 and whose exposition and analysis is the main task of the *Vaiśeṣika-Sūtras* as a whole as proclaimed in *sūtra* 1.1.1 itself, mentions the term *dharma* without clearly indicating the sense in which it is being used. All the six *padārthas* whose *sādharmya-vaidharmya* knowledge is supposed to lead to *tattvajñāna* which, in its turn, is supposed to result in *niḥśreyasa* are themselves supposed to have *sādharmya-vaidharma* determined by what the author of the *sūtras* designates as *dharma-viśeṣas* (1.1.4). But what are these *dharma-viśeṣas*? Surely, they cannot be the *padārthas* themselves, for the similarities and differences amongst the *padārthas* are themselves a creation of the *dharma-viśeṣas*. Nor can they be identified with the *dharma* of the *sūtra* 1.1.1, as it would give rise to the charge of circularity in the foundational definition lying at the very base of the *Vaiśeṣika-Sūtras*. *Dharma* in 1.1.2 is defined at least partly in terms of *niḥśreyasa* and *niḥśreyasa* is defined in 1.1.4. in terms of *dharma-viśeṣas*. It may be said that the difference between *dharma* and *dharma-viśeṣas* saves the situation; but how can we know the *dharma-viśeṣas* without knowing what *dharma* is? If the term *dharma* in the *sūtra* 1.1.4 is to be construed differently from that given in 1.1.1 as has to be done to avoid the charge of circularity, then the author of the *sūtras* would have to be held guilty of not only introducing a term which is deceptively similar to the one used in the *sūtra* 1.1.1 thus giving rise to unnecessary ambiguity in discourse, but also of introducing a *new* term without first defining it in the system. The latter is a serious defect in the *sūtra* style of writing in particular, and the situation becomes even more serious when the author seems, at least on a *prima facie* reading of the text, unaware of it.

However it be, it is fairly clear that the term *niḥśreyasa*, as used in the *Vaiśeṣika-Sūtras*, could hardly be taken in the sense of *apavarga* without not only completely forgetting the context of the *sūtra* 1.1.4, which defines the term *niḥśreyasa* for the system, but also the fact that the *Vaiśeṣika-Sūtras* themselves not only use the term *apavarga*, in a sense different from that of *mokṣa* in *sūtra* 2.2.25, but also give a definition of *mokṣa* in 5.2.18 which is different from that of *niḥśreyasa* given in 1.1.4. This, of course, assumes that *apavarga* is the same as *mokṣa*. In case this is not done, we would have the added problem of distinguishing between *apavarga* and *mokṣa*. All this accords well with the generally accepted position that the *Vaiśeṣika-Sūtras* are not only earlier than the *Nyāya-Sūtras*, but in their earliest form were also anti-Vedic in character. As Kuppuswamy Sastri observes:

> . . . the Nyāya ontology is built upon the atomic theory and pluralistic realism of the Vaiśeṣika. The Nyāya epistemology with its fourfold scheme of *pramāṇas* is distinctly pro-Vedic: and in this respect, it shows a sharp contrast with the Vaiśeṣika scheme of *pramāṇas* which consists of perception and inference and which betrays anti-Vedic leanings.[36] Also, it may not be unreasonable to conjecture that the *Rāvaṇa-bhāṣya* was perhaps dominated by atheistic and pro-Buddhistic proclivities, such as were quite in keeping with the text of the *Vaiśeṣika-Sūtras* and with the spirit of the tradition characterising the Vaiśeṣikas as *ardhavaināśikas* (seminihilists). . .[37]

All of the this, of course, belongs to the earliest period when the so-called systems were only in their formative stage. If we move on to the Gaṅgeśa and post-Gaṅgeśa period in the development of Nyāya, it would be a bold person indeed who would even look to the pursuit of *mokṣa* for their relationship. The period covers almost five hundred years, from the twelfth century to the seventeenth century, and has at least thirty-six known thinkers who are supposed to have actively contributed to the development and refinement of logical thought in India—a development that affected all branches of learning to such an extent that practically no study could lay claims to intellectuality without giving evidence that it had mastered the techniques and methodology of the Navya-Nyāya form of analysis.[38]

Of course, to most writers on Indian philosophy, including Karl H. Potter, these five hundred years are of little consequence. Not only these but all the rest of the facts mentioned earlier do not have sufficient weight to outweigh the self-proclaimed declaration of the purpose of the *sūtras* in the eyes of these writers. These very same people, however, do not show any hesitation in characterizing the whole of western philosophy in terms of its modern period, which, by common consent, is supposed to start with Descartes in the seventeenth century. Prejudices die hard, and the prejudices of scholars die harder still. But when the prejudices of a scholar govern the structure of an *Encyclopedia*, as it does in the case of Potter, it will only ensure that something achieves the status of certain knowledge when, at best, it is uncertain opinion based on arbitrary methods of interpretation which are applied only in the case of the Indian philosophical tradition and never to the one in the west.[39]

NOTES

1. 'Three Conceptions of Indian Philosophy', and 'Three Myths about Indian Philosophy', which are the first two chapters of this book.
2. *Philosophic Exchange*, Vol. i, No. 3 (Summer 1972), pp. 159–74. (*The Journal of the Centre for Philosophic Exchange* of the State University of New York, College of Arts and Science at Brockport, New York, USA).
3. Perhaps there is a radical asymmetry between the lack of any essential nature in all things and the lack of essential nature of self. The latter is far more difficult to envisage or realize than the former. It may be because of this that *nirvāṇa*

primarily means the realization of the 'no-self' nature of self rather than of the 'no-self' nature of objects. It remains a moot question whether the two 'no-selves' in Buddhism are necessarily seen as identical, as they are seen in the Advaitic realization.

4. Karl H. Potter, 'Indian Philosophy's Alleged Religious Orientation,' *Philosophic Exchange*, p. 102.
5. For a similar situation in the field of socio-cultural studies relating to India, see the author's review article 'Anthropology: The Bonded Science?' *New Quest*, May-June 1983.
6. Potter, p. 164.
7. *Ibid.*, p. 164.
8. *Ibid.*, p. 165.
9. *Ibid.*, p. 165.
10. *Ibid.*, p. 165.
11. The following two *ślokas* from the Mahābhārata amongst many others that could be quoted amply confirm this:

    (a) *Trivarga iti vikhyāto gaṇa eṣa svayaṁbhuvā /*
    caturtho mokṣa ityeva pṛthagarthaḥ pṛthaggaṇaḥ ||
    12.59.30.

    (b) *Mokṣasyāpi trivargo'nyaḥ proktaḥ sattvaṁ rajastamaḥ /*
    sthānaṁ vṛddhiḥ kṣyaścaiva trivargaścaiva daṇḍajaḥ ||
    12.59.31.
12. Potter has complained that 'Daya doesn't indicate which texts he has in mind as a basis' for this. Well, the following may perhaps suffice as a small sample to substantiate what is well known to most persons, at least in India. *Kaṭhopaniṣad* (1.2.9, 1.2.23, 2.6.10) and *Muṇḍakopaniṣad* (3.2.3) are some of the well known passages in this connection. The tradition is epitomized in the common Bengali saying *Biśvāse milāy kṛṣṇa tarke bahu dūr* (Only through Faith, one may find Krishna. Far, far is he from all argument and reasoning).
13. Potter, p. 166.
14. *Ibid.*, p. 166.
15. *Ibid.*, p. 166.
16. *Ibid.*, p. 167.
17. *Ibid.* See on this point my article 'Is Īśvarakṛṣṇa's Sāṁkhya-Kārikā Really Sāṁkhyan?' in this book.
18. Potter, p. 166.
19. Potter, *Encyclopedia of Indian Philosophies*, Vol. II, p. 19. With regard to *Mīmāṁsā*, he does accept that 'in ancient times Pūrvamīmāṁsā did not accept liberation as an end, preaching that the ultimate purpose in life was to attain heaven through performance of acts prescribed in Vedic injunctions and avoidance of those acts prescribed by the same sacred scriptures.' (p. 24). However, he does not see the implications of what he has accepted.
20. *Ibid.*, pp. 2–4.
21. *Nyāya-Sūtra* with Vātsyāyana's commentary. Complete English translation by Mrinal Kanti Gangopadhyaya, (Calcutta, 1982).
22. H.P. Sastri, *Journal of the Asiatic Society of Bengal*, 1905, reprinted in Debiprasad

Chattopadhyaya (ed.) *Studies in the History of Indian Philosophy*, Vol. II. (Calcutta, K.P. Bagchi & Co., 1978), p. 88.

23. Potter, *Encyclopedia of Indian Philosophies*, Vol. II, p. 694.
24. *Ibid.*, p. 32.
25. H.P. Sastri, p. 93.
26. Potter, *Encyclopedia*, Vol. II, p. 32.
27. D. N Shastri, *Critique of Indian Realism* (Agra: Agra University, 1964).
28. For some concrete explications of this exegetical principle see 'Is Īśvarakṛṣṇa's Sāṁkhya-Kārikā Really Sāṁkhyan?', 'Adhyāsa—A Non-Advaitic Beginning in Śaṁkara Vedānta' and 'Vedānta—Does It Really Mean Anything?' which are found elsewhere in this book.
29. Potter, *Encyclopedia*, Vol. II. p. 32.
30. *Ibid.*, p. 32.
31. *Nyāya: Gautama's Nyāya-Sūtra with Vātsyāyana's Commentary.*
32. *Ibid.*, p. lxii.
33. *Ibid.*, p. lxii. There are, in fact, many instances where it is clear that *niḥśreyasa* has not been used in the sense of *apavarga*. Besides the *śloka* from Mahābhārata 2.5.24 (critical edn.) which Mrinal Kanti Gangopadhyaya has quoted, there is for example the śloka 5.25.12 in the same text which says:

    mahadbalaṁ Dhāratrāṣṭrasya rājñaḥ,
    ko vai śakto hantumakṣīyamāṇaḥ //
    so'haṁ jaye caiva parājaye ca,
    niḥśreyasaṁ nādhigacchāmi kiñcit //

34. *Ibid.*, p. lxii-lxiv. See on this point the whole argument developed by the author from p. lxii to p. lxv.
35. Of course, the *sūtra* 1.1.4 as given in Śaṅkara Miśra's *Upaskāra* commentary is not found either in the *Sūtrapāṭha* on the basis of Candrānanda's *vṛtti*, published in Gaekwad Oriental Series (No. 136) edited by Muni Sri Jambūvijayajī, or in the *Sūtrapāṭha*, published from Mithilā Vidyāpiṭha, on the basis of a *vṛtti* which is earlier than that of Śaṁkara Miśra but presumably later than that of Candrānanda. But if the *sūtra* 1.1.4 as given in Śaṁkara Miśra's version is not accepted, then we would have the added problem of explaining how the *sūtrakāra* could have committed the procedural absurdity of proceeding with the *vyākhyā* without defining the terms *abhyudaya* and *niḥśreyasa* which were used in the *sūtra* 1.1.2.
36. Debiprasad Chattopadhyaya (ed.), *Studies in the History of Indian Philosophy*, Vol. II, (Calcutta, K.P. Bagchi & Co., 1978), p. 118 from S. Kuppuswami Sastri, *A Primer of Indian Logic* (Madras, 1951). This has been disputed by Sri Ananta Lal Thakur in his *Introduction to the Vaiśeṣika-Sūtra of Kaṇāda* with the commentary of Candrānanda critically edited by Muni Sri Jambūvijayajī, published by Baroda Oriental Institute, 1961, p. 3. He is also of the opinion that 'the word "dharma" in Vs. T.i. 182 means *padārthadharma*' (p. 3).
37. *Ibid.*, p. 119.
38. See M. Chakravarti, 'History of Navya-Nyāya in Bengal and Mithila' in Debiprasad Chattopadhyaya (ed.), *Studies in the History of Indian Philosophy*, Vol. II, pp. 146–82.

39. This may seem unfair to Potter as he *has* referred to positions contrary to those held by him on the subject. But the basic question is whether it was academically proper for him to give a whole perspective to the *Encyclopedia* through his 'Introduction' to the Second Volume when he has such a strong *partisan* position on the subject.

Part II

CHAPTER FOUR

The Vedic Corpus: Some Questions*

The Hard Core of the Vedas

The Vedas are supposed to be, by common consent, the oldest and the most authoritative fountainhead of almost all traditions in India. In fact, it is with respect to the express acknowledgement or denial of their authority that the various traditions tend to define themselves and be defined by others. Except for Buddhism, Jainism and certain forms of Tāntrism, even radical movements against Brahmanism tended to make themselves accepted by claiming derivation from the Vedas or at least by acknowledging their authority. The Vīra Śaiva movement in South India which began in the twelfth century AD is a classic example of this. So is perhaps the movement of Śaiva-Siddhānta which tries to articulate the classical Tamilian thought on philosophical issues, primarily of an ontological kind, without questioning the authority of the Vedas. Dayānandā Sarasvatī's repudiation of all later scriptures, and the response which his call for a return to the Vedas aroused at the end of the last century, is another testimony—if testimony is needed—to the same truth. But when one asks oneself the question as to what it is whose authority is being invoked or being denied, one does not find from the texts or the tradition any clear or definite answer. There is, of course, the famous statement, purporting to give a clear-cut answer to the question, that it is the *Mantras* the *Brāhmaṇas* which constitute the Vedas. But then, which are the *Mantras* and the

* Dr. Mukund Lath, Dr. R. C. Dwivedi, Dr. F. E. Krishna and Dr. R. N. Dandekar have helped in various ways in the completion of this article. It is no exaggeration to say that without their sustained help it would have been almost impossible to complete it.

Though all care has been taken to check the factual accuracy of the statements mede in this article, there may still be marginal inaccuracies at places. However, I do not think they will affect the main conclusion in any substantive manner.

Brāhmaṇas that form the body of the Vedas? Do the *Brāhmaṇas* include or exclude the *Āranyakas* and the Upaniṣads? In case they are taken to include the latter, the question would arise as to whether they include all of them or only some of them. It is difficult to accept—and nobody does—that the Upaniṣads, composed as late as the thirteenth or fourteenth century, are to be included in the Vedic corpus. But, on the other hand, if we include only those Upaniṣads which form an integral part of the *Saṁhitās*, the *Brāhmaṇas* or the *Āranyakas*, then we would have to exclude such well-known Upaniṣads from the Vedic corpus as the *Muṇḍaka*, the *Māṇḍūkya*, the *Praśna* and the *Śvetāśvatara* which are not supposed to form a part of any of them.

Perhaps, one way out of the dilemma might be to draw a date-line and say that Upaniṣads written after the date so chosen, will not be counted as part of the Vedic corpus. But not only would any date-line so chosen be arbitrary, it would also run into the difficulty that some great Ācārya or other has treated the left-out Upaniṣads as a part of *śruti*, that is, the Vedas, assuming the two to mean the same thing. The difficulty might be solved by treating all the Upaniṣads, referred to by any of the Ācāryas, as part of the Vedas, or to delink the notion of *śruti* from its close identification with the Vedas and treat it as including all texts which are regarded as having ultimate authority in the tradition that recognizes the Vedas as authority also. But the problem, then, would be how to distinguish between the so-called non-Vedic *śruti* from what the same tradition regards as *smṛti*, that is, texts of secondary authority. Perhaps, we could think in terms of a hierarchy of authority amongst the texts of the so-called orthodox or mainstream tradition in India with *Saṁhitās*, the *Brāhmaṇas*, the *Āranyakas*, and the Upaniṣads which are an integral part of the first three, at the top. The Upaniṣads, which are independent of these and have been referred to by the Ācāryas as authoritative, could then be treated as occupying the second place in the hierarchy of authority with the *Smṛti* texts occupying the third place.

The notion of a hierarchy of authoritative texts is well known both in legal and non-legal contexts. But if the above formulation were to be accepted, then one would also have to decide who is to be accepted as an Ācārya in the tradition and what is to count as a *Smṛti* text. In other words, what shall be the criteria for any text or person being designated as a *smṛti* or an Ācārya? The issue is important as it has to be decided whether the term Ācārya is to be confined only to the well-known Ācāryas of the Vedānta tradition or it can be considered to include other founders of famous *saṁpradāyas* also. The *saṁpradāyas* extend, as is well known, to all schools—Vedic or non-Vedic. The famous founders of the various Buddhist schools, for example, are all known as Ācāryas. Asaṅga, Vasubandhu, Nāgārjuna, Dignāga and Dharmakīrti are some of the well-known names in that tradition. The same situation obtains in Jainism also. But even if we count the non-Vedic Ācāryas out, we will have to settle the issue with respect to the non-Vedic Ācāryas of the tradition. The simple solution would, of course, be to accept only the so-called Vedāntic Ācāryas, and even amongst them only those who are usually recognized as such. This would leave, besides Gauḍapāda and Śaṁkara, only Yāmunācārya, Rāmānujācārya, Madhvācārya, Vallbhācārya and Nimbārkācārya. But even this extreme extensional restriction, imposed on the term Ācārya in this context, would not serve the purpose as neitherYāmunācārya, Rāmānujācārya, Vallabhācārya nor Nimbārkācārya has written separate, independent *Bhāṣyas* or commentaries on any of the Upaniṣads. Only Madhva has written independent commentaries of his own which happen to be on the same texts on which Śaṁkara is also supposed to have written his commentaries. There is some dispute amongst scholars regarding the attribution of Śaṁkara's commentaries to Śaṁkara himself. Paul Hacker and Sengaku Mayeda are supposed to have done the most careful work in this connection; but, as the same type of work has not even been attempted with respect to the work of the other Ācāryas in the Vedāntic tradition, there can hardly be any significant comparative judgement made about it.

One may argue that it was not necessary for the Ācāryas in the Vedāntic tradition to write independent commentaries on the Upaniṣads, as they had already written commentaries on the *Brahma-Sūtras* which was supposed to contain the quintessence of the Upaniṣads themselves. But if this were really the case, one would be hard put to explain why Śaṁkara or Madhva wrote *Bhāṣyas* on both the *Brahma-sūtras* and the Upaniṣads. On the other hand, it seems equally wrong to think that all the Vedāntic Ācāryas have written commentaries on the *Brahma-sūtras*, even if they have not done so on the Upaniṣads. If Dasgupta's list of the works of Yāmunācārya, given in the third volume of his *History of Indian Philosophy*, is taken to be authoritative, then it can safely be said that he has not written any independent, full-fledged *Bhāṣya* on the full text of the *Brahma-Sūtras*. The same will be true of Nimbārka if the list of his works, given in the *Encyclopedia of Indian Philosophies* (Vol. I, ed. Karl H. Potter), is taken as complete and authoritative.

It may be noted that even the general impression regarding the authoritative character of the so-called *Prasthānatrayī* for the Vedāntic Ācāryas is not sustained by the evidence, as many of them have not only not written any commentaries on the Upaniṣads or the *Brahma-Sūtras*, or even on the Gītā which forms the third text of the triad. Neither Nimbārka nor Vallabha, for example, has written commentaries on the Gītā. The latter has instead written on the *Bhāgavata*, while the former has not done even that. It is only Madhva who has written on the *Brahma-Sūtras*, the Upaniṣads, the Gītā and the *Bhāgavata*. Śaṁkara has commented only on the first three, Rāmānuja on the first and the third, Yāmunācārya only on the third, Vallabha on the first and the fourth Nimbārka on the first. One wonders how, in the light of this evidence, the myth of the *Prasthānatrayī* came to be accepted even by such scholars as Radhakrishnan, who himself wrote commentaries on the first three, falsely imagining that he was following in the footsteps of the great Ācāryas.

One may, of course, give up the criterion of independent commentary on the texts usually supposed to belong to the Vedic corpus, and be satisfied with what may be called authoritative references to them in the works written by the Ācāryas. However, as neither the question regarding the authenticity of the attribution of the various texts to the Ācāryas has been settled nor all the texts allegedly written by them have been published, it is not possible to adopt the alternative and reach any satisfactory conclusions on its basis. But even a cursory glance at the material, wherever available, suggests that no startling results may be expected from the procedure. The Vedic texts considered by Rāmānuja, for example, in his *Śrī Bhāṣya* on the *Brahma-Sūtras* relate mainly to such well-known Upaniṣads as the *Kaṭha*, the *Kauṣītaki*, the *Chāndogya*, the *Taittirīya*, the *Praśna*, the *Bṛhadāranyaka*, the *Muṇḍaka* and the *Śvetāśvatara*.[1]

The question as to whether the Upaniṣads form a part of the Vedic corpus or not has always been there. But even those who have not hesitated to give an affirmative answer to the question, have not generally accepted all the texts that have been known as the Upaniṣads in the tradition as part of the corpus. Nor have they ever been able to give any reason why only some of the Upaniṣads should be included in the corpus and the others excluded. The same has never been the situation with respect to the *Saṁhitās* and the *Brāhmaṇas*. As for the *Āraṇyakas*, nobody seems to have raised any questions about them. Those who have regarded the *Saṁhitās* and the *Brāhmaṇs* as alone forming the genuine Vedic corpus, have ignored both the *Āraṇayakas* and the Upaniṣads, and relegated them to a secondary place in the context of the acceptance of authority in the Vedic tradition of India. On the other hand, those who have opted for the inclusion of the *Āraṇyakas* and the Upaniṣads as essential parts of the Vedic corpus, have tended to emphasize the latter, and treated the former as providing a transition to the latter and thus a sort of no-man's land in which neither the votaries of *karma* in the technical Vedic sense nor those of *jñāna* found any interest whatsoever.

If we forget the *Āraṇyakas* and the Upaniṣads, what remains are the *Mantras* and the *Brāhmaṇas* making up the hard core of the Vedic corpus. And this is what tradition has consecrated as the Vedas. But what is this hard core about which there seems to be little dispute? Perhaps, one should distinguish between the two, and ask about the relative priority with respect to their claim to form the hard core of the Vedic corpus. Perhaps, most would opt for the priority of the *Mantras* over the *Brahmaṇas*, though it is by no means the case that the latter have no votaries of their own against the primacy of the *Mantras*. In fact, the dispute with respect to this issue, as we shall see later on, reaches down to the very heart of the dispute as to what is to be understood as the Vedas even in the tradition.

Sāmaveda: A Book of Melodies

But even supposing we accept, however provisionally, the primacy of the *Mantras* over the *Brāhmaṇas*, the question remains as to which *Mantras* are supposed to constitute the Vedas. The question may seem preposterous, unwarranted and even gratuitous, when everybody has assumed since time immemorial, that there are four Vedas known as *Ṛc, Sāman, Yajuṣ* and *Atharva*, and the *Mantras* contained in them give each its distinctive identity, status and flavour. But this is just not true. The *Sāmaveda*, for example, for the most part does not have any separate *Mantras* of its own, and yet is regarded as a separate, independent Veda in its own right. According to Jan Gonda, only 76 stanzas out of 1810 in the *Kauthuma Saṁhitā* are not found in the *Ṛgveda*.[2] Had he included the *Araṇya Kāṇḍa* which consists of 55 stanzas, the ratio of the non-*Ṛgvedic* part to the *Ṛgvedic* part would be about four per-cent. The *Jaiminīya Saṁhitā* of the *Sāmaveda*, on the other hand, seems to contain only 48 non-*Ṛgvedic* stanzas out of a total of 1678 stanzas as given in Dr Raghu Vira's edition of this work.[3] The ratio of non-*Ṛgvedic* part to the *Ṛgvedic* part in that case would be about three per-cent. One cannot certainly claim that it has the status of an independent text on the basis of only three or four per-cent new material in it. Or, if one wants to do so, one would have to take only this three or four per-cent as constituting the real independent *Sāmaveda* text, and not all that goes under that name and is usually included in it.

But even this three or four per-cent is not as innocent as it looks. First, many of these stanzas are found not only in other Saṁhitās but also in other works on ritual, as Gonda has remarked, even if they are not found in the extant *saṁhitās* of the *Ṛgveda*. Secondly, there is some evidence to suggest that traditionally all the *Mantras* of the *Sāmaveda* were supposed to have been taken from the *Ṛgveda*. The very title of the two parts of the *Sāmaveda—Pūrvārcika* and *Uttarārcika*—as Gonda has noted, suggests this. Gonda has translated these as 'collections of *ṛc* stanzas' and has said that "this name is most appropriate because, 76 excepted (a few of these occur in other *saṃhitās* or works on ritual), all these stanzas are taken from the Ṛgveda-Saṃhitā, mainly from the books VIII and IX of that corpus".[4] But even the so-called exceptions seem only apparent as Sāyaṇa, in his Preface to the *Ṛgvedabhāṣya*, has written that "the *Sāma* verses are all taken from the *Ṛgveda*",[5] and hence it may be taken as established that at least in his time there were no *Mantras* in the *Sāmaveda* which had not been taken from the *Ṛgveda*. The English translation of Sāyaṇa's original[6] is, of course, not as accurate as one would have wished, but the sense, on the whole, seems to remain the same. In fact, one may assume that had exceptions been known in Sāyaṇa's time, he would certainly have mentioned them. The very fact that he has not done so may be taken as fairly strong evidence in favour of the view that traditionally the *Sāmaveda* was not supposed to contain any *Mantras* which were not found in the *Ṛgveda*. The phrase *āśritatvād* may reasonably be taken to mean this.

But, ultimately, even this controversy regarding the fact as to whether there are any independent *Mantras* which belong to the *Sāmaveda* and the *Sāmaveda* alone is irrelevant for, as everyone knows, the *Sāmaveda* is not supposed to be concerned with the content of any *Mantra* or set of *Mantras*, but only with the way they should be sung. As Gonda has clearly stated: "Now, in both books the essential element is not the texts—the *Sāmavedins* are less interested in the meaning of the words than (*sic.* obviously Gonda meant to write 'or' not 'than') in prosodic correctness—but the melody."[7] And, as he adds: "*To teach the melodies is their very purpose*".[8] But if this is the central purpose of the *Sāmaveda*, then it is Veda in a sense which is very different from the sense in which the *Ṛgveda* is regarded as one. The *Mantras* occurring in the *Sāmaveda* could, then, only have an illustrative function, for a melody can be sung to different stanzas without losing its identity. On the other hand, as the same stanza can be sung to different melodies, the uniqueness of identity of the *Mantric* text ceases to be relevant in the musical context. In fact, most texts undergo an alteration because of the requirements of the song, a situation which obtains abundantly in the case of *Sāmaveda* also. Many of the differences between the *Ṛgvedic* verses and their *Sāmavedic* version is attributed to this fact. As Gonda has written: "Some of these Ṛgvedic verses appear with different readings which must be explained as due to alterations introduced when the words of the text were set to music."[9]

It may, of course, be said that, as the *Sāma* singing was an integral part of the Vedic *yajña*, both the *Mantra* and the melody were so integrally and intimately related that, at least in that context, one cannot think of the one without the other. The *Udgātar*, along with his assistants who were usually five in number, formed an integral part of the ceremony constituting the *Śrauta* rites which formed the Vedic sacrifice, and the *Udgātar* was the priest who chanted the hymns which are in the *Sāmaveda*. But if this is accepted, then it would mean that those hymns of the *Ṛgveda* which are not included in the *Sāmaveda* could not be sung to the *Sāma* melodies; or even if they could be so sung, they could not be used in the Vedic sacrifice just because they have not found their way into the collection that goes by the title of the *Sāmaveda* today. In case we accept this conclusion, we would be forced to divide the *Ṛgvedic Mantras* into those which could be used in the Vedic sacrifices, and those which could not. The former would be further divided into those which are sung to the *Sāma* melodies by the *Udgātar* and his associates, and those which are recited by the *Adhvaryu* and are found in the *Yajurveda*. The latter, that is, those which are found neither in the *Sāmaveda* nor in the *Yajurveda*, would be deemed to have no role to play in the *Śrauta* sacrifices, and thus would provide the hard core for that part of the *Ṛgveda* whose meaning has no relation to the sacrifice, and hence has to be understood as being essentially independent of it. This, as we shall see later, would affect the usual understanding of what the Vedas are in a fundamental way.

The *Sāmaveda*, then, cannot be considered a Veda, if by 'Veda' we mean a text with independent *Mantras* of its own. We may, of course, treat the three or four per-cent of the present texts which are not found in the *Ṛgveda* as forming the *Sāmaveda*. But as even these are important only for the melody to which they are supposed to be sung, it is that melody which would constitute the Veda. It should be remembered that even the *Mantras* from the *Ṛgveda* are subjected to relevant modifications, so that they may be suitably sung. The comprehensive term for all these modifications, required for a *Mantra* to be sung according to the *Sāma* pattern, is called *stobha*. As Gonda observes:

> *Stobha* is a comprehensive term for all modifications to which a *ṛc* is subjected when it is sung to a melody of the *Sāmaveda*, viz., modifications (e.g., lengthening) of syllables, repetitions, breaking up of words, insertions of apparently insignificant words or syllables such as *hoyi, hūva, hōi* (so-called 'chanted interjections,' *padastobha*, often briefly *stobha*)—which, admitting of a mystical interpretation, could serve esoteric purposes—and short inserted sentences (*vākyastobha*).[10]

But if even complete sentences could be inserted for melodic purposes, what happens to the sacrosanct character of the *Ṛgvedic Mantras* which were supposed to have been revealed, and were thus not amenable to any modification whatsoever? It may be said that, as the *Sāma* was also revealed, there is no harm in admitting one revelation as modified by another. But if revelation can be modified in such an arbitrary manner, it can hardly be considered a revelation, at least by those who are prepared to modify it. The result of these modifications was, as is well known, not marginal but substantive in character. As Gonda observes: "... it will on the other hand be clear that the luxuriant ornamentation of *sāman* chants affected by repetitions, insertions, ungrammatical mutilations, whatever their significance for the believers, etc., render them abnormal as pieces of literature."[11] It should be remembered that traditionally the *Sāmaveda* is supposed to have about a thousand *śākhās*, though only two of them are extant at present, the *Kauthuma* and the *Jaiminīya* or the *Talavakāra*. But this would imply that there were as many arbitrary modifications or *stobhas*, both *padastobha* and *vākyastobha*, as the *śākhās*, thus rendering the whole notion of Vedic revelation virtually meaningless. Not only this. As the same *Mantra* can be sung to different melodies, it is likely that different *śākhās* would sing the same text to different tunes, and that the modifications introduced might be due to this exigency than to any other. But this would result in there not being just one *sāmaveda*, but as many as there are *śākhās* with all their variations in melody and textual modifications.

In fact, as music was the central concern of the *Sāmaveda*, the actual text of the *Mantras* which were to be sung to those melodies seems to have become less and less important. There is some evidence to suggest that there was a school of *Sāma* which held that the real *Sāma* was independent of the *Mantra*, and in fact, had nothing to do with it. Dr Mukund Lath, the well known scholar on the history of music, has drawn attention to this in one of his recent articles entitled 'Ancient Indian Music and the Concept of Man.'[12] He writes:

> *Sāma* was a revealed form in its own right, just as the *ṛca-s*. Further, in many cases, *sāma* was valued for music alone. An example is that of the *anṛcasāma*. *Anṛcasāma* was a form of *Sāma* that had no *ṛk* base and was sung to meaningless syllables.[13]

The term *anṛca*, literally speaking, can only mean a melody which is not sung to a *Ṛc Mantra*. Dr Lath has, however, taken it to mean a melody which is sung to no text whatsoever. This is an aribitrary interpretation, the justification of which is supposed to lie in the *Jaiminīya Upaniṣad Brāhmaṇa* where, in the *Prathama Khaṇḍa* of the fourth *Anuvāka* of the first *Adhyāya*, it is said that *Sāmnānṛcena svargaṃ lokaṃ prayāteti*; and in the second *Khaṇḍa* of the sixth *Anuvāka* of the third *Adhyāya* it is said that *sa me'śarīreṇa sāmnā śarīrāṇyadhūnot.*[14] The identification of *Anṛca* with *Aśarīra*, though not entirely unjustified, rests on the assumption that *Ṛc* alone can be the body of the *Sāma*. But this obviously is a questionable assumption. For, if *Ṛc* is taken to mean the corpus of *Mantras* which are found in the *Ṛgveda* and if it is accepted that there is no substantive ground *at present* to think that the three or four per-cent of the *Mantras* in the *Sāmaveda* belong to the *Ṛgveda*, then these *Mantras* obviously form the non-*Ṛc* body for the *Sāma* melodies, according to the *Sāmaveda* itself. But the term *Ṛc* may be taken in a wider sense as referring not only to the *Mantras* which are actually found in the *Ṛgveda*, but to any *Mantra* or *Mantras* which display the basic characteristics found in them. But even if this extended sense of *Ṛc* is accepted, it would not necessarily lead to the interpretation which Dr Lath is giving it for the simple reason that any particular melody can be sung to different texts, *Ṛc* or non-*Ṛc*, unless it be established that the *Sāma* melodies can be sung *only* to texts which display the *Ṛc* characteristics. The identification, therefore, that Dr Lath wishes to establish between the *anṛca* and *aśarīra* cannot be established.

Besides this, there are other objections to Dr Lath's attempt to identify the two. First, he seems to assume that only meaningful words and/or sentences could be said to form the body or *śarīrā* of music. But there is no reason for this assumption. The term 'body' here merely means *āśraya* or base and that could be provided by anything, meaningful or meaningless. Secondly, the distinction between meaningful and meaningless is relative, and that which is meaningless in one context or at one time may become meaningful in other contexts or at other times. The so-called meaningless syllables to which *Sāma* came to be sung were later on invested with profound, mystical meanings. The word *Om* is the classical example of this. Thirdly, Dr Lath seems to have overlooked the fact that while the first story refers to

Devas, the second refers to men. Presumably, the *Devas*, usually translated as gods, did not have bodies—at least human bodies. There is, of course, the added question as to why the *Devas* desired heaven when, being *Devas*, they may be presumed to be already there. On the other hand, it may also be noted that in the second story the king did not want to go to heaven but only to meet his friend who had died.

However it may be, the stories do show a desire to assert the independence of the essential *Sāman* from its accidental involvement with the *Mantras* of the *Ṛgveda*. Not only this, there is a strange undercurrent of hostility to the *Ṛgveda* and a desire to show the superiority of the *Sāmaveda* over the *Ṛgveda*. The *Mantras* of the latter are compared to the body, while the *Sāman* is considered to be its soul. After the soul has left, the various parts of the body are supposed to be scattered all over, which are then collected by Prajāpati and given the form of the *Ṛksaṃhitā*. Surely, the denigration of the venerable revealed *Ṛgveda* could not have gone further.

The so-called essence of the *Sāmaveda*, that is, the melodies contained therein, are usually divided in a seemingly non-essential manner. The first division is made on the basis of the place where the melodies may be sung, that is, in a village or a forest. The second division is based on the basis of their use in the sacrifices or rituals of various types. The former are called the *Grāmageyagāna* and the *Āraṇyakagāna*, the latter the *Ūhagāna* and the *Ūhyagāna*. It it obvious that the two bases for division are based on different criteria. In fact, the latter are supposed to be an adaptation of the former for ritual or sacrificial purposes. As Gonda observes:

> The *Ūhagāna* containing the *sāmans* in their ritual order adapts (*ūh*) the melodies of the *Grāmageya* to the exigencies of the ritual praxis. The *Ūhyagāna*—the name is an abbreviation of *Ūharahasyagāna*, *rahasya* 'secret' being synonymous with *āraṇyaka*—has the same relation to *Āraṇyakagāna* with which it is affiliated.[15]

If this is accepted, then it would imply that *Sāmagāna* was used in two radically different contexts, one of pure singing and the other of rituals and sacrifices. The former was distinguished only by the place where one was supposed to sing them, the latter by the sort of sacrifice or ritual one was engaged in. But then not only would it have to be accepted that the context of the sacrifice is contingent for the *Sāmaveda*, but also that the so-called modifications in *Ṛc Mantras* are necessitated by two different kinds of exigencies—one, those arising from the fact of something being sung at a certain place, and the other from the fact of their being used in ritual or sacrifice. The necessity for modification imposed by the former may be regarded as far more intrinsic than those implied by the latter. But it is not quite clear why any modifications should be needed by the fact that something has to be sung in a village or a forest. Similarly, it is not clear why any sacrifice involving a *Ūhyagāna* should be performed in secrecy in a forest.

Also, Gonda's discussion seems to imply that the hard core of the *Sāmaveda* is the *Pūrvārcika*, even though chronologically it may be later, and the important distinction there is between the *Āraṇya Kāṇḍa* and the rest. The *Mantras* in the *Āraṇya Kāṇḍa* are supposed to be sung in a secluded place such as a forest, while the rest require no such secrecy, and may be sung in places where others are present, such as a village. The modifications involved in the *Ṛc Mantras* in these contexts is due to the exigency of singing, though it is not clear what difference, if any, should be made to the style of singing by the fact that it is sung in a forest or a village. The *Uttarārcika*, if Gonda's statement is to be believed, should be the same as the *Mantras* in the *Pūrvārcika*, except that they have added modifications required by their use in rituals and sacrifices. However, it is not clear why these modifications should be needed and whether they can be regarded as musical in nature.

Unfortunately, it is not true that the *Mantras* in the *Pūrvārcika* and the *Uttarārcika* are the same, as would have to be the case if Gonda's statement is correct. From a rough calculation of the *Varṇānukramasūcī* given in the *Sāmaveda Saṃhitā* published from Pardi under the editorship of Satvalekar, it would appear that only 267 of the *Mantras* are repeated at more than one place in the text. Out of these, as many as 259 from the *Pūrvārcika* including the *Āranya Kāṇḍa* and the *Mahānāmnyārcika* are repeated in the *Uttarārcika*, which is supposed to be concerned with rituals and sacrifices. But while this lends some credence to Gonda's claim, it should not be forgotten that the majority of the *Mantras* of the

Pūrvārcika, 391 to be exact, are not repeated in the *Uttarārcika*. The total number of *Mantras* in the *Uttarārcika* being 1225, even if we take out 259 which are mere repetitions from the *Pūrvārcika*, there remains a hardcore of 966 which belong to *Uttarārcika* and *Uttarārcika* alone. Surprisingly, there are repetitions—both full and partial—in the *Uttarārcika* itself. *Mantras* (Nos. 758 and 1331), for example, are repeated in full in those numbering 1264 and 1679 respectively. On the other hand, there are partial repetitions of *Mantras* 651, 1145, 1575, 1576, 1577 and 1578 in 763, 1465, 1703, 1704, 1694 and 1695 respectively.

Gonda is a careful scholar, and it is surprising to find him mistaken, particularly in the context of Vedic studies. What is, however, even more surprising is his explanation of *Ūhagāna* and *Ūhyagāna* as a *modification* of the *Sāmagānas* for ritual and sacrificial purposes. The use of the term 'modification' in this context can only be regarded as misleading in the extreme. Even a cursory look at the text of the *Ūha* and *Ūhyagāna* would show that what is happening is an incredible elaboration, complication and innovation which can hardly be described as modification by any stretch of imagination. The *Ūhyagāna*, for example, is supposed to start from *Mantra* 1160 of the *Uttarārcika*, yet it is preceded by thirty-three full pages of *Ūhyagāna* in the text. Similarly, *Ūhyagāna* is supposed to end with *Mantra* 1159 of the *Uttarārcika*, yet it continues on and on for almost eighteen pages of the text.[16]

The examples can be multiplied, but it is obvious that the situation that obtains in the case of the *Ūha* and *Ūhyagāna* can by no means be described as 'modification', as Gonda seeks to do. Not only this, even his equation between the *Āraṇya Kāṇḍa* and *Ūhyagāna* does not seem to be correct, as the number of *Mantras*, common to the *Āraṇya Kāṇḍa* and the *Uttarārcika* as a whole, hardly add up to ten out of fifty-five if the *Mahānāmnyārcika* is not included, and out of sixty-five if it is included. However, none of these eight *Mantras* of the *Āraṇya Kāṇḍa* repeated in the *Uttarārcika*, is recited in a place where it could be subjected to an *Ūhyagāna* treatment. In fact, the five *Mantras*, which are repeated in the section where they are subjected to *Ūhyagāna* treatment, are taken from those portions of the *Purvārcika* which occur earlier than the *Āraṇya Kāṇḍa*.[17] We may conclude, then, that the presumed relation between the *Āraṇya Kāṇḍa* and the *Ūhyagāna* does not exist.

The styles of singing that may be regarded as the hard core of the *Sāmaveda* need a description other than the one usually offered in terms of *Grāmageyagāna, Āraṇyagāna,* or even *Ūha* and *Ūhyagāna.* Basically, it is a question of the identification of melodies, musical patterns and their distinctive differences from one another. It is strange that it has been usually alleged that there was no written notation for writing music in India till recent times, when there must have been such a system since at least the time when the *Sāmagānas* were reduced to a written form. In fact, the relation of traditional *Sāma* singing to the development of musical tradition in India needs to be explored in greater depth than has been done till now.

The *Sāmaveda*, thus, can hardly be considered a Veda, as not only has it no independent text of its own, but is not even supposed to have one in the strict sense of the term. Once the concepts of *Anṛca* an *Aśarīri Sāma* are accepted, and the emphasis shifts from the text to the melody, the way is opened for the development of pure music for the sake of music. And once the emphasis turns to the music, there develop as many schools as there are styles of singing. The so-called one thousand *śākhās* of the *Sāmaveda* may perhaps be understood in some such way. They might have been like the musical *gharānās* of today—proliferating over centuries and developing and preserving their distinctive styles, and taking pride in them just as they do today.

Divisions of Yajurveda

The *Sāmaveda*, even in tradition, has not been given the same importance as the *Yajurveda*. The *Yajurveda*, in fact, is the heart of the *Yajña* as without it the *Yajña* cannot even be conceived. Sāyaṇa wrote his first *Bhāṣya* on the *Yajurveda* and not on the *Ṛgveda*. Presumably, there were great objections to this, as in his Preface to the *Ṛgvedabhāṣya* he tries to explain why he did this. And his explanation is none other than that of its prime importance for the performance of sacrifice which is the central concern of the Vedas. As he argues: ". . . still the *Yajurveda* is properly explained before it. Because the *Yajurveda* is most important for the sacrifice; and it is in order to perform the sacrifice that we must know the meaning of the Veda."[18] And later he says:

> . . . this being so, the body of the sacrifice is formed in the *Yajurveda*, the Veda of the *Adhvaryu* priest: the hymn and lesson required by the sacrifice as parts of it are filled up by the other two Vedas. Here then the *Yajurveda* is dominant, and it has been properly first explained.[19]

The *Yajurveda*, then, is the body of the sacrifice or rather its very being, if Sāyaṇa is to be believed. But which of the two *Yajurvedas* constitutes this body, for, as everybody knows, there are two *Yajurvedas* and not one, as is the case with the other Vedas. As both have been recognized from the very beginning as the Vedas, the sacrifices may, more properly, be said to have two bodies instead of one.

The *Śukla Yajurveda* and the *Kṛṣṇa Yajurveda* are two Vedas and not one. They are not two *śākhās* of the *Yajurveda*, and have never been treated as such. In fact, each one of them has *śākhās* of its own; and if such be the case, there can be no ground for regarding them as parts of a single Veda and not as two, separate, independent Vedas. But if this is accepted, then even on the traditional reckoning, there would have to be five Vedas and not four, as is usually believed. Usually, the distinction between the *Kṛṣṇa Yajurveda* and the *Śukla Yajurveda* is supposed to lie in the fact that while in the former the *Mantra* and the *Brāhmaṇa* portion is mixed, in the latter it is separated. But if this were the only difference, there would be a close relation between the *Mantra* and the *Brāhmaṇa* portion of the one with the *Mantra* and the *Brāhmaṇa* portion of the other. But this is not the case at all. If we take the *Taittirīya Saṁhitā* of the *Kṛṣṇa Yajurveda* as the point of reference, and compare it with the *Vājasaneyī Saṁhitā* of the *Śukla Yajurveda*, and the *Brāhmaṇa* parts of the former with the *Śatpatha Brāhmaṇa*, which is supposed to belong to the latter, we find that many of the *Mantras* or the *Brāhmaṇa* portions found in the former are not there in the latter. Out of a total of 651 *Mantra* and *Brāhmaṇa* texts of the *Taittirīya Saṁhitā*, only 392 are found in the *Vājasaneyī Saṁhitā* and the *Śatpatha Brāhmaṇa* together. If we delete the *Brāhmaṇa* part and consider only the *Mantras* which are common to the two, then their absolute number would obviously be less. The total number of Mantras in the *Vājasaneyī Saṁhitā* of the *Śukla Yajurveda* is supposed to be 3988, while the total number of *Kaṇḍikās* happens to be 1975. The total number of *Kaṇḍikās*, including the *Brāhmaṇa* portion in the *Taittirīya Saṁhitā* of the *Kṛṣṇa Yajurveda*, now happens to be only 651. The number of *Kaṇḍikās* consisting only of *Mantras*, therefore, is bound to be lower still. Hence there is little likelihood of any fit between the *Mantra* portions of the two *Yajurvedas*, the *Kṛṣṇa* and the *Śukla*. In fact, Keith in comparing the *Taittirīya Saṁhitā* of the *Kṛṣṇa Yajurveda* with the *Vājasaneyī Saṁhitā* and the *Śatapatha Brāhmaṇa* of the *Śukla Yajurveda* finds that only 392 *Kaṇḍikās* of the one are repeated in the other.[20] There is thus a substantive difference between the two *Yajurvedas*; and if one were to cut down the similarity between the *Brāhmaṇa* portions, the difference would look even larger. The prevailing idea, therefore, that the differences between the two amount *only* to the stylistic fact that while the *Mantra* and the *Brāhmaṇa* portions are amalgamated in one, they have been separated in the other, is incorrect. The differences go far deeper and warrant their being treated as separate Vedas.

The *Śukla Yajurveda*, in fact, comprises of many more *Mantras* than are found in the *Kṛṣṇa Yajurveda*. As Gonda observes: "The *mantras* proper, many of which in fact *ṛgvedic* verses, are more numerous and important than in the Black *Yajurveda*."[21] Not only this, "The text has . . . in course of time been much enlarged."[22] In fact, only one to eighteen chapters are supposed to belong to the original part of the *Vājasaneyī Saṁhitā* of the *Śukla Yajurveda* "as they are the only ones that coincide with the ancient parts of the Black *Yajurveda* and are alone in being commented upon in the corresponding first nine books of the *Śatapatha Brāhmaṇa*, no more than a few quotations from the following chapters being found in that voluminous work."[23] But if *twenty-two* chapters out of *forty* are latter additions to the *Saṁhitā* and if they have not even been commented on in the relevant *Brāhamaṇa* related to the text, then how can the *Vājasaneyī Saṁhitā* of the *Śukla Yajurveda* be regarded as authoritative at all? Also, there is supposed to be an "ancient part of the Black *Yajurveda* with which the first eighteen chapters of the *Vājasaneyī Saṁhitā* of the *Śukla Yajurveda* are supposed to coincide." But if that is so, then the hard core of the *Yajurveda* should be regarded as consisting of those texts which are common to the two. But if one looks closely at the list of the *Mantras* which are common to the *Vājasaneyī* and the *Taittirīya Saṁhitās* of the two *Yajurvedas* as given by Keith, one finds that while, by and large, Gonda's statement is correct, it is not as completely true as one would expect it to be from the way he has put it. For example, large parts of Chapters 24 and 25 of the *Vājasaneyī Saṁhitā* are found in Kāṇḍa Vth, *prapāṭhaka* 5, 6 and 7 Similarly, *Kāṇḍa* 7, *Prapāṭhaka* 1 reproduces *Mantra* from *adhyāya* 22 of the *Vājasaneyī Saṁhitā*. Elsewhere, we have *Mantras* from Chapters 33, 22, 19, 39, 38, 27, 29 and 23. In fact, more than sixty *Mantras* from the *Vājasaneyī Saṁhitā* are found in the *Taittirīya Saṁhitā*, according to the list given by Keith.[24]

The *Vājasaneyī Saṁhitā* of the *Sukla Yajurveda*, we are told, borrows at least half of its material from the *Ṛgveda*. According to Gonda: "Half of this *Saṁhitā* consists of verses, most of which (over 700) occur also in the *Ṛgveda*."[25] It is not clear from Gonda's statement whether these verses from the *Ṛgveda* are confined only to the first eighteen chapters of the *Vājasaneyī Saṁhitā* of the *Śuklayajurveda*, or are scattered all over the text. Furthermore it is not clear what Gonda means by a verse in this statement. In case he means a *Mantra*, then he seems to be definitely wrong, for the total number of *Mantras* in the *Vājasaneyī Saṁhitā* happens to be 3988, and 700 is certainly not half of that number. Perhaps, Gonda is referring to *Kaṇḍikās* and not *Mantras*, but even they are 1975, a number substantially higher than twice 700 which he ascribes to them.

The whole problem is further complicated by the fact that there is no single criterion for deciding what constitutes a *Mantra*. Prof. Dandekar has brought to my attention the fact that Sāyaṇa in his Preface to the *Ṛgvedabhāṣya*, has extensively considered this question and concluded 'It is a good definition to say that whatever the sacrificing priest calls a *Mantra* is such.'[26] But what if the *Yājñikas* differ? Sāyaṇa has not considered this possibility. On the other hand, *Āpastamba Śrautasūtra* first defines *Brāhmaṇa* as *Karmacodanā* (24.1.30-35) and *Mantra* as that which is not a *Brāhmaṇa*. But perhaps it is this discrepancy in the criteria used which explains why, even when the printed text is almost the same in two different editions of the *Kṛṣṇa Yajurveda*, the number of *Mantras* given by them differs—a fact which would otherwise be totally inexplicable. Take, for example, the number of *Mantras* contained in 1.1.4, 1.1.5 and 1.1.6 of the *Taittirīya Saṁhitā* of the *Kṛṣṇa Yajurveda* edited by Satvalekar, and the *Mūla Yajurveda Saṁhitā* edited by Maharishi Daivarāta. The former contains 19, 17 and 11 *Mantras* respectively, while the latter gives their numbers as 17, 18 and 12 respectively.[27] It is not as if the text is different in the two editions, but what is conceived of as a *Mantra* differs in the two cases. It is also not the case that the discrepancy is confined to these three *Kaṇḍikās* only. One finds it again in 1.1.10, 1.1.13, 1.6.21, 1.6.4, and so on. It may also be noted that there is no uniformity in the discrepancy. It is not as if one has always more or less *Mantras* than the other, or that the amount by which it is more or less is the same. In fact, Sāyaṇa in his commentary on the very first *Mantra* of the *Taittirīya Saṁhitā* of the *Kṛṣṇa Yajurveda*, wrote that there was a difference of opinion regarding whether it was to be construed as one *Mantra* or two *Mantras*.[28] He writes, अत्र केचित् युष्मच्छब्दावृत्त्या द्वे यजुषी आहुः। It is obvious from the wording that there are two opinions on the matter—some holding that because of the repetition of the word *Yuṣmad* twice, the text should be construed as containing *two Yajuṣ Mantras* instead of one, while others are of a contrary opinion. But it is equally obvious that whatever may be one's opinion on the matter, it is bound to be arbitrary in character and essentially undecidable in principle. The differences regarding the total number of *Mantras* in *Taittirīya Saṁhitā* 1.1.4, for example, do not arise because of the difference of opinion regarding *Yuṣmad* as it does not occur there at all. The first difference, for example, occurs in the treatment of दृँहस्व मा ह्वाः as a separate independent *Mantra* by Satvalekar, while Daivarāta treats it as a part of the previous *Mantra*. The second difference arises because Satvalekar treats वैश्वानर ज्योति as a separate *Mantra* while Daivarāta treats it as forming a part of the earlier *Mantra*. None of these distinctions rests upon the use of *Yuṣmad* about which Sāyaṇa had written in his commentary.*

* Incidentally, Sontakke and Dharmadhikari seem to regard दृँहस्व मा ह्वाः not as an independent *Mantra* but as forming a part of the *Mantra* starting from 'हविर्धानँ' and ending with 'विक्था' (see p. 69). Neither Sāyaṇa nor Bhaṭṭbhāskara seems to have anything to say about this in their commentary on this *Mantra*. The situation thus may be summarized in the following way:

According to Satvalekar, the *mantra* should read as:

1. दृँहस्व मा ह्वाः *Mantra* no. 93 (p. 2).

According to Sontakke and Dharmadhikari as:

2. हविर्धानँ दृँहस्व मा ह्वाः[5] मित्रस्य त्वा
चक्षुषा प्रेक्षे मा भेर्मा सं विक्था (p. 69).

Obviously, the situation is disquieting; but none of the eminent editors of the text seems to feel disconcerted by it as none of them has given any reason as to why *his* construal of the *Mantra* should be accepted rather than that of the others.

Besides this problem of what constitutes a *Mantra*, and that of the relationship between the *Kṛṣṇa Yajurveda* and the *Śukla Yajurveda*, there is the deeper problem of the so-called *Śākhās* of these *Saṁhitās*. After all, there is no such thing as *Kṛṣṇa Yajurveda.* There is either the *Taittirīya Saṁhitā*, the *Kāṭhaka Saṁhitā*, the *Kapiṣṭhala Saṁhitā* or the *Maitrāyaṇī Saṁhitā* and each has a distinctive status and character of its own which is different from the others. Keith has given a comparativc chart of the four *Saṁhitās* of the *Kṛṣṇa Yajurveda* in his well-known work on this Veda, taking the *Taittirīya Saṁhitā* as the standard base and comparing others in relation to it. The comparison reveals that out of a total of 651 *Kaṇḍikās* of the *Taittirīya Saṁhitā*, only 490 are found in the *Kāṭhaka Saṁhitā*, 417 in the *Maitrāyaṇī Saṁhitā* and 229 in the *Kapiṣṭhala Saṁhitā*, Thus the number of *Kaṇḍikās*, missing in the *Kāṭhaka* happens to be 161, while in the case of *Maitrāyaṇī* and *Kapiṣṭhala* it happens to be of the order of 234 and 422 respectively.

This is not a minor or negligible difference, and to treat it as such is to do violence to facts. If one looks at the matter closely, one finds that in the *Kapiṣṭhala Saṁhitā* the whole of the 6th and 7th *Prapāṭhakas* and large parts of the 8th *Prapāṭhaka* of the first *Kāṇḍa* are missing. As for *Kāṇḍa* 2, it is almost totally absent except for ii.5.4, ii.6.4, ii.6.5 and ii.6.6 In *Kāṇḍa* 3, the story repeats itself. Except for iii.1.8, iii.2.10, iii.5.7 and iii.5.8, we draw a completc blank. In *Kāṇḍa* 5, in *prapāṭhakas* IV, V, VI and VII, we again find very few occurrences, the total number coming to nine only. As for *Kāṇḍa* 7, it is almost totally absent from *Kapiṣṭhala Saṁhitā* except for one solitary piece mentioned in vii.2.7. Thus, if we take *Kāṇḍas* 2, 3, 5 and 7 we find that the total number of occurrences comes to about eighteen only.

However, it is not only that large parts of what is found in the

---

And according to Daivarāta as:

3. त्वं देवानामसि सस्नितमं पप्रितमं जुष्टतमं वह्नितमं

देववहूतममहतमसि हविर्धानं दृँहस्व मा ह्वाः[5] (p.4)

Taittirīya Saṁhitā is absent from the *Kapiṣṭhala Saṁhitā*, but also that what is found in the latter is absent in the former. If we take Keith's comparative chart as the basis and reverse the direction of comparison, we find that only twenty-six chapters out of forty-seven have any counterpart in the *Taittirīya Saṁhitā*. Even amongst the chapters that do have a counterpart in the *Taittirīya*, some are only nominally there. Chapter 4, for example, has only one part, that is Section 8, represented in the *Taittirīya*, and that, too, occurs only partially. Similarly, Chapters 34 and 47 have only Sections 1 and 2 respectively, represented in the *Taittirīya*. It is true that the manuscript of this Saṁhitās has been found only in a fragmentary form, but even in such a fragmented form it contains material that is not found in the *Taittirīya Saṁhitā*, and yet was treated as authoritative by the followers of the *Śākhā* as the followers of the *Taittirīya* did theirs.

The situation is no different with *Kāṭhaka Saṁhitā* of the *Kṛṣṇa Yajurveda*. The former does not merely have 161 *Kaṇḍikās* less than the *Taittirīya Saṁhitā* but also has at least three *Sthānakas*, that is, full chapters which are not found in the *Taittirīya Saṁhitā*. These are *Sthānakas* 36, 37 and 38. Even where a *Sthānaka* has a counterpart in the *Prapāṭhakas* of the *Taittirīya Saṃhitā* as *Sthānakas* 14 and 35, the number of *Anuvākas* which are found in the latter are very few. For example, only the first four *Anuvākas* of *Sthānaka* 14 find a place in the *Taittirīya*, when their total number in that *Sthānaka* happens to be ten. The situation is worse if we look at *Sthānaka* 35.[28] Out of it twenty *Anuvākas*, only two are found in the *Taittirīya*, that is, nos. 8 and 13. As for the *Maitrāyaṇī Saṁhitā*, it has not only 234 sections less than the *Taittirīya Saṁhitā*, but its whole fourth *Kāṇḍa* is supposed to be *Khila*, that is, an appendage or addition which is not supposed to be a regular part of the text. But if this is so, then those parts of the fourth *Kāṇḍa* of *Maitrāyaṇī Saṁhitā* which are found in the *Taittirīya Saṁhitā* should also be regarded as *Khila*. But the counterpart material of the fourth *Kāṇḍa* of the *Maitrāyaṇī Saṁhitā* is scattered over all the Kāṇḍas except the 5th and 7th of the *Taittirīya Saṁhitā*. This would make these portions *Khila* also, unless what is regarded as *Khila* in one *Saṁhitā* need not be regarded as *Khila* in another. But normally the *Taittirīya Saṁhitā* is not supposed to have any *Khila* portions in it—a situation that can be explained only on the latter hypothesis. But if it is seriously accepted, it would destroy the very idea of their being *one Kṛṣṇa Yajurveda* and the so-called other *Saṁhitās* being its *śākhās*.

Vedic Śākhās

The whole question of *śākhās* needs to be examined with greater care than seems to have been done until now. Normally, a *śākhā* implies something akin to what is meant by the term 'recension' with respect to a text. There is a large common core and marginal variations in different renderings of the same text. The term *śākhā*, however, has the added connotation of being a school which had branched off from a common source and developed differences because of that. But even though this is the usually accepted story, it does not square with the facts as they are even superficially known. If one asks, for example, which is the *Yajurveda* and what are its *śākhās*, there is no satisfactory answer. First, there is no such thing as the *Yajurveda*. We have either the *Kṛṣṇa Yajurveda* or the *Śukla Yajurveda*. These are not treated as *śākhās* of the *Yajurveda*, but if one were to do so one would have to point to some *Mūla Yajurveda* of which they were the *śākhās*. And there is no such *Yajurveda* extant at present. But do we, then, have a *Kṛṣṇa Yajurveda* or a *Śukla Yajurveda*? As far as I know, there is no such thing either. What we have is the *Taittirīya Saṁhitā* and the *Kāṭhaka Saṁhitā*, the *Kapiṣṭhala Saṁhitā*, and the *Maitrāyaṇī Saṁhitā*. These are all supposed to be *śākhās* of the *Kṛṣṇa Yajurveda*, but then where is the *Kṛṣṇa Yajurveda* of which these are the *śākhās*? Normally, the *Taittirīya Saṁhitā* is treated as being identical with the *Kṛṣṇa Yajurveda* proper, and the rest as its *śākhās*, but no justification seems to be given for it. In fact, if we look at the structure of these four *Saṁhitās* of the *Kṛṣṇa Yajurveda*, they show such variations that it is difficult to see how they could be regarded as *śākhās* of one and the same Veda. The *Taittirīya Saṁhitā* is divided into seven *Kāṇḍas*, each further divided into *Prapāṭhakas* which are then further divided into *Anuvākas* consisting of *Mantras* and *Brāhmaṇas*. The *Kāṭhaka Saṁhitā*, on the other hand, has no *Kāṇḍas* but only *Sthānakas* which happen to be forty in number. These are divided into *Anuvākas* which contain the *Mantras*. The *Kapiṣṭhala Saṁhitā*, which also is supposed to belong to the *Kāṭhakas*, consists of forty-seven chapters containing various sections. The *Maitrāyaṇī Saṁhitā*, on the other hand, consists of only four *Kāṇḍas* containing *Prapāṭhakas* which consist of *Anuvākas* containing *Mantras*.

It is not only that the structure of these texts is different, but also the sequence of the *Mantras* or even the *Anuvākas* is different in different *Saṁhitās*. Even a cursory look at the comparative chart given by Keith reveals this. To give but one example, while 1.6.6 is found in the 5th *Sthānaka* of the *Kāṭhaka Saṁhitā*, 1.6.7 is found in the 31st and 32nd *Sthānaka* of the *Kāṭhaka Saṁhitā*.[29] But if both the structure and the sequence are so different, how can they be regarded as variants of the same Veda? Gonda has admitted, "What is lacking is the original *Yajurveda Saṁhitā*."[30] Not only this, according to him, "the considerable difference between the *śākhās* extant does not even allow us to attempt its reconstruction, except for some sections, among which is that dealing with the horse sacrifice."[31] Gonda's own conclusion is: "So we are led to assume that, while part of these collections developed from one common source, they were after their separation, amplified according to a similar plan or similar principles."[32] But even if the plans or principles behind the amplifications were similar, the contents were not. And it is the difference in content that is crucial for determining whether they are to be regarded as different or just minor variations of a single text. Not only this, Gonda does not even see the significance of the whole activity of addition and amplification on the part of the *Ṛṣis* of a presumably common heritage which had been given to them as a common Vedic patrimony. Obviously, they would not have regarded it as *Apauruṣeya* or *revealed*, or viewed it in any such manner that it was only to be memorized and passed on and nothing altered or added to it.

In fact, the very large proliferation of the *śākhās*, at least as mentioned in the tradition, testifies to the fact that the *Ṛṣis* of those days treated their Vedic patrimony with a degree of freedom that seems sacrilegious when viewed in the perspective of attitudes with which the Vedas have been traditionally looked at for a long time. The *Yajurveda* itself is supposed to have 101 *śākhās*, the *Sāmaveda* 1000, the *Atharvaveda* 9 and *Ṛgveda* 21.[33] The works of most of these *śākhās* are not available today, but the very fact that such was the opinion prevalent in Patañjali's time is sufficient to prove that the Vedas were regarded in a totally different way in Vedic times. At what point and why the development of Vedic *śākhās* ended is an interesting historical question which needs to be investigated further. Perhaps, the interest shifted from the sacrificial ritual to the Upaniṣadic speculation which continued to be written till as late as the thirteenth century AD.

The problem of the *śākhās*, even in their extant versions, deserves more serious attention than has been given till now. Ultimately, it is the differences or the additions, deletions and modifications in the various *śākhās* that are distinctive of them, and these have to be emphasized and brought out in a distinctive manner. It should not be forgotten in this connection that even when there is a repetition of the text between one *Saṁhitā* and another, it is seldom complete or total. Also, normally it is embedded amongst other material which is absent in the text in terms of which the comparison is sought to be made. Keith's table comparing the contents of the *Taittirīya Saṁhitā* with the other texts of the *Yajurveda* is thus systematically misleading; it not only confuses between a *Kaṇḍikā* and *Mantra*, but also gives the impression that the whole of the *Kaṇḍikā* or the *Brāhmaṇa* text has a counterpart in the other texts when, in fact, it has only certain of its parts common with them. Furthermore, for a fuller comparison each of the texts should have been taken as the basis for comparison and not just the *Taittirīya Saṁhitā*, as only then could we have a complete, full-bodied picture of the situation.

The problem of the *śākhās* becomes further complicated by the fact that even the same *śākhā* has several subdivisions which have independent texts of their own. The *kāṭhakas*, for example, are supposed to be divided into twelve *śākhās* which in turn have their own subdivisions. In fact, the *Kapiṣṭhala* and the *Maitrāyaṇī* are both supposed to belong to the *Kāṭhaka* school. But then to which school does the *Kāṭhaka Saṁhitā* belong? And in case it is the original *Saṁhitā* of the *Kāṭhaka* school, then how is it that there are substantial differences, including structural ones, between it and the *Kapiṣṭhala* and the *Maitrāyaṇī Saṁhitās* which are also supposed to belong to the same school? Furthermore, what happens to the *Taittirīya* and to what school does it belong?

There seems little point in ignoring these questions or brushing them aside. In fact, the *Maitrāyaṇī Saṁhitā*, as already pointed out, raises the problem of the whole fourth *Kāṇḍa* which is supposed to be *Khila* in character. Also, the *Saṁhitā* has a total of 1701 *Mantras* taken from the *Ṛgveda* out of which 1062 belong to the forth *Kāṇḍa*. These are taken from all the *Maṇḍalas* of the *Ṛgveda* including the *Pariśiṣṭa* part.[34] But these are not the *Mantras* which are treated as *Khila* in the *Ṛgveda*, and if they are not so treated there, how can they be so treated here? Furthermore, the occurrence of such a large number of *Mantras* from the *Ṛgveda* raises problems of its own. As already discussed in the context of the *Sāmaveda*, it raises the basic question of the unique identity of a text being regarded as a separate Veda by itself.

Ṛg Vedic Repetitions

The problem of repetition, in fact, plagues the *Ṛgveda* itself. Even a cursory glance at Bloomfield's *Ṛgveda Repetitions*[35] would show the enormity and the extent of these repetitions, and the complex problems they pose for any serious student of the subject. It is not only that a very large number of *Mantras* from the *Ṛgveda* are repeated in the other Vedas, but that there are substantive repetitions in the *Ṛgveda* itself. *Ṛgveda Repetitions* is based on Bloomfield's earlier monumental work, *The Vedic Concordance*, published in 1906. As Bloomfield has said in the Introduction to *Ṛgveda Repetitions* the complete picture of Vedic repetitions would emerge only when the *Reverse Concordance* is completed. Unfortunately, no one seems to have completed Bloomfield's unfinished work in this area. Yet, even the *Ṛgveda Repetitions* throws light "on the way in which the poets of the Ṛgveda exercised their art . . . by studying the manner and extent to which *they borrowed from one another, imitated one another, and, as it were, stood upon the shoulders of one another*, (*italics mine*)."[36] But if this was the relation of one Vedic *Ṛṣi* to another, how can that relationship be understood either in terms of *apauruṣeyatva* or revelation, or even in terms of the usual notion of Vedic authority? The problem is even more complicated as the text of the *Ṛgveda* along with the *Saṁhitās* of the other Vedas include portions which are self-consciously proclaimed as *Khila*. Now, if people were prepared to add even to the *Ṛgvedic Mantras* and pass them off as originally belonging to the *Saṁhitā*, then where is that sacrosanct attitude to the Veda about which there is such incessant talk amongst the scholars of the tradition? In fact, there are supposed to be *Khilas* "which found entrance into the *Ṛgveda-Saṁhitā*."[37] According to Gonda: "they are real, though insignificant, Vedic hymns but are considered to be inferior and half-apocryphal."[38]

Gonda does not seem to realize the import of what he himself is saying, a situation not unusual in the field of Vedic scholarship. First, if the Vedas are to be regarded as Vedas, there cannot be a distinction of superior and inferior, or significant and insignificant between its different parts. Also, there can be no such thing as 'half-apocryphal'; either it is apocryphal or it is not. Gonda is misled into characterizing it as such, because the *Vālakhilyas*, unlike those which are just *Khilas*, 'found entrance into the *Ṛgveda-Saṁhitā*.'[39] But that *was* the intention of all the *Khila* compositions; only some succeeded while others failed. Yet, even those who failed found a permanent place in the *Pariśiṣṭa* section of the *Saṁhitā*.

It may be said that we are totally mistaken in our approach, as we are thinking of the Vedas as if they had some distinctive, specific content of their own. It is this presupposition that makes us wonder about the large-scale repetitions which are found in the texts, as they ought not to be construed as contents but rather as different aspects of the Vedic ritual in the context of which alone they have meaning. The *Yajuṣ* formulas, for example, are supposed to be spoken by the *Adhvaryu* at the sacrificial ritual while the *Udgātar* chants the hymns of the *Sāmaveda* to the melodies prescribed in them. The *Hotar*, on the other hand, was supposed to "recite definite consecratory texts (*yājyā*), and the *nividas*".[40] As "the latter represent the oldest prose preserved from the period of the Ṛgveda",[41] it may be taken that the *Hotar* represented the *Ṛgveda* at the Vedic *yajña* just as the *Adhvaryu* represented the *Yajurveda* and the *Udgātar*, the *Sāmaveda*. The *Atharvaveda*, even though having only "slight relation to *śrauta* rites"[42] seems to have got itself there in the role of a priest "who, briefly called the *brahman*, oversees, accompanies (*anumantraṇa*) and corrects by means of expiatory formulas (*prāyaścitta*) possible accidents and blunders of the officiants".[43]

The four-fold division of functions between the *Hotar*, the *Udgātar*, the *Adhvaryu* and the *Brahman* corresponds, we are told, to the four Vedas, and the unity of the sacrifice is the unity of the Vedas. But this idyllic picture hardly corresponds to the facts as attested to by the tradition itself. First, it is well known that the

Atharvaveda never enjoyed the same status as the other three Vedas in the tradition. As Gonda writes:

> Although the doctrine of the fourfold Veda . . . found acceptance, various later texts continued speaking of the Threefold Holy Knowledge. Even in modern times there have been brahmins who refused to recognise the authority of the promulgators of the fourth Veda, because of a certain prejudice prevailing against it. Even today brahmins of the other Vedas do not dine or marry with the atharvanic (*paippalādins*) of Orissa.[44]

The more important point, however, is that even the other two Vedas, that is, the *Sāmaveda* and the *Yajurveda* have borrowed their material from the *Ṛgveda* in such an overwhelming quantity as to make nonsense of the claim that each is performing a different function in the ritual sacrifice. If, for example, *Ṛc* and *Yajuṣ* are totally different, then how can a *Ṛc Mantra* perform the *Yajuṣ* function in the ritual? It is not as if the *Ṛc Mantras* that perform the *Yajuṣ* function do not perform, say, the *Sāma* function in the sacrifice. In fact, when the same text from the *Ṛgveda* is found both in the *Sāmaveda* and the *Yajurveda*, one would be hard put to distinguish its respective functions in the three Vedas or in the sacrifice in which it is used. As most of the *Mantras* of the *Sāmaveda* are from the *Ṛgveda* and a very large portion of the *Mantras* in the various *Saṁhitās* of the *Kṛṣṇa Yajurveda* or the *Śukla Yajurveda* are also from the *Ṛgveda*, it is extremely unlikely that the *Sāmaveda* and the *Yajurveda* have no *Mantras* in common. Even if we forget the *Ṛgveda* for the moment, the occurrence of a *Mantra* both in the *Sāmaveda* and the *Yajurveda* would militate against the view being propounded above. Take, for example, the *Mantra* 1.456 of the *Sāmaveda* (*Indro Viśvasya rājati*) which also occurs in the *Vājasaneyī Saṁhitā* of the *Śukla Yajurveda* as the eighth Mantra of the thirty-sixth *Adhyāya*. Now, shall we treat it as performing a *sāma* function or a *yajuṣ* function? It is true that in the latter it occurs not as the whole *Mantra*, but only as a part of one (*Indro Viśvasya rājati śaṃ no astu dvipade śaṃ catuṣpade*). But then this raises the old question we raised earlier; 'what is a *Mantra*?' Surely, if '*Indro Viśvasya rājati*' forms one complete *Mantra* in the *Sāmaveda*, it cannot cease to do so in the *Yajurveda*.

The *Atharvaveda* itself is supposed to have taken whole sections of the *Ṛgveda* for use by the brahman priest in the sacrifice. According to Gonda:

> '. . .it was for the ritual use of this *brahman* priest, and specially for one of his assistants, the *brāhmaṇācchaṃsin*, that AVS, XX was, as their special collection (*saṁhitā*), added to the corpus. Some portions (13 of the 143 *sūktas*) excepted, this book consists of literal borrowings from the *Ṛgveda Saṃhitā*.[45]

To get some idea of the sort of borrowing that was done, we may take the first *Sūkta* of XXth *Kāṇḍa* of the *Atharvaveda*. It consists of only three *Mantras*, the first taken from the 10th *Sūkta* of the *Maṇḍala* III of the *Ṛgveda*, the second from the 86th *Sūkta* of the *Maṇḍala* I of the *Ṛgveda* and the third from the 46th *Sūkta* of the *Maṇḍala* VIII of the *Ṛgveda*. This, frankly, is not even straight borrowing, but borrowing to cover one's tracks so that none may suspect the act of borrowing. These are borrowings of whole full-fledged *Mantras* from the *Sūktas*. One would be hard put to explain how they undergo a differentiation of function just from the fact of being borrowed in such a clandestine manner from one text to another. In fact, one may easily find from Bloomfield's *Vedic Concordance* scores of instances where the same text occurs in all the four Vedas. The proponents of the sacrificial functional theory would be hard put to account for such a situation. The usual way out is the *ad hoc* injunction that if in any sacrifice a particular *Mantra* is being used from a particular Veda which is presumed to perform the function peculiar to that Veda alone, then the same *Mantra*, even if it occurs in the other Vedas, is not to be used in that sacrifice for the performance of the other functions belonging to those Vedas. But this obviously is an *ad hoc* solution to the problem which must have been adopted by the ritual practitioners to avoid the embarrassment caused by the identity of *Mantras* in what were ostensibly supposed to be different Vedas.

The operational theory of the Vedic texts is deeply enshrined in the Mīmāṁsā way of looking at them. Sāyaṇa's commentary on the Vedas is perhaps a classic example of this. In fact, his decision to write first his commentary on the *Yajurveda* and his defence thereof, as already pointed out, is evidence of this. But this, it is forgotten, would make the *Brāhmaṇas* the centre of the Veda, as it is they and they alone which operationalize the Veda.

The *Mantra* portion would then be subsidiary or ancillary to the *Brāhmaṇas*, as it is through them that they find their meaning, which is contained in the sacrificial operations that they specify. The procedure, followed in the *Taittirīya Saṁhitā*, not to separate the *Brāhmaṇa* portion into independant texts, would then be justified as there is no point in giving the operational meaning separately when it *alone* tells us what is being meant. Also, if it is the *Brāhmaṇas* that provide the meaning to the text, then, strictly speaking, there would be as many Vedas as there are *Brāhmaṇas*. This would be in accordance with our earlier conclusion that it would be more correct to treat the extant texts of the so-called *śākhās* as independent works rather than as variants of a common text, as they are generally held to be. In fact, even when there is a textual repetition between the different *Saṁhitās* of the various *śākhās*, it is very seldom in the same order and almost always embedded in extraneous material. Even a cursory examination of any of the contents of the *Taittirīya Saṁhitā* with the other texts of the *Kṛṣṇa Yajurveda* as given in Keith's work, *The Veda of the Black Yajus School Entitled Taittirīya Saṁhitā*, would convince one of this. But if the sequence itself is changed in an operation or if it is embedded in a different context, it cannot be deemed to have remained the same operation. Thus, the induction of the *Brāhmaṇas* into the central position for understanding what a Veda is would make the Vedas far more in number than most would like to admit.

Also, once the *Brāhmaṇas* are accepted as essential parts of the Vedas or as identical with them, it would be difficult to argue for the so-called *apauruṣeyatva* of the Vedas, for none would seriously maintain that all the ritualistic instructions along with the stories that are meant to emphasize their importance are not of human origin. At least, their conflicting diversity and the attempt to make them acceptable through all the various ways which are included under the so-called *Arthavāda* doctrine evolved by the Mīmāṁsakas, could hardly be ascribed to anyone but the human carriers of the Vedic tradition. And as far as ritual is concerned, it is they and they alone who have any authority in the matter. In fact, for the sacrificial ritual, it is not even the *Brāhmaṇas* which *alone* are sufficient. One needs the *Śrauta* or the *Kalpasūtras* also, and not just them but the whole of what is usually called the *Vedāṅga* literature with them. Thus, along with the *Brāhmaṇas* and the *Kalpasūtras* we have to have the knowledge that is embodied in the texts known as the *Śikṣā, Vyākaraṇa, Nirukta, Nighaṇṭu, Chandas* and *Jyotiṣa* in order to perform the sacrificial rituals as they are supposed to be ordained by the *Saṁhitās* and the *Brāhmaṇas*. But no one has ever maintained that the *Vedāṅgas* are not of human origin. In fact, they have always been treated as *smṛti*, and not *śruti*. But if this is so and if it is also true that without their knowledge one cannot perform the prescribed sacrifices correctly, and if the injunction for performing those sacrifices is the essence of the Vedas, it follows necessarily that the Vedas cannot, in principle, be *apauruṣeya* in character.

The Need for Revision

According to tradition, it was the sage Vyāsa who gave shape to the present collection which is known as the Vedas. It is difficult to believe this of all the *śākhās* of the different *Saṁhitās*, or of the various *Brāhmaṇas* that are supposed to be associated with them. As for the Upaniṣads, particularly those which are selections out of pre-existent Vedic texts,[46] it is difficult to believe that the same person, who made the first arrangement, made the second selection also. The latter activity presupposes the former and hence, most probably, would have been undertaken by someone other than Vyāsa. But however it may be, the whole thing is so unsatisfactory that a new arrangement of the whole Vedic corpus is urgently needed. There is nothing sacrosanct in what somebody collected thousands of years ago, and in the format that he gave to that collection. We need a new Vyāsa for modern times who would undertake the work keeping in view the needs of the times.

For far too long the problems relating to the Vedic texts have been swept under the carpet. Even when formulated, they have been seldom squarely faced. The tradition has been accepted too unquestioningly, as if what somebody arranged and edited has to be taken as the final word in the matter. That there are four Vedas, and that they are the *śruti* or the final authority for all orthodox Hinduism is axiomatically accepted by everybody who writes on the subject. Also, that they form a unity, a musical harmony like that of a string quartet,[47] the so-called *śākhās* are nothing but rescensions of the same text, and there are no problems in this best of all possible worlds.

The truth, however, is very, very different. Instead of the proclaimed harmony, there is a continuous one-upmanship amongst the specialists of the different Vedas. It is not only the *Sāmavedin* who relegates the *Ṛksaṁhitā* to the realm of the lifeless body whose soul is the *Sāma*, as pointed out earlier in our discussion. The *Atharvavedin* "explicitly asserts that those who study the three-fold Veda will reach, it is true, the highest heaven, but yet the *atharvans* and *aṅgirases* go beyond to the great worlds of Brahman."[48] Not only this, in order to assert their supremacy over the other three Vedas, the *Atharvavedin* resorted to "the spread of legends and allegorical stories in which the other Vedas are represented as incompetent and the *Atharvaveda* appears as superior to them."[49] As for the *Yajurveda*, it places itself not only in the centre of the sacrificial ritual, but by making the ritual itself as central to the Veda it relegates all the non-ritual parts of the other Vedas to a secondary status and dismisses them as *arthavāda*.

As for the *śākhās* being recensions, one can only say that the use of the term in this context is systematically misleading. It tends to suggest that there are various manuscripts of the same text from which the original may possibly have been reconstructed. This, obviously, is not the case. Each *śākhā* may have its own variant manuscripts out of which the original Saṁhitā of the *śākhā* may possibly be reconstructed. On the other hand, the text belonging to a particular *śākhā* cannot be regarded as a 'recension', even in the literal, technical sense given to it in *The Shorter Oxford English Dictionary*. The latter gives the meaning of 'recension' as 'the revision of a text, est. in a careful or critical manner; a particular version of a text resulting from such revision'. Now the *śākhās* are not the result of any attempt at '*careful* or *critical revision*' of a pre-existent text on the part of anybody. Further, there is so much of addition, omission and change of sequence that they cannot be regarded as even 'revisions' of the text, for any revision in order to be called a 'revision' must be only marginal in character.

The Vedas, thus, have to be rescued from the age-old forms in which they have been imprisoned and immobilized. For this, a new way of looking at the texts is required. It is hoped that this essay will provide a small, first step in this direction.

NOTES AND REFERENCES

1. Diwan Bahadur V.K. Ramanujachari, *Vedic Texts Considered in the Śri Bhāshyam* (Kumbakonam, 1930).
2. Jan Gonda, *Vedic Literatures* (Wiesbaden: Otto Harrassowitz, 1975), p. 313.
3. Raghu Vira, *Sāmveda of the Jaiminīyas: Text and Mantra Index* (Lahore: The International Academy of Indian Culture, 1938).
4. Gonda, p. 313.
5. *Sāyaṇa's Preface to the Ṛgvedabhāṣya*, trans. Peter Peterson (Poona: Bhandarkar Oriental Research Institute, 1974), p. 5.
6. Sāyaṇa has written, साम्नामृगाश्रितत्वात् which may be translated as 'because of the fact that Sāmaveda is completely based on the Ṛgveda.' Dr Lath has suggested that the term *Ṛc* here should not be taken to mean the *Ṛgveda* but rather the *Ṛc Mantras* which may be found in the *Ṛgveda* or in any of the other *Saṁhitās*. This would have been plausible if those *Mantras* of the *Sāmaveda* which are not found in the *Ṛgveda* were to be from any of the other *Saṁhitās*. Also, it raises the problem of finding the essential characteristics which constitute a *ṛc mantra*.
7. Gonda, p. 314.
8. *Ibid*., p. 314.
9. *Ibid*., p. 314.
10. *Ibid*., p. 316.
11. *Ibid*.
12. Mukund Lath, 'Ancient Indian Music and the Concept of Man' (*NCPA Quarterly Journal*, Vol. XII, nos. 2 and 3, June–September, 1983).
13. Lath, p. 5.
14. Bellikoth Ramchandra Sharma, *Jaiminīya Ārṣeya-Jaiminīya Upaniṣad Brāhmaṇas* (Tirupati: Kendriya Sanskrit Vidyapeetha, 1967), p. 21 and p. 125.
15. Gonda, pp. 317–18.
16. Ramnath Dịkshit, *Ūhagānam and Ūhyagānam* (Varanasi: Banaras Hindu University, 1967).
17. The *mantras* that are so repeated are 108, 122, 184, 320 and 465.
18. Peter Peterson (trans.), *Sāyaṇa's Preface to the Ṛgvedabhāṣya* (Poona: Bhandarkar Oriental Research Institute, 1974), p. 3.
19. *Ibid*., p. 5.
20. A.B. Keith, *The Veda of the Black Yajus School Entitled Taittiriya Samhita* (pt. 1), (Delhi: Motilal Banarsidass, 1967), pp. xlvii-lxvi.
21. Gonda, p. 328.
22. *Ibid*., p. 328.
23. *Ibid*., p. 328.
24. Keith, *op. cit*.
25. Gonda, p. 328.
26. Sāyaṇa, Peter Peterson, p. 44.
27. Śrīpāda Dāmodara Satavalekara, *Kṛṣṇayajurvedīya Taittirīya Saṁhitā*, 4th ed. (Pardi: Svādhyāya Maṇḍala), pp. 2–3 and Maharishi Daivarata, *Mūla Yajurveda-Saṁhitā* (Varanasi: Banaras Hindu University Sanskrit Series, Vol. VII, 1973), pp. 4–5.
28. Sontakke, N.S. and T.N. Dharmadhikari (eds.), *Taittirīya Saṁhitā*, Vol. I (Poona: Vaidika Saṁśodhana Maṇḍala, 1970), p. 12.

29. Keith, p. 9.
30. Gonda, p. 323.
31. *Ibid.*, p. 323.
32. *Ibid.*, p. 324.
33. All of these estimates are based on Patañjali's statement in the *Mahābhāsya*. See Bhagvad Dutta, *Vaidika Vāṅmaya Kā Itihāsa*, (Delhi: Praṇava Prakashana, 1978).
34. Satvalekar (ed.), *Maitrāyaṇī Saṁhitā* (Vikram Samvat 1998), p. 515.
35. Maurice Bloomfield, *Ṛg-Veda Repetitions*, pts, 1, 2 and 3 (Cambridge, Mass.: Harvard University Press, 1916).
36. Bloomfield, p. 3.
37. Gonda, p. 37.
38. *Ibid.*, p. 37.
39. *Ibid.*, p. 37.
40. *Ibid.*, p. 36.
41. *Ibid.*, p. 36.
42. *Ibid.*, p. 268.
43. *Ibid.*, p. 269.
44. *Ibid.*, p. 268.
45. *Ibid.*, p. 269.
46. See on this point my article 'The Upaniṣads—What Are They?' in this book.
47. 'The functions of the four Vedas being comparable, to quote Caland, to the parts of the players of a string quartette the role of the *hotar* cum suis (i.e. the *hautra*) must be learnt from the *sūtras* of the Ṛgveda, the office of the chanters (*audgātra*) from those of the Sāmaveda, the activities of the *adhvaryu*—the officiant who is in charge of the manual operations and mutters the sacrificial formulas (*yajus*) and his assistants (i.e., the *ādhvaryava*)—from the Yajurveda; as to the task of the *brahman* priest (*brahmatva*), he owes his dignity to the 'sap extracted from the other Vedas', although the Atharvavedins claim his close connection with the atharvanic tradition'. See Gonda, *The Ritual Sutras*, pp. 471–72.
48. Gonda, *Vedic Literature*, p. 271.
49. *Ibid.*, p. 271.

CHAPTER FIVE

The Upanisads—What are They?

The Upanishads[1] are perhaps the most famous of the sacred texts of India. Only the Gītā may presumably dispute this place. Besides being acknowledged as sacred, and thus surrounded by an aura of religious authority, they are also the fountain-head of one of the major schools of Indian philosophy usually designated as Vedānta. The history of the discovery of these texts along with that of their translation and publication is well known. But what is perhaps not so well known, except amongst the very specialized scholars of the subject, is the history of the texts themselves, and how they have come to be known and designated as the Upaniṣads. Even amongst the specialists, the awareness of the problem and the issues related thereto is only marginal. It would be no exaggeration to say that the tradition concerning what are regarded as the Upaniṣads is largely accepted uncritically and repeated as read or heard from the so-called 'authorities' who, in the context of the Indian tradition, one has learnt not to question.

The number of texts constituting the Upaniṣads is not settled, and most scholars make a distinction between the major and the minor Upaniṣads. Yet, the dominant tradition in India treats them as a part of the *Śruti*, that is, as an integral part of the Vedas, without noticing the incompatibility between the two contentions. If they are an integral part of the Vedas, how can there be a distinction into major and minor between them, or a dispute about their exact number? It may be urged that the situation with respect to the Vedas is no different, as the status of one of the Vedas, that is, the *Atharvaveda* is not generally regarded as equal to those of the other Vedas. Even amongst the other three, there is what may be called an order of priority or hierarchy amongst the *Ṛg*, *Yajur* and *Sāma* in that order. Even if this is conceded, it would be accepted that there is, in the case of the Vedas, such a thing as a closure of the canon, which does not seem to have been the case with respect to the Upaniṣads, as they continued to be composed long after the Vedic corpus was finalized. Everyone talks about the *Allopaniṣad*, but no one seems to see the significance of it. If one could think of writing such an Upaniṣad, then obviously the Upaniṣads could not have been regarded as an integral part of the Vedas, as is taken for granted today. The same is true of the 'sectarian' Upaniṣads. The very fact that they continued to be written is ample proof that no one thought of the Upaniṣads in the same way as they thought of the Vedas.

It is, of course, a matter of dispute even within the tradition as to what is to be regarded as the Veda in the strict sense of the term. The dispute concerns the *Brāhmaṇas* and the *Āraṇyakas*, besides the Upaniṣads. But whether the former two are regarded as an integral part of the Vedas or not, they did not continue to be composed beyond a certain period which was reached early in the tradition, a situation far different from that of the Upaniṣads which continued to be composed till almost the thirteenth century. It may, therefore, be safely surmised that the *Brāhmaṇas* and the *Āraṇyakas* were treated as having reached a final state within the Vedic corpus in the sense that nothing more could be added to them, a situation which was absent in the case of the Upaniṣads. To provide a spurious continuity with the Vedic tradition, and to treat them as an integral part of the Vedic corpus, all Upaniṣads which were written later were ascribed to the *Atharvaveda*, thus indirectly confirming the slightly inferior status which had been given to it from the very beginning as compared with the other three Vedas, which have been distinctively referred to as *Trayī*.

In fact, though the term Upaniṣad is found even in the *Ṛgveda* as a title in Hymn No. 145 of the tenth Maṇḍala, it was not regarded as so sacred or sacrosanct as not to be used in profane contexts. Kauṭilya's *Arthaśāstra* uses it in the sense of secret weapons to destroy the enemy, and Vātsyāyana's *Kāmasūtra*, according to Keith, uses it in an analogous manner. If the fact of this usage is taken into account along with the continuing production of Upaniṣads as late as the end of the thirteenth century, or even the first half of the sixteenth century, depending upon the date assigned to the commentary of Lakṣmīdhara on

Saundaryalaharī, the *Sākta* Upaniṣads seem, by common consent, to have been written very late. Yet, if the Upaniṣads not only continued to be composed but also to be accepted and included in the orthodox canon, then they cannot be regarded as *śruti* in the same sense as the Vedic *Saṁhitās* or even the *Brāhmaṇas* and the *Āraṇyakas*.[2]

In fact, even in traditional times, that is, the period of the Vedic *Saṁhitās*, *Brāhmaṇas* and *Āraṇyakas*, it was not clear as to what is to be considered as an Upaniṣad and on what grounds. True, the so-called eleven major Upaniṣads have continued to be accepted as a part of the authoritative Vedic corpus from almost the very beginning of the tradition. But even with respect to these, it is not clear why they have been traditionally so accepted or, in other words, what have been the grounds for their acceptance. It is well known, at least amongst the specialists, that many of these Upaniṣads are not independent works, but selections from existent texts. But if that is so, someone must have made the selection. It is not quite clear what was the basis for the selection, as presumably there must have been some basis for the selection that was made. It is also not quite clear why during the long period of time since the first selection was made, no one has made a different or alternative selection.

Take, for example, one of the oldest Upaniṣads, the *Aitareya*, which forms a part of the *Aitareya Āraṇyaka* and must have been selected out of it to be treated separately for certain purposes. Chapters 4, 5 and 6 of the second *Āraṇyaka* are usually known as the *Aitareya Upaniṣad*. Yet, in none of these chapters is the word Upaniṣad mentioned anywhere, nor does it refer to itself as an Upaniṣad. This would have little significancc if there were no statement to this effect in any other part of the *Āraṇyaka*. But the third *Āraṇyaka* begins by proclaiming itself to be an Upaniṣad. It says clearly अथातः संहिताया उपनिषत्. Moreover, the fifth paragraph of the second chapter of the third *Āraṇyaka* starts with the statement "अथ खल्वियं सर्वस्यै वाच उपनिषत्। सर्वा ह येवेमाः सर्वस्यै वाच उपनिषत् इमां त्वेवाचक्षते।" which is translated by Keith as follows, "Now comes this Upaniṣad of the whole speech. All these indeed are Upaniṣads of the whole speech, but this they so call." It is strange that in the face of this clear-cut statement within the *Āraṇyaka* itself, the *Aitareya Upaniṣad* is not usually taken to include the third *Āraṇyaka* which proclaims itself to be such, and includes Chapters 4, 5 and 6 of the second *Āraṇyaka* which says nothing about itself being an Upaniṣad. Keith is aware of the difficulty, and in fact entitles his discussion of the issues as 'The three Upaniṣads of the *Aitareya Āraṇyaka*.[3] He writes, "Book III bore the special title of *Saṁhitā* Upaniṣad which is given to it in Śaṁkara's commentary and which it claims for itself by its opening words."[4] But the so-called *Saṁhitā* Upaniṣad has almost never been treated or listed separately as an Upaniṣad, nor has it been regarded as important. And this in face of the fact that it proclaims itself to be an Upaniṣad. The same is true of the so-called *Mahā-aitareya Upaniṣad* which is supposed to consist of *Āraṇyakas* II and III and would thus include the portions which proclaim themselves as Upaniṣads in this *Āraṇyaka*. First, there is a dispute about what this *Mahā-aitareya* actually includes. As Keith writes, "the term Mahaaitareya or *Bahvṛca-brāhmaṇa* Upaniṣads though it sometimes applies to both *Āraṇyaka* II and III, sometimes is confined to *Āraṇyaka* II."[5]

The very fact that the usage of the term was so fluctuating proves our point that the criteria for what was to be considered an Upaniṣad was not fixed. Still, it is surprising that what proclaimed itself as an Upaniṣad should have been the subject of controversy, a situation that casts grave doubts on the veneration and infallibility with which *Śruti* is supposed to have been regarded in the orthodox Indian tradition. It should be noted that if the term *Mahā-aitareya* is confined only to *Āraṇyaka* II, it would still exclude the self-proclaimed Upaniṣadic portions of the *Āraṇyaka*, while if it is supposed to include both *Āraṇyaka* II and III, we will have to face the problem as to why it has not usually been commented upon or treated or listed as a separate Upaniṣad. And, why should we accept that "there is no doubt that the term *Aitareya Upaniṣad* especially belongs to II, 4–6',[6] as Keith contends? Surely, if we accept the texts to be integrated wholes, it would be more logical to expect that the meaning of Chapters 4–6 cannot be understood except in the context of what has gone before and what comes later in the *Āraṇyaka*.

Of course, Keith argues that the doctrines developed in Chapters 1–3 of *Āraṇyaka* II are different from those developed in Chapters 4–6 and that the latter are a further development of the doctrine. And, according to him, the doctrine contained in Chapters 1 and 2 of *Āraṇyaka* III is a step backward from the one contained even in Chapters 1–3 of *Araṇyaka* II. But if this is the case, and here he seems to agree with what Śaṁkara and Sāyaṇa have to say on the subject, then the whole sequence of the *Āraṇyakas* has to be rearranged if they are to be meaningful from the philosophical point of view. Or, at the least, the selection that we are to make regarding what is to be regarded as significant in the *Aitareya* Upaniṣad has to be arranged differently from what tradition has handed down to us.

The problem is not confined to the *Aitareya* Upaniṣad only; it simply highlights the problem which is endemic to almost all the Upaniṣads. Take, for example, the *Īśa Upaniṣad*, which is supposed to be an integral part of the *Śukla Yajurveda*, *Vājasaneyi Mādhyandina Saṁhitā* itself. It is supposed to be the fortieth chapter, the last of the *Saṁhitā*. But as even a cursory glance would reveal, it has no connection with the other thirty-nine chapters nor any continuity with them. The *Īśa Upaniṣad* has nothing to do with *Yajña* with which the rest of the text is directly concerned. Keith has rightly observed, "...the *Īśa* Upaniṣad has succeeded in obtaining entry as a book (xl) of the *Vajasaneyī Saṁhitā*, with which it has nothing really to do..."[7]. But if an extraneous text can smuggle itself into the Vedic *Saṁhitā* and manage to pass itself off as an integral part of the *Saṁhitā*, what happens to the much-vaunted sacrosanct character of the Vedic texts whose transmission through an infallible oral tradition is praised by scholars and laymen alike? Further, if all this is true, how can one accept their so-called revelatory character which gives them the aura of supernatural authority? If the text could be tampered with, it could not have been regarded as a revelation by those who tampered with it. The Upaniṣads are now regarded by most people as revelatory in the same sense as the Vedic *Saṁhitās*. In that case, either an exception will have to be made in the case of the *Īśa Upaniṣad* or the revelatory character of the *Śukla Yajurveda*, of which it forms an integral part, will have to be regarded as dubious.[8]

There is another problem to which not much attention has been paid in the literature on the subject. Unfortunately, the *Yajurveda* itself is divided into two parts called the *Śukla* and the *Kṛṣṇa* or the White and the Black *Yajurveda*. Now there is no counterpart of the *Īśa Upaniṣad* in the *Kṛṣṇa Yajurveda*, not even with a variant reading. It may be said that the *Taittirīya Saṁhitā* which constitutes the so-called *Kṛṣṇa Yajurveda* has no parallel with the text of the *Śukla Yajurveda*, except that in both the *Saṁhitās*, unlike the Ṛgveda and the *Sāmaveda*, the name of the *ṛṣi* with whom the *Mantra* is associated is not given. But if the two are so different, what is the point of calling them by the same name? It only misleads us into thinking that there are four Vedas when, in fact, there are five. Either we should treat the two *Saṁhitās* of the *Yajurveda* as completely different in essentials, and deceptively unified through the accident of a common name, or some parallel between the two has to be established in significant detail.[9] If the latter course is adopted and if the *Īśa Upaniṣad* is accepted as an integral part of the *Śukla Yajurveda Saṁhitā*, then we shall have to ask the question as to why there is no parallel to the *Īśa Upaniṣad* in the *Kṛṣṇa Yajurveda Saṁhitā*.

The *Kṛṣṇa Yajurveda* which consists of the *Taittirīya Samhitā* has another peculiarity which has not been noticed. The *Saṁhitā* has three separate Upaniṣads embedded in it, some of which are supposed to be an integral part of the *Taittirīya Āraṇyaka* and others a part of the *Taittirīya Brāhmaṇa*. The *Taittirīya Upaniṣad* is supposed to consist of parts 7, 8 and 9 of the *Taittirīya Āraṇyaka* while the *Mahānārāyaṇa Upaniṣad* is supposed to be part 10 of the same *Āraṇyaka*. On the other hand, the *Kāṭhaka* or *Kaṭha Upaniṣad* is supposed to be part of the *Taittirīya Brāhmaṇa*, a situation different from the diverse *Aitareya Upaniṣads* all of which form part of the *Aitareya Āraṇyaka* only.

The *Kṛṣṇa Yajurveda* itself is supposed to have another *Saṁhitā* called the *Maitrāyaṇī Saṁhitā* which has an Upaniṣad attached to it called the *Maitrāyaṇī Upaniṣad*. But then what is the relationship between the *Taittirīya* and the *Maitrāyaṇī Saṁhitās*? Is it that between two recensions occasioned by the fact that it was handed down in two different schools or is the difference a deeper one as, say, between the *Kṛṣṇa* and the *Śukla Yajurveda*? Whatever the case, it should be noted that the *Maitrāyaṇī Saṁhitā* has no *Brāhmaṇas* or *Āraṇyakas* associated with it, but only an Upaniṣad. This raises doubts about the theory that each Vedic *Saṁhitā* has its own *Brāhmaṇa* and *Āraṇyaka* and the Upaniṣads are embedded in either of them. The *Sāmaveda*, of course, is not supposed to have *Āraṇyakas*, but still it has *Brāhmaṇas* associated with it. The *Maitrāyaṇa Upaniṣad*, then, will have to be understood on the pattern of the *Īśa Upaniṣad* which managed to incorporate itself as an integral part of the text in the *Śukla Yajurveda Saṁhitā*. While there is little dispute about the antiquity of the *Īśa Upaniṣad*, almost everyone thinks that the *Maitrāyaṇī Upaniṣad* is a later work both in terms of its style and content. Keith writes, "... in the case of the *Maitrāyaṇīya*, which Max Müller wrongly believed early in date, the language is obviously closely allied to classical Sanskrit, which it follows in the introduction of greater development and complexity of style."[10] Deussen, on the other hand, tries to account for the spuriously archaic character of this Upaniṣad which misled Max Müller into thinking that it belonged to an earlier period. According to him:

> The orthographic and the euphonic peculiarities of this *śākhā* recur in the Upaniṣad which, on that account, preserves an ancient appearance. But this character of the Upaniṣad which is not, indeed, itself ancient or archaic but on the contrary *which is contrived to have been archaic* had misled Max Müller (with whom L.V. Schroeder agrees) to ascribe this Upaniṣad to 'an early rather than to a late period'. The numerous quotations literally borrowed not only out of *Chandogya* and *Bṛhadāranyaka Upaniṣads* but also out of *Kāṭhaka, Śvetāśvatara, Praśna* ... and indeed, out of still later other copious literature ... makes the late character of the work indubitable...[11]

It is strange that a *śākhā* which possesses a Vedic *Saṁhitā* itself should commit a forgery and try to pass on an Upaniṣad as belonging to that *Saṁhitā* when it does not belong to it. If Deussen's phrase 'which is contrived to have been archaic', is taken seriously, it would cast grave doubts on the so-called role of the *śākhās* in preserving the sacred texts intact. The evidence points to a competition amongst the *śākhās* in which each one staked a claim to antiquity and tried to win by all means, fair or foul. The claim in this case does not appear to have succeeded, for Śaṁkara did not consider the Upaniṣad important enough to write a commentary on it.

But then even when Śaṁkara has written commentaries on some Upaniṣads, they are alleged to have been falsely ascribed to him. Potter, in the third volume of his *Encyclopedia of Indian Philosophies* devoted to Advaita Vedānta up to Śaṁkara and his pupils, treats only the commentaries on *Bṛhadāranyaka*, *Taittirīya*, *Chāndogya*, *Aitareya*, *Īśa*, *Kaṭha*, *Kena*, *Muṇḍaka*, *Praśna* and *Māṇḍūkya Upaniṣads* amongst those allegedly attributed to him. Even amongst these, only the commentaries on *Bṛhadāraṇyaka*,

Taittirīya, *Aitareya*, *Chāndogya*, *Muṇḍaka* and *Praśna* are supposed to be authentic. He argues:

> . . . the following may without question be accepted as the work of the author of the *Brahmasūtrabhāṣya*: the *Bṛhadarāṇyakopaniṣadbhāṣya*, the *Taittirīyopaniṣadbhāṣya*, and the *Upadeśasāhasrī*. There seems no real reason to question the inclusion of the *Aitareyopaniṣadbhāṣya*, the *Chāndogyopaniṣadbhāṣya*, the *Muṇḍakopaniṣadbhāṣya* and the *Praśnopaniṣadbhāṣya* on this list. Beyond this point, however, is only speculation.[12]

If we accept the distinction which Potter seems to be making here, then we can be sure about Śaṁkara's *bhāṣyas* only on the *Bṛhadāraṇyaka* and the *Taitirīya Upaniṣads*. As is well known, "The most careful work on the criteria for deciding which works are Śaṁkara's has been done by Paul Hacker, with application by Sengaku Mayeda."[13] But, firstly, most of the Upaniṣads ascribed to Śaṁkara have not been examined for their authenticity according to Hacker's criteria and, secondly, even when some alleged work has been found to be correct with respect to Hacker's criteria it has been accepted as Śaṁkara's by many scholars, including Potter himself. Śaṁkara's alleged *bhāṣya* on *Māṇḍūkya Upaniṣad*, for example, is a case in point. Potter, after conceding the argument that this Upaniṣad fulfils all the criteria proposed by Hacker, still refuses to accept its ascription to Śaṁkara. He writes, "Vetter, Hacker and Mayeda all utilize Hacker's criteria. Hacker finds no serious discrepancy between the style of this work and that of Śaṁkara's genuine works. . ."[14] But, "despite these considerations, I retain serious doubts about the work's authenticity."[15] One way out of this difficulty would be to regard Hacker's criteria as necessary, though not a sufficient condition for accepting the genuineness of any work alleged to be ascribed to Śaṁkara.

Hacker's criteria are primarily substantive and doctrinal rather than formal or linguistic in nature. And though they have been applied only to determine the genuineness of ascription of any work to Śaṁkara, they or any of their variants could also be used to determine what is to be regarded as an Upaniṣad. At places, Śaṁkara himself is supposed to have used such a criterion. For example, Chapter III of the *Aitareya Āraṇyaka* which proclaims itself to be the *Saṁhitā Upaniṣad* is not regarded as an Upaniṣad because it is not concerned with the doctrine of the *Ātman*, and with those who seek freedom through knowledge. The difference between the three Upaniṣads of the *Aitareya* derives from their being concerned with different types of persons who desire different things. "There are three class of men", says Sāyaṇa in the Introduction to Book III, "those who desire immediate freedom through knowledge of Brahman, and accordingly find it by aid of Book II, 4–6, those who desire to become free gradually by attaining to the world of *Hiranya-garbha*, for whom II, 1–3 is intended, and those who care only for prosperity, for whom the third *Āraṇyaka* serves."[16] This certainly makes some sense, but it still fails to answer the question why, if it is all a question of graded desire or aspiration, the third *Āraṇyaka* comes after, and not before, the second. Surely, a discussion of the means for the fulfilment of desire for prosperity should precede those that deal with gradual and immediate liberation. Also, as the third *Āraṇyaka* calls itself an Upaniṣad, it is clear that at that time at least, the term 'Upaniṣad' was not confined only to those texts or treatises which dealt with matters which according to a Śaṁkara or a Deussen they should be exclusively concerned with.

Even if we take the content-criterion seriously, and seek to apply it to what are usually regarded as Upaniṣads, we would still have to do a lot of pruning. Both the *Bṛhadāraṇyaka* and the *Chāndogya* have large parts which have little to do with doctrinal matters relating to *Ātman* or *Brahman*. In fact, they remind one more of the *Brāhmaṇas* or the *Āraṇyakas* which have never been treated as Upaniṣads by tradition. True, there are portions of these texts which are preeminently upaniṣadic in the technical sense of the term, but then they should be delinked from the other parts which are not, and treated separately as the Upaniṣads proper. In fact, large portions of the early parts of the *Bṛhadāraṇyaka* could be treated as an *Āraṇyaka* only and not as an Upaniṣad. The same could be done with the *Chāndogya*, even though *Sāmaveda* is not supposed to have an *Āraṇyaka* of its own. In fact, Keith does remark that 'the first two sections of the work are of the *Āraṇyaka* type"[17] but does not see the implication of what he has said. Instead of suggesting that they should not be treated as part of the *Chāndogya Upaniṣad* proper, he ascribes the reason why they are not regarded as *Āraṇyakas* to the general fact that "texts attached to the *Sāmaveda* generally do not bear that name".[18] But Keith knows very well that even when a text has both *Āraṇyakas* and Upaniṣads, it is not always the case that what traditionally forms a part of one could not, with more justice, be treated as belonging to the other. The same is true even of the *Brāhmaṇas* which sometimes have a part which should go to the *Āraṇyakas* or even to the Upaniṣads, and vice versa.

The problem arises because everybody has treated the traditional classification as sacrosanct, forgetting that the person who did the classification in the past might have made a mistake, or that his criteria might have been different from ours, or overlapping and even conflicting. The latter seems more often the case and, if so, what we need to do is to disentangle the situation and not continue as helpless victims of what someone did in the past.

Most of the Upaniṣads are not independent works, but selections made out of a pre-existing text which is explicitly referred to at the beginning of the Upaniṣad concerned. Then the obvious questions are, who made the selection, and what was the criteria? Furthermore, if the selections were made from a pre-existing text, can they be understood by themselves without reference to the text of which they formed an integral part? On the other hand, if once the idea of making the selections was accepted, why were alternative selections not attempted? The acceptance of a particular selection for millennia seems strange indeed, especially when they gradually replaced the real functioning authority of those very texts from which the selections had been made for at least one of the most important spiritual and intellectual traditions of the country, that is, Vedānta.

These questions have not been raised by scholars who have paid intellectual attention to these sacred texts of the Hindu tradition. To give but one example, Arun Shourie, whose book *Hinduism: Essence and Consequence* is a fairly detailed study of the Upaniṣads, the *Brahma-Sūtras* and the Gītā, and was published as recently as 1979, does not show even an awareness of the issues involved in the questions we have raised.[9] Nor, for that matter, does Karl H. Potter whose third volume of the *Encyclopedia of Indian Philosophies*[20] is devoted specifically to Advaita Vedānta up to Śaṁkara and his pupils, and was published as recently as 1981.

One reason for this may perhaps lie in the usual contention that the Upaniṣads are the last part of the Vedas, a situation epitomized in the tradition by calling the philosophy embedded in them as Vedānta and treating the *Brahma-Sūtras* as their summary. But as most students of the subject know, or should know, this is not always the case. The *Aitareya Upaniṣad*, one of the oldest, forms part of the middle of the *Aitareya Āraṇyaka*. The *Kena Upaniṣad* is a part of the *Jaiminīya Upaniṣad-Brāhmaṇa* and occurs as its tenth chapter, followed by two more chapters, the eleventh and the twelfth. The *Tattirīya Upaniṣad* occurs as Part 7, 8 and 9 of the *Taittirīya Āraṇyaka*, but it is followed by Part 10, which is treated as a separate and independent Upaniṣad. It is called the *Mahānārayaṇa Upaniṣad* and is not only far longer than the *Taittirīya* but also different in content and spirit. But it is doubtful that it is on this ground that it has been treated as a separate Upaniṣad, for even those that are treated as one Upaniṣad do not display a unified character within themselves. The first part of the *Taittirīya*, for example, has little relation with the other two.

The *Kaṭhopaniṣad* which also belongs to the *Kṛṣṇa Yajurveda*, seems to stand almost in a class apart, for though it does occur in the eighth *Anuvāka* of the eleventh *Prapāṭhaka* of the third chapter of the *Tattirīya Brāhmaṇa*, it only occurs in an attenuated seed form, and not in the independent, full-fledged form in which it is found in the text bearing that name. According to Keith, "it is really a rewriting, from a philosophical as opposed to a ritual point of view, of the story, found in the *Taittirīya Brāhmaṇa*, of Nachiketas and the winning of boons from death by him."[21] But this only establishes the lineage of the Upaniṣad; it does not tell us where it is to be found. And in case it is not present in its full form, it would share this characteristic, among the major Upaniṣads, with *Śvetāśvatara* which, however, is more the work of a single author and cannot be ascribed, according to Deussen, to "any Vedic School furnished with *Śaṁhitā* and *Brāhmaṇas*."[22] The *Kaṭha*, on the other hand, definitely belongs to a school which is designated by the name, *Kāṭhaka*. The *Kāṭhakas* are supposed to have a *Saṁhitā* of their own,[23] though Deussen considers it more as an "extensive Brāhmaṇa-work."[24] In any case, whether it is regarded as a *Saṁhitā* or a *Brāhmaṇa*, it consists of "an admixture of *Mantras* and *Brāhmaṇas*", running "in general parallel to the

Tattirīya Saṁhitā."[25] But if it is so like the *Taittirīya Saṁhitā* in its admixture of *Mantras* and *Brāhmaṇas*, it is difficult to understand why Deussen refuses to call it a *Saṁhitā*.

In the case of all these terms, their reference is not indicated as clearly as one would like it to be done for intellectual purposes. One can, of course, accept an extensional definition of the terms, or tell oneself that the situation is the same with all definitions which are not stipulative in character. Even with extensional definitions, one would have to have a closed universe to feel completely secure, as any new member would raise the difficulty of ascriptive classification once again. On the other hand, stipulative definitions may show unwelcome implications leading to a situation requiring us to change the stipulation. Yet, even though there may be some problem or other with all terms, we bear with the situation only when it does not lead to cognitive difficulties which we regard as serious, or if they do not lead to intellectual confusions which are harmful in their consequences. The situation with respect to what goes by the name of the Vedic corpus is such that it leads both to cognitive difficulties and intellectual confusion which needs to be rectified. As is well known, even the tradition does not agree whether the Upaniṣads or the *Āraṇyakas* should be counted as an integral part of what is to be considered as the Vedas.[26] But why the *Brāhmaṇas*? And, if the *Brāhmaṇas*, why not the *Āraṇyakas* and the Upaniṣads?

There may be substantive reasons either way, but they have to be spelt out and brought into the open. Perhaps, the line of division falls between those who opt for what is called the *jñāna pakṣa* (ज्ञान पक्ष) of the Vedic corpus and those who opt for the *karma pakṣa* (कर्म पक्ष). The traditional debate between the Mīmāṁsaka and the Vedāntin seems to support this. But this would be to assume that the hard core of the Vedic corpus, that is, the *Mantras*, have meaning only in the context of the sacrificial ritual adumbrated in the *Brāhmaṇas* on the one hand, and in the *Śrauta-Sūtras* on the other. This obviously is not the case, as to do so would not only be to do violence to the innumerable *Mantras* of the Ṛgveda which have no necessary relation to any specific sacrificial ritual but also to adopt an ultra-operational theory of meaning of both observational and theoretical terms which has proved inadequate even in the context of modern science.

Besides the generalized problem referred to above, the

problem with respect to the Upaniṣads has other dimensions which have been mentioned earlier in the course of this essay but have not been discussed seriously by major scholars in the field until now. Till questions are not raised about what the Upaniṣads are, one may remain satisfied with what tradition has handed down to us in this regard. But once such questions are raised, we cannot close our eyes to the arbitrariness of the manner in which what are now known as the Upaniṣads have come to be so known. And once the 'accidental arbitrariness' of the selection presently designated as Upaniṣads is realized, the way is open for a new selection based on an explicitly formulated criteria, or even a number of selections made for different purposes based on different criteria.

It may be objected that all the texts which are known as Upaniṣads at present are not selections from pre-existing texts, and at least in their case what we are suggesting has no relevance whatsoever. The Upaniṣads ascribed to the *Atharvaveda* all share this characteristic. Even such well-known Upaniṣads as the *Muṇḍaka*, the *Māṇḍūkya* and the *Praśna* do not belong to any *Brāhmaṇa* or *Āraṇyaka* or even *Saṁhitā*. Regarding the *Muṇḍaka*, Deussen says that it does not belong to a definite Vedic school but is, as the name signifies, "the Upaniṣad of those who have shaved their heads clean"[27]. In fact, all the Upaniṣads which are ascribed to the *Atharvaveda* have been done so in a residual manner. As Deussen remarks, "when all these Upaniṣads were joined to the *Atharvaveda* the reason for it lay mostly not in an inner connection with the same but only in the fact that this fourth Veda, originally half apocryphal, was not preserved or protected like the three other Vedas through a competent surveillance by their *śākhās* in the face of alien intruders."[28] The *Atharvaveda* itself enjoys only a dubious authority, and the Upaniṣads linked to it may be supposed to share the same fate. In a sense this is true, for except for *Muṇḍaka, Praśna* and *Māṇḍūkya*, hardly any of them enjoys any venerable authority in the tradition. Thus, the very fact that they are independent works seems to have militated against their being accepted as being authoritative. As for the exceptions, the *Praśna* in its frame of narration appears, according to Deussen, "an imitation of *Satp.* Br. 10.6.1 ff, of Chānd. 5.11.1 ff with the only difference that there in those passages . . . the six *Brahmanas* inquire of Aśvapati about one and the same common theme; while in the *Praśna Upaniṣad* everybody asks something different. . . ."[29] As for *Māṇḍūkya*, even though it is assigned to *Atharvaveda* it "bears the name of a half-lost school of the *Ṛgveda*."[30] Also, its importance is because it "gave rise to one of the most remarkable monuments of Indian philosophy, viz., the *Kārikā* of Gauḍapāda,"[31] a foundational work of Advaita Vedanta. It may be interesting to note that, according to Deussen, all the four parts of the *Kārikā* are "usually regarded as four Upaniṣads" even though it is only the first which includes the *Māṇḍūkya Upaniṣad*. Deussen must have had some evidence for his assertion, but I have not been able to corroborate it from any other source. However, it confirms once again the arbitrariness with which a particular text or part of a text is called an Upaniṣad or regarded as such.

But whatever may be one's view regarding the three well-known Upaniṣads of the *Atharvaveda*, there can be little doubt that Upaniṣads, which are really independent works, are not regarded as of major importance by anyone, and those that are so regarded are mostly not independent works at all, but selections from pre-existing texts made on the basis of criteria which are neither clear nor uniform to our comprehension. An alternative selection made on the basis of clearly formulated criteria which are also philosophically relevant from the contemporary point of view may meet the current needs better than the one that was made long back with a view perhaps to meet the needs of those times.

NOTES AND REFERENCES

1. The term 'Upaniṣad' has usually been written without the usual diacritical marks except when used in quotations.
2. The situation is even more complicated by the fact that texts whose theme is not even remotely connected with what the Upaniṣads are usually supposed to be concerned with call themselves by that name. The latest to be published with such a title is *Vāstusūtra Upaniṣad* (ed., Alice Boner, Sadāśiva Ratha Śarmā and Bettina Baümer, (Delhi: Motilal Banarsidass, 1982.)
3. A. B. Keith, *The Aitareya Āraṇyaka*, (Oxford University Press, 1909), 1969, p. 39.
4. *Ibid.*, pp. 39–40.
5. *Ibid.*, p. 39. Laxmana Shastri Joshi treats the *Aitareya Upaniṣad* as consisting of *Āraṇyakas* II and III on the ground that Śaṁkara has treated them as such in his commentary on the Upaniṣad. But he does not discuss the points raised by Keith

nor does he give any reason why the latter thinkers treated only the Chapters 4, 5 and 6 of *Āraṇyaka* II as constituting the *Aitareya Upaniṣad*, See Lakṣmaṇa Shastri Joshi, *Dharma Kośaḥ, Upanishatkāṇḍam*, Vol. II, Part II, Wai, 1949.

6. See on this question the whole discussion by Keith, *Aitareya Āraṇyaka*, pp. 39–52.
7. A. B. Keith, *The Religion and Philosophy of the Veda and Upanishads* (Cambridge, Mass.: Harvard University Press, 1925), p. 499.
8. Dr. R. C. Dwivedi, in a personal communication, informs me that Chapters 28–29 of the *Súkla Yajurveda* are also supplement and later addition. If so, the situation even with respect to the *Saṁhitās* is far worse than is commonly imagined.
9. Normally, the distinction between the *Śukla* and the *Kṛṣṇa Yajurveda* is drawn on the basis that while in the former the *Mantra* and the *Brāhmaṇa* portions are seperated, in the latter they are combined. But the more important question is not whether the two are separate or mixed, but whether they are the same, or similar to a substantial extent. Unless they are two recensions of the same text, there is no point in calling them by the same name.
10. Keith, p. 500.
11. Paul Deussen, *Sixty Upaniṣads of the Veda*, translated by V. M. Bedekar and G. B. Palsule, Vol. I (Delhi: Motilal Banarsidass, 1980), pp. 328–9. (Italics mine).
12. Karl H. Potter, (ed.), *Encyclopedia of Indian Philosophies*. Vol. III, (Delhi: Motilal Banarsidass, 1981), p. 116.
13. Potter, p. 115.
14. *Ibid.*, p. 309.
15. *Ibid.*, p. 309.
16. Keith, *The Aitareya Āraṇyaka*, p. 40.
17. Keith, *The Religion and Philosophy of the Veda and Upanishads*, p. 499.
18. Keith, p. 499.
19. Arun Shourie, *Hinduism: Essence and Consequence* (Delhi: Vikas Publishing House, 1979).
20. Karl H. Potter, (ed.), *Encyclopedia of Indian Philosophies*, Vol. III (Delhi: Motilal Banarsidass, 1981).
21. Keith, p. 499.
22. Deussen, p. 301.
23. Keith, p. 499.
24. Deussen, p. 269.
25. *Ibid.*, p. 269.
26. मन्त्रब्राह्मणयोवेदनामधेयम् ।
27. Deussen, Vol. II, p. 569.
28. *Ibid.*, p. 555.
29. *Ibid.*, p. 589.
30. *Ibid.*, p. 605.
31. *Ibid.*, p. 606.

CHAPTER SIX

The Text of the *Nyāya-Sūtras*—Some Problems*

The Indian intellectual and literary traditions are not known for any special concern for discovering the originals of their texts. In fact, normally the question itself does not arise, and hence the problem of additions, modifications, deletions, interpolations, etc., is not even seen as a problem which needs to be tackled. The recent search for the so-called *Ur texts* and their reconstruction on the basis of diverse criteria is due to the demands which western scholarship has imposed in the field of all classical studies, including those relating to India. It is therefore surprising to find that even in classical times attempts had been made to fix the authoritative text of the *Nyāya-Sūtras*, the foundational work for Nyāya in the Indian tradition. Till now little thought has been given to these attempts to ascertain why they were attemp in the first place, and to assess their significance.

This exercise in fixing the text of the *Nyāya-Sūtras* becomes even more intriguing if we remember that *Nyāya* has had a more continuous and sustained tradition of thought and discussion than any other philosophical school, not only in India but,

* This paper owes a great deal to Pt. R. Thangaswami Sarma, without whose sustained help in sorting out problems by replying to my incessant queries and sending me xeroxed material bearing on the issues, it could never have been written. I have also been helped by Dr. Tripathi, Director, Ganganatha Jha Research Institute, who generously supplied photocopies of some articles which otherwise I would never have seen. Prof. R. C. Dwivedi and Dr. Mukund Lath have, as always, been continuously associated with the discussions regarding the problems this paper deals with. It was the former, in fact, who drew my attention to the text of the *Nyāyasūtroddhāra* in the *Nyāya-mañjarī* edited by Pt. Sūrya Nārāyaṇa Śukla. And, it was Dr. Mukund Lath who brought to my attention the works of Keśava Miśra and Bhaṭṭa Vāgīśvara edited by Dr. Kishore Nath Jha discussed later in the paper. While every care has been taken to see that the details given are as accurate as possible, some mistakes in computing might still be there. But they do not affect the main contentions of the article.

perhaps, elsewhere also. From Gautam to Gadādhara or Baccā Jhā[1] or Badrīnātha Shukla[2] is certainly a long period of sustained intellectual inquiry to be found anywhere in the world. The first attempt to settle the text of the *Nyāya-Sūtras* was made by no less a person than Vācaspati Miśra I who, in his *Nyāya-Sūcī-Nibhandha*, not only fixed the text of the *Nyāya-Sūtras*, but also divided them in proper order. This fact is well known to scholars, yet no one seems to have asked himself the simple question as to why Vācaspati Miśra I felt the necessity of fixing the text of the *Nyāya-Sūtras*, specially when sensitivity to textual purity does not seem to have been a distinctive characteristic of traditional Indian scholarship, then or now. Vācaspati Miśra himself does not seem to have undertaken this exercise with respect to the text of any other philosophical school on which he had also written his commentaries. He was also not the first commentator on the *Sūtras*, as both Vātsyāyana and Uddyotakara had already written their *Bhāṣya* and *Vārttika* on them. As Vācaspati Miśra's own work on Nyāya is supposed to be a *ṭīkā* on Uddyotakara's *Vārttika*, it may be assumed that he was basing himself on Uddyotakara's text as it was available to him. The relation between Uddyotakara's *Vārttika* and Vātsyāyana's *Bhāṣya* is not quite clear. Is the first an independent work on the *Nyāya-Sūtras*, or is it a work primarily on Vātsyāyana's *Bhāṣya* and thus only indirectly on the *Sūtras* themselves? As a *Vārttika* is not supposed to be a full commentary like the *Bhāṣya*, it would be interesting to know what were the special issues chosen by Uddyotakara to write his *Vārttika* upon. The same thing applies to the work of Vācaspati Miśra I as well as to those of subsequent writers on Nyāya. Unfortunately, neither the traditional pandits, nor modern scholars of Indian philosophy have been interested in undertaking this task.

It has been said that Vātsyāyana had no *Sūtrapāṭha* before him to write his *Bhāṣya* upon, or that there is even a 'hidden *vārttika*' in 'the *Bhāṣya* itself.'[3] The suggestion seems to be that there was a 'floating body of *sūtras*' from which he picked out some and treated them a authoritative. In other words, he first did what Vācaspati Miśra I was to do later, though more explicitly and clearly than Vātsyāyana ever did. But, then, why not reconstruct the *sūtras* out of Vātsyāyana's *Bhāṣya*? There are supposed to be technical difficulties in this as the way in which the *sūtras* are referred to is not such as to clearly demarcate them from those that are not part of the original *Sūtras*. In fact, there seems to be a lot of confusion even about such a simple fact as the manuscripts of the *Nyāya-Sūtras* themselves. H. P. Sastri, in his article entitled *An Examination of the Nyāya-Sūtras,* published in 1905, has stated that "ninety-nine percent of the manuscripts of this work are accompanied with some commentary or other. Manuscripts giving the *sūtra* only are extremely rare."[4] However, Gaṅgānātha Jhā has referred to at least three manuscripts containing only the *sūtras* which he had consulted for his own translation of the text along with the *Bhāṣya* of Vātsyāyana and the *Vārtika* of Uddyotakara. He refers to "A palm-leaf Manuscript of the Sūtra only," "Paper manuscript of the *sūtra* only belonging to Jagadish Mishra," and "Paper Manuscript of *Sūtra* only belonging to Babu Govindadasa."[5] He does not mention any discrepancies in the manuscripts. Instead, according to him, "Every one of these manuscripts was found to be quite correct."[6] Gopīnātha Kavirāja, in his Introduction to this monumental work of translation of Pt. Gaṅgānātha Jhā, seems to be unaware of any problem regarding the paucity of manuscripts containing the text of the *Nyāya-Sūtras* only. Instead, he writes that "a critical edition of the *Sūtra-Pāṭha* of Nyāya, based upon a collection of all available manuscripts of different recensions and of the *Sūtras* as accepted by the various glosses and commentaries still existing, is the greatest desideratum of the day, and until this is done it is vain to endeavour to determine the *sūtratva* of a particular aphorism."[7] This obviously implies that it is not the absence of manuscripts of the *Nyāya-Sūtras* which has made their collation impossible, but only the fact that nobody has tried to undertake it. In fact, Karl Potter in his bibliographical entries under Gautama refers to a host of editions of the *Nyāya-Sūtras* published between 1821 and 1977, and it may be assumed that at least some of them would have consulted the original manuscripts of the work.[8] The references in the *New Catalogus Catalogorum* X, p. 276 at the beginning of the bibliography on the *Nyāya-Sūtras* may be treated as additional evidence for this assumption.

Yet, though the *Nyāya-Sūtras* seem to have been edited and translated a number of times, no one appears to have made an exhaustive list of the variant readings of the text, or of their significance. Even H.P. Sastri, who writes of discrepant readings, does not give any concrete examples of the discrepancies he is referring to. What is, perhaps, even more surprising is the fact that nobody accepts the text of the *Nyāya-Sūtras* as given in the *Nyāyasūcīnibandha* of Vācaspati Miśra I as finally authoritative, though no one has given reasons for doubting either their authenticity or his authority. Pt. Gopīnātha Kavirāja, for example, has said in his Introduction to Gaṅgānātha Jhā's work that "in the translation efforts have been made to determine this, as far as possible. From the very nature of the present work, the translation has had to rely upon the verdict, direct or implied, of the *Bhāṣya*, the *Vārttika*, the *Tātparya* and also upon Vācaspati Miśra's *Nyāyasūcīnibandha*; but help was also derived from two old manuscripts, obtained from two different sources."[9]

This statement is surprising in more ways than one. Firstly, it does not indicate in what ways the sources he has cited differ between themselves with reference to the text of the *Nyāya-Sūtras*. Normally, one would have expected either Gopīnātha Kavirāja or Gaṅgānātha Jhā to have pointed out the issue, discussed the discrepancies, and given reasons for their choice or reconstruction of what they considered to be the correct rendering of the *sūtras*. Gaṅgānātha Jhā has not given even the Sanskrit version of the *sūtras* so that one could do the required exercise oneself. Not only this, Gopīnātha Kavirāja finds no problem in referring both to the *Tātparya* and the *Nyāyasūcīnibandha* as independent sources for the determination of the text of the *Nyāya-Sūtras*. By the *Tātparya*, he presumably means the *Nyāya-Vārttika-Tātparyaṭīkā*. But if this is so, then as everybody knows, both the *Tātparya* and the *Nyāyasūcīnibandha* are works of one and the same person, that is, Vācaspati Miśra I, and it would be strange to think that there are discrepancies between the two. The *Nyāyasūcīnibandha*, it should be remembered, was itself written to establish the authentic *sūtras* and must have been based not only on Uddyotakara's *Varttika* on which the *Tātparyaṭīkā* is ostensibly written, but also on Vātsyāyana's *Bhāṣya* to which the *Vārttika* is related and which must have been available to him independently. The only reason for postulating a divergence between the text as given in the *Nyāyasūcīnibandha* and those found in the works of Vātsyāyana and Uddyotakara would lie in the assumption that the texts of these works which were available to Vācaspati Miśra I were different from those that are available to us today. But, then, it should have been the task of Gaṅgānātha Jhā, if not Pt.

Gopīnātha Kavirāja, to have pointed out the discrepancies between the text of the *Nyāyasūcīnibandha* and those found in the texts of the *Bhāṣya* and the *Vārttika* as they are found today.

What is, however, even more surprising is the total lack of any reference to the *Nyāyasūtroddhāra* either by Gaṅgānātha Jhā or Gopīnātha Kavirāja when that work also tries to fix the text of the *Nyāya-Sūtras* like the *Nyāyasūcīnibandha* to which they refer to. It is inconceivable that either of these scholars, justifiably renowned in their times, did not know of this work. Gopīnātha Kavirāja explicitly refers to Haraprasada Sastri's article published in 1905[10] which specifically refers to the *Nyāyasūtroddhāra*. The translation of the *Nyāya-Sūtras* by Gaṅgānātha Jhā was originally published in *Indian Thought* (Vols. IV-XI) from 1912 to 1919. Thus, a careful scholar such as Jha also may be assumed to have known of H. P. Sastri's article. But even if he did not, he should have known independently of the work as it had already been published in the Vizianagaram Sanskrit Series in 1896 as their publication No. 9 along with the *Nyāya-Bhāṣya* of Vātsyāyana. Pt. Gopīnātha Kavirāja does write about it later in his work entitled *Gleanings from the History and Bibliography of the Nyāya-Vaiśeṣika Literature*, but even there he neither mentions where it has been published, nor discusses its discrepancies with the text of the *sūtras* as given in the *Nyāyasūcīnibandha*. He treats it only as a Maithila recension of the *Sūtras*. In his own words, "this booklet was intended to determine the number and true readings of the genuine *sūtras* as distinguished from those which have been interpolated into the text from time to time. This work is therefore in its object, of a similar nature with its predecessor, the *Nyāyasūcīnibandha* of Vācaspati Miśra I. Its principal interest however consists in the fact that it represents the Maithila rescension of the *Sūtrapāṭha*."[11]

It is unbelievable that a scholar of Pt. Gopīnātha Kavirāja's eminence should have failed to see the problems raised by this statement. He did not ask himself the simple question as to why Vācaspati Miśra II felt even the necessity of settling the text of the *Nyāya-Sūtras* when Vācaspati Miśra I had already done so, or what were the interpolations that he thought needed to be rectified, and what were the discrepancies between the text as established by Vācaspati Miśra I and the text as established by

Vācaspati Miśra II.* His conclusion seems even stranger, for if his intention was "to determine those which have been interpolated into the text from time to time" then how can it be treated as a mere Maithila recension of the text? And, what is the evidence of its being such a recension? Has the whole Maithila school accepted it? And is not Vācaspati Miśra I himself supposed to belong to Mithilā?

Not only does Pandit Gopīnātha Kavirāja fail to raise these questions, he does not give any indication of the text of the *Nyāyasūtroddhāra* he is referring to, whether in published or manuscript form so that one could establish the truth of what he is saying.

Haraprasad Sastri is himself, of course, mistaken in his reference to the *Nyāyasūtroddhāra*. First, though writing in 1905, he is under the mistaken impression that the work has not been published at all till it was given by him to Dr. Venis who published it in Benaras. He writes: "I got one from Midnapore, and gave a copy of it to my friend Dr. Venis, and it was published at Benaras."[12] Secondly, he seems to be under the impression that both the *Nyāyasūcīnibandha* and the *Nyāyasūtroddhāra* are the works of the same person. He writes, "The difficulty which I feel

* Recently, Dr. Kishor Nath Jha has disputed the ascription of the authorship of the *Nyāyasūtroddhāra* to Vācaspati Miśra II on the grounds that many of the *sūtras* accepted in the *Nyāyasutroddhāra* have neither been mentioned nor commented upon in the *Nyāyatattvāloka* which is also ascribed to Vācaspati Miśra II. In his own words: '*yato hi nyāyasūtroddhāraparigṛhītāni bahūni sūtrāṇi nyāyatattvāloke na vyākhyatāni na vollikhitāni. tasmādekatra tadanupasthitiraparatra tadupasthiteḥ pramādikatāmeva sādhayati, ekasyaiva viduṣaḥ dvayoḥ kṛtyoḥ parasparaviruddhalekhanaṁ kathaṁ nāma sambhavet.*' (*Dr. V. R. Sharma Felicitation Volume*, Kendriya Sanskrit Vidyapeeth, Tirupati, 81, p. 71–72). Dr. Jha has forgotten that one's 'not mentioning' a *sūtra* or 'not commenting upon' it may just be a sign that one does not think it sufficiently important to mention or comment upon. On the other hand, one may also do it because one may not have anything important to say upon it. Further, if this criterion were to be accepted then one would have to deny the ascription of the authorship of the *Nyāyasūcīnibandha* to Vācaspati Miśra I, as there are *sūtras* in it which have not been commented upon in the *Nyāyavārṭikatātparyaṭīkā*. But even if one were to accept the contention of Dr. Kishore Nath Jha, it will only raise another issue, *viz*., who is the author of the *Nyāyasūtroddhāra* and why he felt the necessity of establishing the text of the *Nyāyasūtras* once again after it had already been established by Vācaspati Miśra I in the *Nyāyasūcīnibandha* assuming, of course, that whoever was the author of the *Nyāyasūtroddhāra* came after him. For the present, we will assume that it is the work of Vācaspati Miśra II, as even if it were not so, it would not affect the substance of our argument in this paper.

in regard to the *Nyāya-Sūtras* was also felt about a thousand years ago, when Vācaspati Miśra, who flourished about the end of the tenth century, twice attempted to fix the number of *Sūtras* and their readings, namely, the *Nyāyasūtroddhāra* and in *Nyāyasūcīnibandha*, both of which go by his name. If both are the works of one man, as they profess to be, it is apparent that the author did not feel sure of his ground."[13] It is obvious that the writer is not aware of the existence of Vācaspati Miśra II, who flourished centuries after Vācaspati Miśra I, the author of the *Nyāyasūcīnibandha*.

The neglect of the *Nyāyasūtroddhāra* by such outstanding scholars even after its publication as early as 1896 in one of the most prestigious Sanskrit Series defies all explanation. The facts about this work seem to have been wrongly given even in prestigious bibliographical reference works. Potter's classic reference work on Indian philosophies published as late as 1983 does not seem to be aware of the fact that the *Nyāyasūtroddhāra* had already been published, and that too as early as 1896. The entry under *Nyāyasūtroddhāra* only states "(Partly in ms., acc. to DB, 147; cf. also UM, 292)."[14] Similarly, in the Volume on *Nyāyā-Vaiśeṣika*, the only reference to Vācaspati Miśra II occurs not with reference to his work entitled *Nyāyasūtroddhāra* but in connection with the name of the author of the *Ratnakośa* mentioned by him.[15] There is a reference to the publication No. 9 of the Vizianagaram Sanskrti Series, but without any mention of the fact that it published the text of the *Nyāyasūtroddhāra* for the first time.[16]

Dinesh Chandra Bhattacarya has tried to deny the authenticity of the text as being the text of *Nyāyasūtroddhāra* of Vācaspati Miśra II. He writes, "the so-called *Gautamasūtras* printed along with the *Nyāyabhāṣya* in pp. 28 with the introductory verse, *Śrīvācaspatimiśreṇa mithaleśvarasūriṇā likhyate munimūrdhanyaśrīgautamamatam mahat*, is not an edition of the *Nyāyasūtroddhāra*, as is sometimes supposed but only a text of the *Nyāyasūtras* prepared by the editor of the *Bhāṣya* after consulting various books including a copy of the *Sūtroddhāra*."[17] However, this is a statement unsubstantiated by any evidence whatsoever. Not only this, he does not state as to what is the authentic text of the *Nyāyasūtroddhāra* in manuscript or published form, and how this text departs from it. Furthermore, as he has not here given exact references to the edition of the *Bhāṣya* he is referring to, it is not easy to check what he is referring to. Later, of course, in his article entitled *Nyāya Works of Vācaspati Miśra* II of *Mithilā*, he does give the reference in the footnote as *Viz*. ed. 1896[18] which obviously refers to Gaṅgādhara Śāstrī's edition of the *Nyāyabhāṣya* published in that series. But if it refers to that, then it has to be explained as to why the *Sūtrapāṭha* given therein has been preceded by the verse he has quoted, for it ascribes it to Vācaspati Miśra and not to the editor Gaṅgādhara Śāstrī Tailaṅga. Secondly, in case he is the compiler of the *Sūtra-Pāṭha*, as alleged by Dinesh Chandra Bhattacarya, why should he have given such extensive footnotes to the *Sūtras* claiming in the case of many of them that the *pramāṇa* of their *sūtratva* does not seem to be available, a point we will discuss in detail later on. Also, though the editorial statement in the beginning (*pṛthak sūtrapāṭhaśca Vācaspatimiśrakṛta sūtroddhāranāmakaṁ baṅgākṣaralikhitam nātiprācī-naṁ pustakamālocya saṁyojitāḥ*) is capable of being interpreted the way Dinesh Chandra Bhattacharya has done, it generally has not been so interpreted. And there is no reason to do so, unless someone produces a more authentic text of the *Nyāyasūtroddhāra* based on manuscripts which have been critically edited. However, even if there were to be such a text, it will only prove our main point that not only the text of the *Nyāya-Sūtras* has been repeatedly sought to be fixed by eminent Naiyāyikas in the past, without having given sufficient grounds for their choice, but that the practice continues in the present with the added anomaly that the present scholars do not seem to be aware of each other's works or even of the implication of their statements.

The scholar who takes the *Nyāyasūtroddhāra* seriously for the first time is, perhaps, Pandit Śrī Sūrya Nārāyaṇa Śukla who, in his edition of Jayanta Bhaṭṭa's *Nyāyamañjarī* has not only printed the text of the *Nyāyasūtroddhāra* at the end of the work but also compared it with other renderings of the *Sūtras* or their existence or non-existence in other standard texts on the subject. It is perhaps the most comprehensive comparative statement of the *Nyāya-Sūtras* as rendered by different texts.[19] However, as the appendix is neither listed in the table of contents of the book, nor discussed by the author in his Preface, it seems to have escaped the attention of most scholars of the subject. This could also be the reason why Potter, though mentioning it in the Bibliographical section on Jayanta Bhaṭṭa, fails to include it under the bibliographical references on Gautama's *Nyāya-Sūtras*.

In fact, even earlier, Rāma Bhavana Upādhyāya had published the variant readings along with the deletions and additions of the *Sūtras* in an article in the *Pandit* New Series.[20] However, it had confined itself only to the text of Viśwanāth's *Vṛtti* on the *Nyāya-Sūtras* as found in the Sarasvati Bhavan Library Manuscript on a *tāḍapatra*, referred to in his article as अ० वृ०, an edition of the same as edited by Jīvānanda Vidyāsāgara and published in Varanasi, referred to as मु० वृ० and as given in Vātsyāyana's *Bhāṣya* published in the *Pandit* Series itself referred to as मु० भा० along with the *sūtras* as given in the published text of the *Nyāya Vārtika* edited by Pt. Vindhyeshwarī Prasad Shastrī in 1888 A.D. referred to as मु० वा०. Thus the article compares the *sūtras* as given in the manuscript of Viśwanātha's *Vṛtti* found in the Saraswati Bhavan Library with the published version of the text edited by Jīvānanda Vidyāsāgara, along with the *Bhāṣya* and the *Vārttika* published earlier.

However, though the article was written around 1922, the author who himself edited and published Viśwanātha's *Vṛtti* on the *Nyāya-Sūtras*, did not refer either to the *Nyāyasūcīnibandha* or the *Nyāyasūtroddhāra*, the two known texts which earlier had tried authoritatively to fix the text of the *Sūtras*. In fact, there seems to be an extreme arbitrariness amongst scholars regarding what shall be accepted as the source of *pramāṇa* for the *sūtratva* of a *sūtra* in the Nyāya tradition. If we take, for example, the text of the *Nyāyasūtroddhāra* as first published by Pt. Gaṅgādhara Śāstrī Tailanga in 1896 as a text of the *Nyāya-Sūtras* with Vātsyayāna's *Bhāṣya* in the Vizianagaram Sanskrit series, Vol. IX, we find that, according to him, no *pramāṇa* is available for as many as 184 *sūtras* out of a total of 531 *sūtras* given in the text. That this is a surprisingly large number needs to be emphasized. Yet, what is perhaps even stranger is the fact that the learned editor of the text is not bothered about it nor, for that matter, is anyone else. The situation becomes even more intriguing if one remembers that there is not a single *sūtra* out of the first chapter whose *pramāṇatva* has been questioned by him. And as the whole of the second part of the fifth chapter is problematic in a special sense, the real proportion of the non-*prāmāṇik sūtras* is found amongst Chapters 2 to 5.1 that is, the first *Āhnika* of Chapter V. Even amongst these the distribution of the *non-prāmāṇik sūtras* varies as will be evident from the following list:

Chapter	*Total No. of sūtras*	*The number of non-pramāṇic sūtras*
2.1	68	17
2.2	66	19
3.1	73	20
3.2	77	32
4.1	68	38
4.2	51	30
5.1	43	27

It is obvious from the above that in Chapters 4.1, 4.2 and 5.1 the proportion of the non-*prāmāṇik sūtras* is above 50%, while in Chapter 3.2, it is not very far from it. How could any text have been taken seriously in such a situation, and why did Pt. Gaṅgādhara Śāstrī Tailang waste so much time over it, and publish it in the beginning of his scholarly edition of the *Nyāya-Sūtras* in 1896? What is, however, even more surprising is the fact that inspite of his considering so many of the *sūtras* as un-*prāmāṇik*, he treats them as a part of the *Nyāya-Sūtras* in the main body of the text. All the 183 *sūtras* about each of which he writes '*nopalabhyate asya pramāṇam*' are reproduced in the main body of the published text without giving any reason as to why, if there is no authentic foundation for treating them as genuine *sūtras*, as he has explicitly stated, they should be treated as the *sūtras* on which Vātsyāyana had written his *Bhāṣya*. And in case the latter is treated as a *Bhāṣya* on those *sūtras*, then is it not sufficient ground for treating them as genuine? The lack of any discussion on the part of the learned Pandit makes it difficult to answer these questions. In fact, even when he departs from the reading of the *Sūtra* as given in the *Nyāyasūtroddhāra* text published by him in the main body of the work, as he does in the case of *sūtras* 5.1.17 and 5.1.34, he does not give any reasons for the change, or why he prefers the variant version, and on what basis.[21]

The problem is even more complicated by the fact that when Pandit Śrī Sūrya Nārāyaṇa Śukla tries to find the *pramāṇas*, for those *sūtras*, he finds them either in *Nyāyatattvāloka* or *Nyāyasūcīnibandha* or *Anvīkaṣānayatattvabodaḥ*. While one may accept the possibility of Pandit Gaṅgādhara Śāstrī Tailang not being aware of *Nyāyatattvāloka*, as the only known copy of it is in the India

Office Library in London, and that too in incomplete form,[22] it is inconceivable that he did not know of *Nyāyasūcīnibandha* which is the most well-known compilation of the *Nyāya-Sūtras* done by Vācaspati Miśra I who had himself written the famous *Ṇyāya-Vārttika-Tātparyaṭīkā*, or of *Anvīkṣānayatattvabodaḥ* about which, according to the entry in *New Catalogus Catalogorum*, mention had been made in the Princess of Wales Sarasvati Bhavan Studies, III, p. 133–34.[23] Even if it is assumed that the latter work was not known to Pt. Gaṅgādhara Śāstrī Tailang, the neglect of *Nyāyasūcīnibandha* remains a problem which can only be solved by assuming that he did not accept its *prāmāṇik* character. But as he does accept Vācaspati Miśra's *Tātparyaṭīkā* as *prāmāṇik*, it is surprising why he should not have accepted the *pramāṇic* character of his *Nyāyasūcīnibandha* also, particularly when it was ostensibly written to fix the text of the *Nyāya-Sūtras*, and classify them according to the topics dealt with. The only way this anomaly could be dealt with would be to assume that, in his opinion, these two texts were not written by the same person or, in other words, that the *Nyāyasūcīnibandha* and the *Tātparyaṭīkā* were written by two different persons. This, however, will be an even more radical position to take, and one would have to explicitly justify it on cogent grounds rather than just assume it, as seems to have been done by Pt. Gaṅgādhara Śāstrī Tailaṅg.

But if one does accept the identity of the authors of the two texts, as most authorities do, then it is incomprehensible as to how one can cite them as *independent pramāṇa* for the *sūtratva* of a *sūtra*. But that is just what Pandit Sūrya Nārāyaṇa Śukla does in his attempt to find *pramāṇa* for the *sūtras* given in the text of the *Nyāyasūtroddhāra*. He gives both *Tātparyaṭīkā* and *Nyāyasūcīnibandha* as *pramāṇa* for the *sūtratva* of a *sūtra*, forgetting that as they are written by the same person they cannot be independent *pramāṇas*. In fact, it is not clear why, if one of these texts provides a basis for the authenticity of a *sūtra*, the other would not do the same unless one were to assume that there was variation in what are counted as *sūtras* in the two texts. However, if one were to assume this, one would have the problem of explaining how the two could then have been written by the same person.

In fact, Pandit Sūrya Nārāyaṇa Śukla not only cites both *Tātparyaṭīkā* and *Nyāyasūcīnibandha* as sources for the authenticity of the *sūtras* as given in the *Nyāyasūtroddhāra*, but also *Tattvāloka* which is supposed to be a work written by the author of the *Nyāyasūtroddhāra* itself. But this he could have done only if he did not know the identity of the authorship of the two texts. But to have known the text and not to have known the author would be strange indeed, particularly as it is not considered to be an anonymous work. There is, of course, the further problem as to how Pt. Sūrya Nārāyaṇa Śukla could have seen the work in such detail as the only manuscript of the work, according to the *New Catalogus Catalogorum*, is in the India Office Library.[24] He, of course, could have got a photocopy of the manuscript, but considering the facilities available in the early thirties, it is extremely unlikely that it was so. There was perhaps, a manuscript of the *Tattvāloka* in the Saraswati Bhavan Library at Benaras, not known to the compilers of the *New Catalogus Catalogorum*.

In any case, it is baffling as to why Pt. Sūrya Nārāyaṇa Śukla had to go to unpublished sources for establishing the *pramāṇatva* of the *sūtras*, when most of them could have been easily found in the *Nyāyasūcīnibandha*. To give but one example, the *pramāṇa* for *sūtras* 2.1.47 and 2.1.48 is given as *Tattvāloka* on p. 7 of the Appendix to his edition of the *Nyāyamañjarī*. But both 2.1.47 and 2.1.48 can be found in the *Nyāyasūcīnibandha*, the former with a little modification and the latter with none. The *sūtrapāṭha* in the *Nyāyasūtroddhāra* is *'nāpratyakṣe gavaye pramāṇārthamupamānasya paśyāmaḥ'* (2.1.47) and *'tathetyupasaṁhārādupamānasiddhernāviśeṣah'* (2.1.48). In the *Nyāyasūcīnibandha* they are given as *'nāpratyakṣe gavaye pramāṇārthamupamānasya paśyāma iti'* and *'tathetyupasaṁhārādupamānasiddhernāviśeṣaḥ'* (p. 12–13). Of course, the numbering of the *sūtras* in the *Nyāyasūcīnibandha* is not 2.1.47 and 2.1.48, but 2.1.48 and 2.1.49 respectively. But that hardly matters, and is easily explained by the fact that while there are only 68 *sūtras* in the first *Āhnika* of the second *Adhyāya* in the *Nyāyasūtroddhāra*, the corresponding number of *sūtras* is 69 in the *Nyāyasūcīnibandha*. In fact the situation is the same even with the remaining ones where *Tattvāloka* alone is given as a *pramāṇa*. Why this has been done and what purpose it serves is beyond all comprehension. The situation is even more baffling if one remembers that the author has given in the case of many *sūtras* more than one source of authentication. *Sūtras* 2.1.59 to 2.1.64, for instance, provide one such example where both

Tattvāloka and *Nyāyasūcīnibandha* are cited as *pramāṇa* for the *sūtratva* of these *sūtras*.

In fact, as only 10 *sūtras*[25] of the *Nyāyasūtroddhāra* are missing from the *Nyāyasūcīnibandha*, all the rest may be authenticated from the *Nyāyasūcīnibandha*, if its *prāmaṇik* character is accepted by a thinker. In case variant readings are also taken into account, about eleven *sūtras*[26] in the *Nyāyasūttroddhāra* have a variant reading (including additions, deletions, etc.) from the one found in the *Nyāyasūcīnibandha*. Hence, all in all we would have only a problem of about 21 *sūtras* if we confine our attention to these two texts only. On the other hand, if we take the *Nyāyasūcīnibandha* as our base, we find 8 *sūtras* of the *Nyāyasūcīnibandha* missing in the *Nyāyasūtroddhāra*.[27] Thus, there is a discrepancy of 18 *sūtras* between the two texts. In case we include the variant readings also, it would all come to 29 *sūtras*.

However, the story does not end with these two texts alone. If we forget the pre-*Nyāyasūcīnibandha* attempts to fix the text of the *Nyāya-Sūtras*,[28] there are a number of post-*Nyāyasūtroddhāra* attempts which cannot be ignored. The most prestigious of these is, of course, the *Vṛtti* of Viśvanātha Bhaṭṭācārya, originally published in 1922 in *Pandit* New Series 2.2. edited by Rāma Bhavana Upādhyāya and reprinted in 1985 in the Anandashram Sanskrit Series, No. 91. If we take the *sūtra-pāṭha* as given in the appendix to the work as the base, we find that 11 *sūtras* of the *Vṛtti* are missing in the *Nyāyasūcīnibandha* and 6 *sūtras* in the *Nyāyasūtroddhāra*.[29] Conversely, we find 3 *sūtras* of the *Nyāyasūcīnibandha* missing in the *Vṛtti* (2.1.20, 2.2.43 and 3.1.73). As for the *Nyāyasūtroddhāra*, it appears that none of its *sūtras* is missing in the *Vṛtti*. If we take the *sūtras* with the variant readings from the *Nyāyasūcīnibandha* (with additions etc.) their number comes to about 16.[30] If we take them from the *Nyāyasūtroddhāra*, the variant readings in the *Vṛtti* are also around 16, though this time they relate to different *sūtras*.[31] Thus, in all, Viśvanāth's *Vṛtti* has a difference in about 30 *sūtras* (missing or variant reading with additions, etc.) from the *Nyāyasūcīnibandha* and of about 22 *sūtras* from the *Nyāyasūtroddhāra*.

Viśvanātha's *Vṛtti* is a well-known work and the discrepancies in the *sūtra-pāṭha* from both the *Nyāyasūcīnibandha* and the *Nyāyasūtroddhāra* may be deemed to be important. The same can hardly be said about the *Nyāya-Sūtra* text given by Rādhāmohana

Gosvāmī Bhaṭṭācārya published in the *Pandit* New Series, 23, 24, and 25 in 1901, 1902 and 1903 along with his commentary on them entitled *Vivaraṇa* by S.T.G. Bhattacharya.[32] Though it was brought to the notice of the scholarly world at the very beginning of this century, it has been little discussed in any significant way be the scholarly community. In this respect, it seems to have had the same fate as the *Nyāyasūtroddhāra* which was published only a little earlier, in 1896. However, if the *Nyāyasūtroddhāra* had the good fortune of having caught the attention of Pt. Gaṅgādhara Śāstrī Tailang and Pt. Sūrya Nārāyaṇa Śukla whose work we have discussed earlier, the text of Rādhāmohana Gosvāmī has had the good fortune of finding an advocate in Śrī T. K. Gopalaswamy Aiyangar who has written a couple of articles trying to draw attention to its importance in the context of the question as to what exactly is the text of the *Nyāya-Sūtras*. In his article entitled *A Critique of the Nyāya-Sūtra Text* (*as interpreted in the Nyāya-Sūtra Vivaraṇam*),[33] he has given in the Appendix to the article a detailed comparison of the readings of the *sūtras* between the *Vivaraṇa* and the *Nyāyasūcīnibandha* where the two differ. According to him, seven *sūtras* of the *Nyāyasūcīnibandha* are missing in the *Vivaraṇa* and six *sūtras* of the *Vivaraṇa* are missing in the *Nyāyasūcīnibandha*.[34] The variant readings between the two texts, on the other hand, seem to be unbelievably large. If we take *Vivaraṇa* as the base of comparison, then the *sūtras* that have a variant reading come to about 85, while if we make the *Nyāyasūcīnibandha* as the base, they come to about 87. These are rather large discrepancies, and should have been the subject of intensive discussion and investigation by scholars interested in Nyāya philosophy in the country. But, as far as I know, nothing of the kind seems to have taken place even after the publication of Gopalswamy Aiyanger's article.

However, Gopalswamy Aiyangar compared the *Vivaraṇa* text only with the *Nyāyasūcīnibandha* and not with the *Nyāyasūtroddhāra* or with Viśvanātha's *Vṛtti*, though he does mention both in the list of editions of the *Nyāya-Sūtras* which were available at that time. One reason for this seems to be his belief that both the *Nyāyasūcīnibandha* and the *Nyāyasūtroddhāra* were written by the same Vācaspati Miśra, an opinion he derives from Pt. Hara Prasad Sastri whom he quotes to this effect. But while there might have been some justification for Pt. Hara Prasad Sastri to have made the mistake in 1905, there could have been none in Aiyangar's case in the year 1947. Surprisingly, he does not even know of the *Nyāyatattvāloka* and thinks that the references to it by the editor of *Vivaraṇa* is the result of some confusion. He writes: "I wish to draw the attention of the readers to the fact that the editor of the *Nyāya-Sūtra-Vivaraṇam* refers to a *Nyāya-Sūtra* text known as *Nyāyatattvāloka* as being ascribed to Vācaspati Miśra . . . and very frequently refers to the book to point out the variations in the reading with reference to *Nyāyasūcīnibandha*. He does not refer to *Nyāyasūtroddhāra* at all. So it is doubtful whether the editor identifies *Nyāyatattvāloka* with *Nyāyasūtroddhāra* or refers to a separate work of Vācaspati Miśra. Perhaps, *Nyāyatattvāloka* is an outcome of a third attempt of Vācaspati Miśra in collecting the *Nyāya-Sūtras*. Anyhow no such work is available."[35] It is obvious that he has not seen the *Nyāyasūtroddhāra* text published by Pt. Sūrya Nārāyaṇa Śukla in the text of the *Nyāyamañjarī*, which he edited and published in 1936. Otherwise, it would have been obvious to him that *Tattvāloka* was not only a different work from the *Nyāyasūtroddhāra*, but also that it was well known to scholars in Kashi. However, the fact that the editor of the *Nyāyasūtravivaraṇa* made a reference to it in 1901 suggests that the information given about *Tattvāloka* in both the *New Catalogus Catalogorum* and the *Darśanamañjarī* is incomplete as some other manuscript of it, besides the one in the India Office Library at London, must have been available at Banaras. As for the information in Potter's *Encyclopedia of Indian Philosophies*, Vol. I, it is doubly wrong as it not only identifies *Nyāyasūttroddhāra* with *Tattvāloka*, but assumes that it is available only in manuscript form, and that too only partly.[36] In a sense, it appears that Gopalswamy Aiyangar has not even carefully seen Dr. Gaṅgādhara Śāstrī's text in the Vizianagaram Sanskrit Series, No. 9 to which he refers in the article mentioned above. For had he done so, it is unbelievable that he would not have been struck by the fact that according to the learned editor no *pramāṇa* was available for so many *sūtras* in the text of the *Nyāyasūtroddhāra* which he had published therein. His reference to *Nyāya Koṣa* seems even more otiose as there is no discussion about the text of the *Nyāya-Sūtras* in it except for stating that there are in all five *adhyāyas* in the *Nyāya-Sūtras* each consisting of two *Āhnikas*, and the total number of *sūtras* being 537.[37] Surprisingly, in his article on the same subject published 23 years later, he does not show any awareness of the gross confusions and downright mistakes of which he is guilty in this article.[38]

The two subsequent works that surprisingly show a self-conscious awareness of the problem are the *Gautamīya-Sūtra-Prakāśaḥ* of Keśava Miśra and the *Nyāya-Tātparya-Dīpikā* of Bhaṭṭa Vāgīśvara, both edited by Dr. Kishore Nath Jha and published by Ganganath Jha Kendriya Sanskrit Vidyapeeth, Prayaga, in 1978 and 1979 respectively. In his Introduction to the first volume, Dr. Kishore Nath Jha quite clearly states that in any discussion about the text of the *Nyāya-Sūtras*, one would have to take into consideration besides the *Nyāyasūcīnibandha* and the *Nyāyasūtroddhāra* of the elder and the younger Vācaspati Miśra, the *Vivaraṇa-Pañjikā* of Aniruddha, the *Pariśuddhi* of Udayana, the *Prakāśa* of Keśava Miśra, the *Vṛtti* of Viśvanātha Pañcānana, the *Khadyota* of Gaṅgānātha Jhā, the corrected *Bhāsya* of Phaṇibhūṣaṇa Tarakavāgīśa, the *Nyāya-Bhūsaṇa* of Bhāsarvajña, the *Nyāyamañjarī* of Jayanta Bhaṭṭa and other relevant works where the *Nyāya-Sūtras* have been explicitly stated and counted. It is not quite clear why he has not included Rādhāmohana Gosvāmī Bhaṭṭācārya's *Vivaraṇa* in it, as it is unlikely that he is unaware of it, or of *Tattvāloka*, specially when so much had already been written about them. In any case, Dr. Jha has shown a considerable degree of awareness about the complexity of the problem, and he is perhaps the first person who has taken into account a work written in a language other than Sanskrit, that is, the outstanding work of Pt. Phaṇibhuṣaṇa Tarkavāgīśa in Bengali.

But though he has indicated the enormity of the task, he has confined himself to noting the problems raised for the *sūtrapāṭha* only by the text he is editing, that is, the *Gautamīya-Sūtra-Prakāśaḥ* of Keśava Miśra Tarkācārya.[39] Pt. Ananta Lal Thakur, on the other hand, says in his Introduction to the *Nyāya-Tātparya-Dīpikā* that for determining the text of the *Nyāya-Sūtras* it would be best to take the *Nyāya-Tattvāloka* of the younger Vācaspati, the *Nyāyasūtravṛtti* of Vaṁśīdhara, the *Gautmīyasūtraprakāśa* of Keśava Miśra and the *Nyāya-Tātparyā-Dīpika* of Bhaṭṭa Vāgīśvara.[40] It is not quite clear if the learned pandit is once again confusing *Tattvāloka* with the *Nyāyasūtroddhāra* of Vācaspati Miśra II, for if he is talking of the *Tattvāloka* whose manuscript is supposed to be in the India Office Library, London, then it can hardly serve as the basis for establishing the text of the *Nyāya-Sūtras* as it is supposed to be incomplete. And, pray, why not the *Nyāyasūcīnibandha* of Vācaspati Miśra I which, as far as we know, is the earliest known attempt at fixing the text of the *Nyāya-Sūtras*? In any case, the self-consciousness of these two scholars about the problem as displayed in their Introduction to these two recently edited works is a welcome change and needs to be pursued more systematically by others.

If we compare the *sūtrapāṭha* given in these two recently edited texts, we find that 13 *sūtras* of the *Nyāyasūtroddhāra* are missing in the *Gautamīya-Sūtra-Prakāśa* and 39 *sūtras* in the *Nyāya-Tātparya-Dīpikā* of Keśava Miśra and Bhaṭṭa Vāgīśvara respectively. Conversely, 5 *sūtras* of *Prakāśa* and 29 *sūtras* of *Dīpikā* are missing from the *Nyāyasūtroddhāra*. The variant readings between the *Nyāyasūtroddhāra* and the *Prakāśa* are roughly about 14, while those between the *Nyāyasūtroddhāra* and the *Dīpikā* are about 53. Thus the total *sūtras* missing between the *Dīpikā* and the *Nyāyasūtroddhāra* comes to 60, while that between the *Prakāśa* and the *Nyāyasūtroddhāra* comes to 18. The comparison of these two texts with the *Nyāyasūcīnibandha* reveals that 40 *sūtras* of the *Nyāyasūcīnibandha* are missing in the *Nyāya-Tātparya-Dīpikā* and 8 *sūtras* in the *Gautamīya-Sūtra-Prakāśa* of Keśava Miśra. On the other hand, 25 *sūtras* from the *Nyāya-Tātparya-Dīpikā* are missing in the *Nyāyasūcīnibandha*, while only 3 *sūtras* from the *Gautamīya-Sūtra-Prakāśa* are not found therein. The variant readings between the *Nyāyasūcīnibandha* and the two texts is about 31 and 12 respectively. (For details see Appendices I, II, III and IV).

The comparative situation between the six texts that we have examined up till now may be summarized thus:

1. 8 *sūtras* of the *Nyāyasūcīnibandha* are not found in the *Nyāyasūtroddhāra*.
2. 10 *sūtras* of the *Nyāyasūtroddhāra* are not found in the *Nyāyasūcīnibandha*. (Total 18.)
3. The variant reading in the existing *sūtras* between the *Nyāyasūcīnibandha* and the *Nyāyasūtroddhāra* occurs in the case of about 11 *sūtras* only.
4. 3 *śutras* of the *Nyāyasūcīnibandha* are not found in the *Vṛtti* of Viśvanātha.
5. 11 *sūtras* of the *Vṛtti* are not found in the *Nyāyasūcīnibandha*. (Total 14.)

6. No *śutra* of the *Nyāyasūtroddhāra* seems to be missing in the *Vṛtti*.
7. 6 *sūtras* of the *Vṛtti* are missing in the *Nyāyasūtroddhāra*. (Total 6.)
8. The *Vṛtti* has about 16 *sūtras* which have a variant reading from that of the *Nyāyasūcinibandha*.
9. The *Vṛtti* has variant readings from the *Nyāyasūtroddhāra* in about 16 *sūtras* also, though they are not the same as have the variant reading when compared with the *sūtras* in the *Nyāyasūcinibandha*.
10. 7 *sūtras* of the *Nyāyasūcinibandha* are missing in the *Vivaraṇa*.
11. 6 *sūtras* of the *Vivaraṇa* are missing in the *Nyāyasūcinibandha*- (Total 13.)
12. The variant readings between the *Vivaraṇa* and the *Nyāyasūcinibandha* seem to range between 85 and 87.
13. 13 *sūtras* of the *Nyāyasūtroddhāra* are not to be found in the *Gautamīya-Sūtra-Prakāśa*.
14. 5 *sūtras* of the *Gautamīya-Sūtra-Prakāśa* are not found in the *Nyāyasūtroddhāra*. (Total. 18.)
15. The variant readings between the *Nyāyasūtroddhāra* and the *Gautamīya-Sūtra-Prakāśaḥ* are roughly about 14.
16. 8 *sūtras* of the *Nyāyasūcinibandha* are missing in the *Gautamīya-Sūtra-Prakāśa*.
17. 3 *sūtras* of the *Gautamīya-Sūtra-Prakāśa* are missing in the *Nyāyasūcinibandha*. (Total. 11)
18. The number of variant readings between the *Nyāyasūcinibandha* and the *Gautamīya-Sūtra-Prakāśa* comes to about 12.
19. 31 *sūtras* of the *Nyāyasūtroddhāra* are not to be found in the *Nyāya-Tātparya-Dīpikā*.
20. 29 *sūtras* of the *Nyāyatātparyadīpiktā* are not to be found in the *Nyāyasūtroddhāra* (Total. 60).
21. The variant readings between the *Nyāyasūtroddhāra* and the *Nyāya-Tātparya-Dīpikā* come to about 53.
22. 40 *sūtras* of the *Nyāyasūcinibandha* are missing in the *Nyāya-Tātparya-Dīpikā*.
23. 25 *sūtras* of the *Nyāya-Tātparya-Dīpikā* are missing in the *Nyāyasūcinibandha*. (Total 65).
24. The variant readings of the *sūtras* in the *Nyāyasūcinibandha* and the *Nyāya-Tātparya-Dīpikā* occur in about 32 *sūtras* of the two texts.

If we treat the *Nyāyasūcīnibandha* as the reference point, we find the following situation obtaining in respect of the texts we have examined in the article:*

	NST	*Vṛtti*	*Vivaraṇa*	*Prakāśa*	*Dīpikā*
Missing total	18	14	13	11	65
Variant Readings	11	16	85 to 87	12	32

On the other hand, if we take the *Nyāyasūtroddhāra* as our base, we find the following situation:

	NST	*Vṛtti*	*Vivaraṇa*	*Prakāśa*	*Dīpikā*
Missing total	18	6	—	18	60
Variant Readings	11	16	—	15	53

NOTE: The comparison of the *Nyāyasūtroddhāra* with the *Vivaraṇa* has not been done as we have not been able to procure a copy of the latter.

The two tables reveal that the most radical situation obtains in the case of the *Dīpikā* and the *Vivaraṇa* which seem to be very unorthodox in their approach to the text of the *sūtras*. The *Dīpikā* has a difference of as many as 65 *sūtras* from the *Nyāyasūcīnibandha* and of 60 from the *Nyāyasūtroddhāra*. Even if we take into account the editor's contention that many of these additional *sūtras* are statements taken from the *Bhāsya* and elevated to the status of the *sūtras*, the difference still remains substantial as the total number of what may be called the *Bhāsya-Sūtras* is only 13. So, even if we ignore them, the total difference will still amount to 52 and 47 respectively. The variant readings in the case of the *Dīpikā* are also unusually high: they run to around 32 when compared with

*The abbreviations stand for the following texts:
(i) NS = Nyāyasūcīnibandha (ii) NST = Nyāyasūtroddhāra, (iii) Vṛtti = Viśvanātha Bhaṭṭācārya's Vṛtti on Gautama's *Nyāya-Sūtra* (iv) Vivaraṇa = Nyāyasūtra-Vivaraṇa of Rādhāmohana Gosvāmī Bhaṭṭācārya, (v) Prākaśa = Gautamīyasūtraprakāśa of Keśava Miśra and (vi) Dīpikā = Nyāyatātparyadīpikā of Bhaṭṭvāgīśvara.

the text of the *Nyāyasūcīnibandha*, and to about 53 when compared with the text of the *Nyāyasūtroddhāra*. The only comparable situation is found in the case of the *Vivaraṇa* where the variant readings come to about 85 or 87. This is almost the combined variant readings of the *Dīpikā* with respect to both the *Nyāyasūcīnibandha* and the *Nyāyasūtroddhāra*. Surprisingly, the total number of missing *sūtras* in the *Vivaraṇa* is only 13, though we should remember that it is perhaps only a one-way comparison between the *Nyāyasūcīnibandha* and the *Vivaraṇa*, and does not include the reverse comparison which is necessary to get a complete picture of the situation.

The author of the *Dīpikā*, according to Pt. Ananta Lal Thakur, seems to belong to a period before Udayana and is in the tradition of older Nyāya.[41] As for the author of the *Vivaraṇa* he is supposed to belong to the seventeenth century and is well-versed in Navya-Nyāya, according to T. K. Gopalswamy Aiyangar.[42] From the tenth century (if we accept Udayana's date as eleventh century)[43] to the seventeenth century is a long period, and yet the freedom with respect to what to accept or not as a *sūtra*, or which reading of the *sūtra* to adopt, seems to remain the same. It is not as if the older author is more concerned with accepting the so-called authority of the venerable elders than the younger—a situation one would have normally expected given the way the Indian intellectual tradition is usually presented to us in the text-books on the subject. It is instead the elder who seems more independent, as he does not hide what he accepts or rejects or modifies under the guise of finding a new manuscript of the text.

Keśava Miśra Tarkācārya's *Prakāśa* comes in between the two as, according to Potter's *Bibliography*, he flourished around 1525.[44] *Prakāśa's* variant readings or the missing *sūtras* are not very different in number from those in the other texts, though it seems closer to the *Nyāyasūcīnibandha* than to the *Nyāyasūtroddhāra*, at least in numerical terms. Viśvanātha Pañcānana's *Vṛtti* belongs to a slightly later period than Keśava Miśra as the former is supposed to have flourished around 1540, according to the same source.[45] If we accept the date of Vācaspati Miśra II, the author of the *Nyāyasūtroddhāra*, as 1450 A.D.[46] and of Vācaspati Miśra I as 960 A.D.[47] then the chronological order of the six texts we have considered would be the following:

(1) *Nyāyasūcīnibandha,*
(2) *Nyāyatātaparya-Dīpikā,*
(3) *Nyāyasūtroddhāra*
(4) *Gautamīyasūtraprakāśaḥ,*
(5) *Viśvanātha's Vṛtti* and
(6) Rādhāmohana Gosvāmī. Bhaṭṭācārya's *Vivaraṇa.*

It should, however, be remembered that the *Dīpikā* is a text only recently discovered and edited, and that its author's date is only conjecturally suggested by Pt. Ananta Lal Thakur in his Introduction to the text on the basis of internal evidence. In fact, the text is not listed either in the *New Catalogus Catalogorum* or in Potter's *Bibliography* or Thangaswami Sarma's *Darśanamañjarī*. The only work referred to by that name both in the *New Catalogus Catalogorum* and the *Darśanamañjarī* is one by Jayasiṁhasūrī, being a commentary on Bhāsarvajña's *Nyāyasāra.*[48] As for *Vivaraṇa*, it is primarily a commentary on a *Nyāya-Sūtra* text supposed to have been found by Rādhāmohana Gosvāmī Bhaṭṭācārya, and as no one else seems to have seen the original text, neither its dating nor its author is known. In fact, if the authenticity of that text is accepted, then one would have to believe that in some essential respects the Nyāya tradition from Vātsyāyana onwards has been essentially mistaken. In T. K. Gopalaswamy Aiyangar's words, "So in the light of a clear deviation of the readings of many *sūtras*, and of the disclosure of some new *Nyāya-Sūtras* unknown as yet to the world of the Nyāya scholars, and of the unflinching fidelity on the part of the commentator to a different text, it can be admitted that the *Nyāya-Sūtra* text as found edited in the *Nyāya-Sūtra-Vivaraṇa* belongs to a different recension of the *Nyāya-Sūtras* unknown either to the Bhāṣyakāra, Vārttikakāra, or Vācaspati Miśra or Udayana."[49] He is, of course, aware that "most of the critics may contend that Rādhāmohana Gosvāmī Bhaṭṭācārya, who flourished somewhere in the seventeenth century A.D. even perhaps subsequent to Viśvanātha Pañcānana might have interpolated some into the body of the text to suit his line of Nyāya conception."[50]

He rejects this possibility, but does not explore or even show any awareness of the problems raised by such a situation. If Rādhāmohan Gosvāmī has not interpolated the *sūtras* and the variant readings, then either the writer of the manuscript did, or we would have to hold Vātsyāyana guilty of deleting, modifying and interpolating the *sūtras*, and the *sūtra*-variations in his text. The other alternative of two recensions with such divergent readings would only push the problem still further back, and also raise the question as to why there is no prior evidence of the other recension till Rādhāmohana Goswāmī Bhaṭṭācārya in the seventeenth century. Furthermore, the whole notion of 'recension' is so loosely applied in scholarly writings relating to classical Indian studies that one is usually unaware of the many problems hidden under this rubric.[51]

However, the question of the missing *sūtras* or the variant readings is, as we have already seen, and as T. K. Gopalaswamy Aiyangar should have known, not confined to Rādhāmohana Gosvāmī Bhaṭṭācārya's *Vivaraṇa* alone. The only unique thing about his additions, omissions and variations is their supposedly radical difference from the accepted Nyāya position, but even that would have to be established by a comparative study of the other additions, omissions and variations found in different texts, only some of which we have noted in the course of this essay. Why, for example, are the omissions, additions and variations in the *Dīpikā*, which are far greater in number than in the *Vivaraṇa*, considered to be of less significance, is not clear. Unfortunately, the editor of the *Dīpikā* has not even referred to the work of Rādhāmohana, let alone compared it with the *Dīpikā*.

In fact, the lackadaisical manner in which classical scholarship in this field has functioned is truly unbelievable. How could one possibly account for the fact that Pt. Gaṅgādhara Śāstrī Tailaṅg, who perhaps was the first person to edit and publish the text of the *Nyāyasūtroddhāra*, has nothing to say about how he found the manuscript, where it was located, what problems it raised for the text of the *Nyāya-Sūtras*, what variations it has and what are their philosophical importance. The only thing he says is that he has separately given the *sūtra-pāṭha* of a text named *Sūtroddhāra* written by Vācaspati Miśra found in a not very ancient book written in Bengali script after having critically edited it.[52] This is perhaps the same text about which Hara Prasāda Śāstrī had written in 1905: "Manuscripts giving the *sūtra* only are extremely rare. I got one from Midnapore and gave a copy of it to my friend Dr. Venis, and it was published at Benaras. It is known as the *Nyāyasūtroddhāra*." If the two works are the same, as is most likely, then it is surprising that even after nine years of its publication, the learned pandit does not know that this is not the work of the author of the *Nyāyasūcīnibandha* with whom he confuses him. Not only this, he does not even care to compare the two texts and discuss the differences therein. And though he refers to Rādhāmohana Gosvāmī in the article, he not only places him in the nineteenth century, but also shows no awareness of those supposed radical variations in the readings of the *sūtras* or of those new *sūtras* which are alleged by T. K. Gopalaswamy Aiyangar to lead to the postulation of a totally different recension of the *Nyāya-Sūtras*, even though the *Vivaraṇa* commentary had been published in the *Pandit* New Series 23 (1901), 24 (1902) and 25 (1903).[54] Furthermore, surprisingly if the *New Catalogus Catalogorum* entry under *Nyāyasūtroddhāra*[55] is to be believed, he has entered it as a commentary, and that too incomplete, assuming, of course, that he is the author of the *Notices of Sanskrit Manuscripts, Second Series*, published in 4 volumes by the Government of Bengal, Calcutta in 1900, 1904, 1907 and 1911. The anomaly is even more incomprehensible if we remember that while the article was published in 1905, the relevant notice of the manuscript of the *Nyāyasūtroddhāra* is supposed to be in Vol. II of the *Notices* which was published in 1904. This is perhaps a different manuscript from the one claimed to have been given by Pt. Hara Prasad Sastri to Dr. Venis.* In any case, what is surprising is that no one has tried to check the veracity of the statements of Pt. Hara Prasad Sastri made in his article of 1905, or the correctness of the entry in the *Notices of Sanskrit Manuscripts*, Vol. II, published in 1904 or that of the entry in the *New Catalogus Catalogorum* published in 1978.

The problems relating to the works of Pt. Gaṅgādhar Śāstrī Tailaṅga, Pt. Sūrya Nārāyaṇa Śukla, and Shri T. K. Gopalaswamy Aiyangar in this connection have already been referred to earlier. So also have been those arising from the Introduction by Pt. Gapīnātha Kavirāja.[56] One may say that the traditional Indian pandit did not have much interest in textual or historical matters. He was primarily concerned with the philosophical issues, and only secondarily with historical questions relating to the authenticity of the text. In fact, it may be urged that it was the intrusion of the western way of looking at the texts and their

* I say 'claimed', as Pt. Gaṅgāhara Śāstrī Tailaṅga has made no mention of this fact in his *Introduction* to the V.S.S. 9 publication of the *Nyāyasūtroddhāra*.

tradition that, in a sense, forced Indian scholars in this century to work in this field and as their heart was not in it, they produced the kind of inexcusably shoddy work we have seen them doing.

But, then, what about the modern scholars? They do not seem to show any awareness of the problem either. Instead, they seem to be blind to things before their eyes, which perhaps is even more inexcusable than that of the pandits. Debiprasad Chattopadhyaya, for example, seems completely unaware of the falsity of the statements made by Hara Prasad Sastri in his article '*An Examination of the Nyāya-Sūtras*' which he has included not only in the second volume of *Studies in the History of Indian Philosophy* edited by him and published in 1978, but also referred to approvingly in his long Introduction to Mrinal Kanti Gangopadhyaya's translation of the *Nyāya-Sūtra* with Vātsyāyana's commentary published in 1982. Similarly, Matilal in his discussion of the *Sūtras* in his recent work, *Perception,* shows hardly any awareness of the problem. Not only this, though he refers to Jayanta's *Nyāyamañjarī*, edited by Sūryanārāyaṇa Śukla and published by Chowkhamba from Banaras in 1936 he does not seem to have seen the text of the *Nyāyasūtroddhāra* published therein, or noted the problems we have referred to in our discussion of it earlier.[57]

Thus the traditional and the modern scholars both seem to be either uninterested or unaware of the problems that we have tried to highlight in this essay. And the situation with respect to one of the most ratiocinative, argument-oriented schools of Indian philosophy today is that there is no standard, authoritative edition of its basic work, that is, the *Nyāya-Sūtras* giving all the additions, deletions and variant readings with an assessment of their philosophical significance, if any. Even such a prestigious publisher of classical works of Indian philosophy as Motilal Banarasidas has not taken the opportunity to ask an outstanding scholar in the field to survey the problems relating to the text when recently reprinting Gaṅgānātha Jhā's well-known work, *The Nyāya-Sūtras of Gautama*. Perhaps, the Indian Council of Philosophical Research and the Rashtriya Sanskrit Sansthan could undertake this work jointly with the help and collaboration of the well-known Nyāya scholars in the country.

Any such work, however, will first have to come to terms with the following:

1. What is the manuscript on the basis of which Pt. Gaṅgādhara Śāstrī Tailaṅga published his version of the *Nyāyasūtroddhāra* in V.S.S. 9?
2. What is the exact nature of the entry under *Nyāyasūtroddhāra* in the second volume of *Notices of Sanskrit Manuscripts* by Hara Prasād Sastri and published by the Government of Bengal in 1904?
3. Where is the manuscript of the *Nyāyasūtroddhāra* referred to under this entry?
4. Is this the same as has been published in VSS. volume, IX or is it a commentary as mentioned in the *New Catalogus Catalogorum*?
5. What are the grounds for the assertion that the *Nyāyasūtroddhāra* is the work of Vācaspati Miśra II, and not of Vācaspati Miśra I?
6. What is the manuscript of the *Nyāyatattvāloka* said to be in the India Office Library, London, about? Is it the same as the *Nyāyasūtroddhāra*, as is asserted by Potter in his *Encyclopedia of Indian Philosophies*, vol. I? In case it is different, what are the grounds for believing it to be the work of Vācaspati Miśra II?
7. What could be the grounds for Pt. Gaṅgādhara Śāstri Tailaṅg's denying the *prāmāṇikatva* of so many *sūtras* in the footnotes to the *Nyāyasūtroddhāra* as given in V.S.S. 9?
8. What could be the possible reasons for his accepting almost all the *sūtras* whose *pramāṇatva* he could not discover, as genuine *sūtras* in the main body of the text?
9. What could be the possible reasons for Pt. Sūrya Nārāyaṇa Śukla giving *Tattvāloka* as a *pramāṇa* for *sūtras* in the *Nyāyasūtroddhāra* in his 1936 edition of *Nyāyamañjarī*, when the two are usually supposed to be works by the same person?
10. Where is the manuscript on the basis of which Shri S.T.G. Bhattaccarya edited and published Rādhāmohana Gosvāmī Bhaṭṭācārya's *Vivaraṇa* on the *Nyāya-Sūtras* in *Pandit* New Series 23, 24 and 25 in 1901, 1902 and 1903 (according to Potter in the Vol. I of his *Encyclopedia of Indian Philosophies*?
11. Did Shri S.T.G. Bhattaccarya write any editorial note giving information about the manuscript he had found,

and the radical character of the additions, omissions and variant readings pointed out later by T. K. Gopalswamy Aiyangar?

12. Why are *Nyāyasūcīnibandha* and *Nyāya-Vārttika-Tātparyaṭīkā* mentioned separately as authoritative sources when they are supposed to be the works of the same person, that is, Vācaspati Miśra I?
13. If Vācaspati Miśra I's *Nyāya-Vārttika-Tātparyaṭīkā* is supposed to be a *ṭīkā* on Uddyotakara's *Nyāyavārttika* then how can it reject the *sūtratva* of those *sūtras* which have been accepted as such in the *Vārttika*?
14. The problem of something occurring in Vātsyāyana's *Bhāṣya* being taken as a *sūtra* should be distinguished from someone accepting as a *sūtra* something which does not occur in the *Bhāṣya*.
15. The variant readings should be divided into those which are philosophically significant from those that are only linguistic in character, or where *sūtra-pāṭha* has been separated or combined to make one *sūtra* read as two *sūtras*, or two *sūtras* as one. Special attention should be paid to *sūtras* where the variant readings include or exclude the negative prefix, which makes its sense totally different.

NOTES AND REFERENCES

1. Baccā Jhā, 1860.
2. Perhaps, the most outstanding *Naiyāyika* in 20th Century India. He recently passed away. Sometime back he had propounded the theory of *Dehātmavāda* within the Nyāya framework at a gathering of more than a hundred Nyāya scholars at Sarnath, Banaras. The text of the lecture along with his reply to the objections raised is proposed to be published by the Indian Council of Philosophical Research, New Delhi. An English translation by Dr. Mukund Lath has been published in *JICPR*, Vol. V, No. 3, 1988.
3. Karl H. Potter, (Ed.), *Encyclopedia of Indian Philosophies: Indian Metaphysics and Epistemology: The Tradition of Nyāya Vaiśeṣika upto Gaṅgeśa* (Delhi: Motilal Banarsidass, 1977), p. 239.
4. Debiprasad Chattopadhyaya (ed.), *Studies in the History of Indian Philosophy*, Vol. II (Calcutta: K. P. Bagchi & Co., 1978), p. 88.
5. Ganganatha Jha, *The Nyāya-Sūtras of Gautama*, Vol. I, Preface (Delhi: Motilal Banarsidass, Reprint 1984), p. ix. Originally published in *Indian Thought* from 1912–1919.
6. *Ibid.*, p. ix.

7. *Ibid.*, p. xvi.
8. Kral H. Potter (Ed.) *Encyclopedia of Indian Philosophies*, Vol. I: Bibliography (Delhi: Motilal Banarsidass, Second Revised Edition, 1983). p. 46–47.
9. Ganganatha Jha, p. xvi.
10. Ganganatha Jha, p. xii, xv.
11. Gopinatha Kaviraja, *Gleanings from the History and Bibliography of the Nyāya-Vaiśeṣika Literature*, in *Indian Studies: Past and Present* (Calcutta: Firma K. L. Mukhopadhyaya, 1962), p. 46. Originally published in Princess of Wales, Saraswati Bhawan Studies, Banaras from 1924 to 1927 in Vols. 3,4,5, & 7.
12. Debiprasad Chattopadhyaya, p. 88.
13. *Ibid.*, p. 99.
14. Potter, Vol. I. p. 234. Potter's reference to *History of Navya-Nyāya* in Mithila by Dinesh Chandra Bhattacharya does not exactly corroborate what he has written as nowhere on p. 147 is it said that the text is partly in ms. It only says "It appears that the late Mahamahopadhyaya V. B. Dwivedi had access to a ms of this work copied in Caitra 1418." Reference under DB on p. x also needs correction for the year of publication; it is 1958 and not 1959 as given in Potter's *Encyclopedia*.
15. Potter Vol. II on *Nyāya-Vaiśeṣika*, p. 684.
16. Potter, Vol. I, p. 43, No. (788).
17. Dinesh Chandra Bhattacharya, *History of Navya-Nyāya* in *Mithila* (Darbhanga: Mithila Institute of Post-graduate Studies and Research in Sanskrit Learning, 1958) p. 147.
18. *Journal of the Ganganatha Jha Research Institute*, Vol. IV, 1947, p. 300
19. Sri Surya Narayana Sukla (ed.), The *Nyāyamañjarī* of Jayanta Bhaṭṭa, (Kashi Sanskrit Series, No. 106, Chowkhamba, Benaras, 1936); p. 1–28 (at the end of the work).
20. Ram Bhavan Upadhyaya, Pan-Ns. 2–1, 1922. I owe this reference to Pt. Thangaswami Sarma, the outstanding scholar who has compiled perhaps the most exhaustive reference bibliography on *Nyāya-Vaiśeṣika* published under the title *Darśanamañjarī*, Part I by the University of Madras in 1985.
21. 5.1.17 reads in the main body of the text as: *pratipakaṣātprakaraṇasiddheḥ pratiṣedhānupapattiḥ pratipakṣopapatteḥ* (p. 240), while in the *Nyāyasūtroddhāra* it reads as: *pratipakṣātprakaraṇasiddheḥ pratiṣedhānupapattiḥ* (p. 25). Similarly 5.1.34 reads in the main body of the text as: *dṛṣṭānte ca sādhyasādhanabhāvena prajñātasya dharmasya hetutvāttasya cobhayathābhāvānna viśeṣaḥ* (p. 253) while in the *Nyāyasūtroddhāra* it reads as: *dṛṣṭānte ca sādhyasādhanabhāvena dharmasya hetutvāttasya cobhayathābhāvānna viśeṣaḥ*. (p. 26).
22. R. Thangaswami Sarma, *Darśanamañjarī*, Pt. I, p. 34.
23. V. Raghavan, *New Catalogus Catalogorum* (University of Madras, 1968, Vol. I), p. 242.
24. See *New Catalogus Catalogorum*, Vol. X. p. 247. The entry mentions, 'in 2 chs. by Vācaspati Miśra. IO 1968'. First, it may be pointed out that according to the detailed indication regarding the abbreviation IO on p. ix of the first volume there is no such catalogue published in 1868. It specifically says 'A catalogue of Sanskrit and Prakrit manuscripts in the India Office Library. By Julius Eggeling. 2. parts (London, 1887, 1896) and Vol. II in 2 parts by A. B. Keith, with a

supplement—Buddhist Manuscripts—By F.W. Thomas, London, 1935. This may be regarded as a printing mistake, but it is inexcusable on the part of the Editor not to have indicated whether it was Vācaspati Miśra I or Vācaspati Miśra II who is supposed to be the author of the work. By the year 1978, when the tenth volume was published, it was generally accepted that there were two different Vācaspati Miśras and that the *Tattvāloka* is the work of the later one. It is not that the *New Catalogus Catalogorum* does not know of the fact as it refers to the author of the *Nyāyasūtroddhāra* as 'Vācaspati Miśra (Junior) of Mithila (15 cent.)'. (p. 280). But even here the entry is wrong in two respects. One, it classifies the text as a commentary, which it certainly is not. Secondly, it mentions it as incomplete which also is mistaken. The editor relies on what is written by Hara Prasad Sastri in his *Notices of Sanskrit Manuscripts*, Second Series, published in 4 volumes by the Govt. of Bengal, Calcutta in 1900, 1904, 1907 and 1911 which is cited as the authority for the statement. But the *Nyāyasūtroddhāra*, as we know, had already been published by Pt. Gaṅgadhara Śāstrī Tailaṅg in 1896, a fact, which does not seem to be known either to Hara Prasad Sastri in 1904 or to Prof. Kunjunni Raja, the editor of Vol. X of the *New Catalogus Catalagorum* in 1970. If we remember that the text of the *Nyāyasūtroddhāra* had once again been published in between by Pt. Sūrya Nārāyaṇa Śukla in 1936 with new footnotes, the situation is unbelievable indeed. Or, is there another *Nyāyasūtroddhāra* which is a commentary on the *Nyāya-Sūtras* to which Hara Prasad Sastri refers to in his *Notices of Sanskrit Manuscripts* published in 1904. Strangely, even Pt. Thangaswami Sarma who in his *Darśanamañjarī*, Part I, published in 1985, mentions the 1896 publication of *Nyāyasūtroddhāra* in VSS 9, does not question the correctness of its classification as a commentary in the *New Catalogus Catalogorum*.

25. The missing *sūtras* of the *Nyāyasūtroddhāra* in the *Nyāyasūcīnibandha* are 3.1.15, 3.1.38, 3.1.63, 3.1.69, 3.1.70, 3.2.34, 3.2.38, 3.2.47, 3.2.69 and 3.2.70.
26. The following *sūtras* of the *Nyāyasūttrodhāra* have variant readings (with additions etc.) in the *Nyāyasūcīnibandha*: 2.1.47, 2.2.17, 2.2.52, 3.2.14, 3.2.26, 3.2.48, 5.1.17, 5.1.18, 5.1.19, 5.1.20 and 5.1.24.
27. The missing *sūtras* of the *Nyāyasūcīnibandha* in the *Nyāyasūttrodhāra* are 2.1.20, 2.2.28, 2.2.43, 2.2.49, 3.1.29, 3.1.30 and 3.1.73.
28. Prof. Thangaswami Sarma informs me in a personal communication that even Uddyotakara's *Nyāyavārttika* tries to do this to some extent.
29. The *sūtras* in the *Vṛtti* missing in the *Nyāyasūcīnibandha* are 3.1.15, 3.1.38, 3.1.53, 3.1.63, 3.1.69, 3.1.70, 3.2.40, 3.2.44, 3.2.47, 3.2.69 and 3.2.70. The *sūtras* missing in the *Nyāyasūtroddhāra* are: 3.1.29, 3.1.30, 3.1.31, 3.1.53, 3.2.10 and 3.2.44.
30. The list of the *sūtras* in the *Vṛtti* which have a variant reading (with additions, etc.) from the *Nyāyasūcīnibandha* are: 2.1.25, 2.1.53, 2.2.13, 2.2.17, 2.2.48, 2.2.49, 2.2.52, 2.2.61, 3.1.62, 3.2.10, 3.2.14, 3.2.25, 4.1.49, 4.1.61, 4.2.10 and 5.2.15.
31. The variant readings in the *Vṛtti* and the *Nyāyasūtroddhāra* relate to the following *sūtras*: 2.1.25, 2.1.44, 2.1.53, 2.2.13, 2.2.48, 2.2.61, 3.1.62, 3.2.10, 3.2.14, 4.1.49, 4.1.61, 4.2.10, 5.1.18, 5.1.19, 5.1.20, 5.1.24 and 5.2.15.
32. Potter, *Encyclopedia*. Vol. I, p. 43, entry 790.
33. T. K. Gopalaswamy Aiyangar, *Journal of the Shri Venkatesvara Oriental Research Institute*, Tirupati, Vol. VIII, 1947, p. 34–47.
34. The *sūtras* of the *Nyāyasūcīnibandha* missing in the *Vivaraṇa* are: 2.1.20, 2.2.37,

2.2.43, 3.1.38, 3.1.55, 4.2.7, and 4.2.8. The *sūtras* of the *Vivaraṇa* which are not to be found in the *Nyāyasūcīnibandha* are: 3.1.15, 3.2.10, 4.1.45, 4.1.49, 4.2.50m and 5.2.20.

35. T.K. Gopalaswamy Aiyangar, Footnote. p. 35. Italics mine.
36. Potter. p. 334.
37. Bhīmācārya, *Nyāyakośaḥ* (Poona: Bhandarkara Oriental Research Institute, 1978), p. 2.
38. T. K. Gopalaswamy Aiyangar. 'Lost *Nyāya-Sūtras* as restored by Radhamohana Gosvami Bhattacarya'. *The Journal of the Ganganatha Jha Research Institute*, Vol. XXVI, No. 14., (Oct. 1970), pp. 41–44.
39. Though the editor has not added '*Tarkācārya*' to his name it is necessary to do so to distinguish him from Keśava Miśra, the author of the *Tarkabhāṣā*.
40. Kishore Nath Jha (ed.), *Nyāyatātparyadīpikā* by Vāgīśvara Bhaṭṭa (Allahabad: Ganganath Jha Kendriya Sanskrit Vidyapeeth, 1979), p. tha. da.
41. Kishore Nath Jha, p. 2.
42. T. K. Gopalaswamy Aiyangar, 'Lost *Nyāya-Sūtras* as restored by Radhamohana Gosvami Bhattaccarya'. *The Journal of the Ganganatha Jha Research Institute*, Allahabad, Vol. XXVI, No. 4 (Oct. 1970), p. 41.
43. On Udayana's date, see Potter (ed.), *Encyclopedia of Indian Philosophies*, Vol. II (Delhi: Motilal Banarsidas, 1977), p. 523.
44. Potter, p. 345.
45. *Ibid.*, p. 411.
46. Potter, p. 334.
47. Potter, p. 205.
48. *New Catalogus Catalogorum*, Vol. X, p. 248. Also, *Darśanamañjarī*, p. 74.
49. T.K. Gopalaswamy Aiyangar, 'A Critique of the Nyāya-Sūtra Text', p 41.
50. *Ibid.*, p. 41.
51. See for a further illustration and discussion of this point my article 'The Vedic Corpus: Some questions' in this book.
52. The only thing he says about it is '*pṛthak sūtra-pāṭhaśca vācaspatimiśrakṛtasūtroddhār-anāmakam vaṅgākṣaralikhitamekaṁ pustakamālocya saṁyojitaḥ*'.
53. H. P. Sastri, p. 88.
54. There does not seem to be any mention of these in the *New Catalogus Catalogorum*.
55. Vol. X. p. 280.
56. Interestingly, Ganganatha Jha refers to three different manuscripts consisting of the *Sūtra-pāṭha* only. These are (i) A palm-leaf Manuscript of the *sūtra* only, (ii) Paper manuscript of the *sūtra* only belonging to Jagadish Mishra, and (iii) Paper manuscript of *sūtra* only belonging to Babu Govindadasa.' (p. ix of the Preface)'. This is in contrast to the statement by Hara Prasad Sastri in the 1905 article already referred to. The *New Catalogus Catalogorum* seems to refer to a number of manuscripts without commentaries (Vol. X. p. 276) but none seems to have collated or checked the standard reading of the *sūtras* with them.
57. Bimal Krishna Matilal, *Perception: An Essay on Classical Indian Theories of Knowledge* (Oxford: Clarendon Press, 1986), p. 429.

APPENDIX I

A

Sūtras in the *Nyāyasūtroddhāra* missing in the *Nyāya-Tātparya-Dīpikā* of Bhaṭṭa Vāgīśvara.

1. 2.1.61
2. 3.1.15
3. 3.1.18
4. 3.1.54
5. 3.1.71
6. 3.2.14
7. 3.2.16
8. 3.2.21
9. 3.2.34
10. 3.2.37
11. 3.2.38
12. 3.2.39
13. 3.2.46
14. 3.2.47
15. 4.1.15
16. 4.1.16
17. 4.1.33
18. 4.1.49
19. 4.1.60
20. 4.2.6
21. 4.2.11
22. 4.2.12
23. 4.2.14
24. 4.2.17
25. 4.2.20
26. 4.2.21
27. 4.2.22
28. 4.2.25
29. 4.2.27
30. 4.2.28
31. 4.2.29
32. 4.2.30
33. 4.2.32
34. 4.2.33
35. 4.2.34
36. 4.2.37
37. 4.2.42
38. 5.1.20
39. 5.1.34

Total: 39

B

Sūtras in the *Nyāya-Tātparya-Dīpika* of Bhaṭṭa Vāgīśvara missing in the *Nyāyasūtroddhāra*.

1. 2.1.20
2. 2.1.21
3. 2.1.27
4. 2.1.34
5. 2.1.56
6. 2.1.60
7. 2.1.64
8. 2.2.7
9. 2.2.10
10. 2.2.11
11. 2.2.50
12. 2.2.51
13. 2.2.52
14. 3.1.1.
15. 3.1.18
16. 3.1.28
17. 3.1.30
18. 3.1.31
19. 3.1.32
20. 3.1.41
21. 3.2.16
22. 3.2.19
23. 3.2.20
24. 3.2.22
25. 3.2.37
26. 3.2.42
27. 3.2.60
28. 4.2.22
29. 4.2.30

Total: 29

C

Variant readings of the *sūtras* in the *Nyāyasūtroddhāra* and the *Nyāya-Tātparya-Dīpikā* of Bhaṭṭa Vāgīśvara.

1. 1.1.28
2. 1.1.40
3. 1.2.17
4. 2.1.1
5. 2.1.24
6. 2.1.25
7. 2.1.43
8. 2.1.44
9. 2.1.46
10. 2.1.55 (variant reading with न)
11. 2.2.7
12. 2.2.8
13. 2.2.9
14. 2.2.11
15. 2.2.15
16. 2.2.17
17. 2.2.31 variant reading with अ 2.2.34)
18. 2.2.56
19. 3.1.16 (Variant reading with न)
20. 3.1.13 (Variant reading without न)
21. 3.1.28
22. 3.1.34
23. 3.1.38
24. 3.1.46
25. 3.1.53
26. 3.1.65
27. 3.1.12 (Variant reading with अनुपलब्धि)
28. 3.2.24
29. 3.2.29
30. 3.2.45
31. 3.2.48 (Variant reading with न)
32. 3.2.54 (Variant reading with न)
33. 3.2.65 (Variant reading without न)
34. 3.2.74
35. 3.2.76
36. 4.1.4
37. 4.1.7
38. 4.1.10
39. 4.1.36
40. 4.1.39
41. 4.1.40
42. 4.1.47
43. 4.1.62
44. 4.2.10
45. 4.2.15
46. 4.2.23
47. 4.2.35 (4.2.19)
48. 4.2.47
49. 4.2.49
50. 5.1.17
51. 5.1.38
52. 5.2.3
53. 5.2.15

Total: 53

APPENDIX II

A

Sūtras of the *Nyāyasūtroddhāra* missing in the *Gautamīya-Sūtra-Prakāśa* of Keśava Miśra.

1. 1.1.8
2. 2.1.25
3. 3.1.15
4. 3.1.54
5. 3.1.60
6. 3.1.65
7. 3.1.71
8. 3.2.38
9. 3.2.47
10. 3.2.71
11. 3.2.73
12. 4.2.7
13. 4.2.8

Total: 13

B

Sūtras of the *Gautamīya-Sūtra-Prakāśa* missing in the *Nyāyasūtroddhāra.*

1. 2.1.20
2. 3.1.28
3. 3.1.29
4. 3.1.30
5. 3.2.10

Total: 5

C

Variant readings of the *sūtras* in the *Nyāyasūtroddhāra* and the *Gautamīya-Sūtra-Prakāśa.*

1. 2.1.55 (Variant reading with न)
2. 3.1.6 (Variant reading with न)
3. 3.1.30
4. 3.1.36
5. 3.1.38
6. 3.1.50
7. 3.1.53
8. 3.2.54 (Variant reading with न)
9. 4.1.7
10. 4.1.24
11. 4.2.44
12. 4.2.45
13. 5.1.17
14. 5.1.20

Total: 14

APPENDIX III

A

Sutras in the *Nyāyasūcīnibanda* missing in the *Nyāya-Tātparya-Dīpika* of Bhaṭṭa-Vāgīśvara.

1. 2.1.25
2. 2.1.46
3. 2.1.61
4. 2.2.28
5. 2.2.43
6. 2.2.51
7. 2.2.52
8. 3.1.17
9. 3.1.38
10. 3.1.55
11. 3.1.71
12. 3.2.14
13. 3.2.16
14. 3.2.35
15. 3.2.44
16. 4.1.15
17. 4.1.16
18. 4.1.33
19. 4.1.48
20. 4.1.59
21. 4.2.6
22. 4.2.11
23. 4.2.12
24. 4.2.14
25. 4.2.17
26. 4.2.20
27. 4.2.21
28. 4.2.22
29. 4.2.25
30. 4.2.27

31. 4.2.28
32. 4.2.29
33. 4.2.30
34. 4.2.32
35. 4.2.33
36. 4.2.34
37. 4.2.37
38. 4.2.42
39. 5.1.20
40. 5.1.34

Total: 40

B

Sūtras in the *Nyāya-Tātparya-Dīpikā* of Bhaṭṭa Vāgīśvara missing in the *Nyāyasūcīnibandha.*

1. 2.1.21
2. 2.1.27
3. 2.1.34
4. 2.1.35
5. 2.1.49
6. 2.1.56
7. 2.1.60
8. 2.1.64
9. 2.2.7
10. 2.2.15
11. 3.1.1
12. 3.1.18
13. 3.1.28
14. 3.1.41
15. 3.1.42
16. 3.1.68
17. 3.2.16
18. 3.2.19
19. 3.2.20
20. 3.2.42
21. 3.2.60
22. 3.2.69
23. 4.1.42
24. 4.2.22
25. 4.2.30

Total: 25

C

***Sūtras* with variant readings in the *Nyāyasūcīnibandha* and the** *Nyāya-Tātparya-Dīpikā* of Bhaṭṭa Vāgīśvara.

1. 1.2.8
2. 1.2.17
3. 2.1.26 (A mixture of 2.1.25 and 2.1.26)
4. 2.1.46
5. 2.1.58
6. 2.2.8
7. 2.2.10 & 11 (combined into 2.2.9)
8. 2.2.18
9. 2.2.34 (Variant reading without अ)
10. 2.2.55
11. 2.2.57
12. 3.1.14 (Variant reading with न)
13. 3.1.29
14. 3.1.38
15. 3.1.50
16. 3.1.63
17. 3.2.22
18. 3.2.30
19. 3.2.47
20. 3.2.63 (Variant reading with न)
21. 3.2.71
22. 4.1.4
23. 4.1.7
24. 4.1.36
25. 4.1.37
26. 4.1.38
27. 4.1.44
28. 4.2.9
29. 4.2.17
30. 4.2.34
31. 5.1.18

Total: 31

APPENDIX IV

A

Sūtras in the Nyāyasūcīnibandha which are missing in the *Gautamīya-Sūtra-Prakāśa* of Keśava Miśra.

1. 1.1.8
2. 2.1.26
3. 3.1.38
4. 3.1.55
5. 3.1.61
6. 3.1.71
7. 4.2.7
8. 4.2.8

Total: 8

B

Sūtras in the *Gautamīya-Sūtra-Prakāśa* of Keśava Miśra missing in the *Nyāyasūcīnibandha*.

1. 2.1.32
2. 3.2.10
3. 4.1.45

Total: 3

C

Variant readings of the *sūtras* in the *Nyāyasūcīnibandha* and the *Gautamīya-Sūtra-Prakāśa* of Keśava Miśra.

1. 1.1.27
2. 3.1.32
3. 3.2.46 (Variant reading with न)
4. 3.2.48
5. 4.1.17
6. 4.1.24 (Variant reading with अ)
7. 4.1.36
8. 4.2.42
9. 4.2.43
10. 5.1.33
11. 5.2.11
12. 5.2.15

Total: 12

CHAPTER SEVEN

Is Īśvarakṛṣṇa's *Sāṁkhya-Kārikā* Really Sāṁkhyan?

Īśvarakṛṣṇa's *Sāṁkhya-Kārikā* is the 'oldest known text of Sāṁkhya philosophy that we possess. There are undoubtedly references to the philosophical doctrine known as Sāṁkhya in texts dated earlier, but they are scattered references and do not form a full, independent text expounding the doctrines of the system. How do we know, then, that these scattered references are Sāṁkhyan in character? Is it only because they agree with what is written in the *Sāṁkhya-Kārikā*, the standard work for understanding what the Sāṁkhya means in the Indian philosophical tradition? If, however, there is some disagreement between them, shall we hold them to be non-Sāṁkhyan or only partially Sāṁkhyan in character? In case we decide on the latter alternative, how do we determine that the divergences are not of such a radical character as to destroy the very Sāṁkhyan nature of the thought so designated? Or, shall we think in terms of an evolution of Sāṁkhyan thought, as one of the writers on the subject, Dr. Anima Sen Gupta, seems to suggest? But then, how do we determine the elements of continuity and growth in the history of the doctrine, and why do we stop at Īśvarakṛṣṇa's *Sāṁkhya-Kārikā*, and not consider the commentary on it by Vācaspati Miśra, or the writings of Vijñānabhikṣu and the author of the *Sāṁkhya-Sūtras*?

The problem, in a sense, remains the same whether we treat *Sāṁkhya-Kārikā* in relation to the pre-*Kārikā* Sāṁkhya or the post-*kārika* Sāṁkhya. Supposing there are relevant philosophical differences in the work of Īśvarakṛṣṇa and those of Vācaspati Miśra, Vijñānabhikṣu and the author of the *Sāṁkhya-Sūtras*, shall we then give preeminence to the *Sāṁkhya-Kārikā* alone and treat all divergent elements as non-Sāṁkhyan in character, or treat Īśvarakṛṣṇa as only a precursor who held some non-Sāṁkhyan views? Īśvarakṛṣṇa, or course, claims that he himself has merely summarized the teachings handed down through a succession of teachers and disciples beginning with Kapila in ancient times.[1] But, in a sense, the same claim is also made by Vācaspati Miśra, Vijñānabhikṣu, and the author of the *Sāṁkhya-Sūtras*. The *Tattva-Kaumudī* of Vācaspati Miśra is a straightforward commentary upon the *Sāṁkhya-Kārikā*. The *Sāṁkhya-Sūtras* ostensibly try to pass themselves off as the work of Kapila, the mythical founder of Sāṁkhya, and Vijñanabhikṣu's *Sāṁkhya-Pravacana-Bhāsya* is a commentary upon them. Yet, as everybody knows, there are significant, even radical, differences between the way Vijñānabhikṣu tries to interpret the *Sāṁkhya-Sūtras* and the *Sūtras* themselves. Equally, if we accept the usual contention that there was a theistic pre-*kārikā* Sāṁkhya, then the claim of the author of the *Sāṁkhya-Kārikā* to summarize the ancient teaching is as false as that of Vijñānabhikṣu with respect to the *Sāṁkhya-Sūtras*. The theistic interpretation of the latter is as unwarranted as the atheistic interpretation of the former, provided we accept the usual characteristic of pre-*kārikā*, or rather pre-*Pañcaśikha* and pre-*cārvāka* Sāṁkhya as theistic in character.

The claim for continuity of interpretation is, thus, deceptive if we consider it seriously. The so-called Sāṁkhya was itself understood differently, even in classical times, by different thinkers and it would be difficult to find grounds for preferring one philosopher's interpretation to another's. Why should we prefer Īśvarakṛṣṇa's interpretation to that of Vijñānabhikṣu's or vice versa? Furthermore, in the case of Sāṁkhya we do not even know what they are interpreting. There is no complete text available earlier than the *Sāṁkhya-Kārikā*, and if it too is regarded as an interpretation, it is difficult to see how in the absence of that which presumably is being interpreted, we can judge the adequacy or inadequacy of the interpretation. In case we are supposed to judge it by comparing it with the statements made about this school in the Mahābhārata and the Gītā, the question would arise as to what we are to compare these statements themselves with. The chain has to be broken somewhere, and the perspective of interpretation in which Indian philosophy has usually been presented discarded as illusory. There is just no point in asking whether the interpretation is correct or incorrect, adequate or inadequate. The individual philosopher is just propounding his view, and the pose of interpretation is simply a mask, or rather a cultural style of presentation, a *façon de parler* which deceives none except those who are distanced from the age and culture where it was current usage.

The problem, then, remains as before as to what exactly is meant by Sāṁkhya in relation to which we could decide whether a particular philosopher's thought is or is not Sāṁkhyan. In a certain sense, the problem is the same with respect to all the schools of Indian philosophy, even though in this paper we are directly concerned only with the issue of Sāṁkhya. What, for example, is Vedānta, Nyāya or Mīmāṁsā, or any of the schools of Buddhism and Jainism? Are they characterized by the distinctive philosophical positions they hold on various issues and in terms of which they are distinguished from one another? Are they something like the various philosophical 'isms' of the western tradition, which are differentiated by the positions they hold on diverse philosophical issues? Are they, so to say, something like 'idealism', 'realism', 'empiricism', 'dualism', 'monism', etc.? Or, are they just proper names which do not connote any specific philosophical positions? Are they something as indeterminate as the traditional *Brahman* of Indian thought, which may be designated and symbolized by any and everything, without being in reality designated by any or even all of them together? Or, are they all just separate names for the same ultimate which basically cannot be named at all?[2]

Whatever be one's choice among these alternatives, the only one which is philosophically relevant is the one that treats them as connoting diverse philosophical positions. Unless they are treated in this way, they can be of no interest to the practicing philosopher today, whatever their interest may be for the student of cultures and civilizations. Sāṁkhya, then, is to be understood as the name of a philosophical position which is different from that of the Vedānta, Nyāya, Vaiśeṣika, Mīmāṁsa, Cārvāka, Bauddha, or Jaina position.[3] The distinctiveness of its philosophical position should be articulated in such a way that it does not depart too far from the traditional texts usually associated with this school in the Indian tradition. But it need not be too diffident in this respect either. The particular texts may not agree fully with the spirit of the school, and every thinker would have his own idiosyncratic variation on the central theme, but there may also be aspects or tendencies of a philosopher's thought which are counter to the core of the distinctive philosophical position worthy of being given the name of a school. There is always a certain departure which is a violation, and not a variation of the theme. A certain philosophic temper may see everything as a variation on some basic indeterminate theme, but by that very fact it counts itself out of the arena of all debate and controversy.

If we take this point of view, we would have to ask ourselves in an almost *a priori* manner what could not be, or ought never to be called, a Sāṁkhyan position. If the term Sāṁkhya is basically held to characterize a philosophical position which asserts the ontological reality of both *puruṣa* (i.e., self or subject) and *prakṛti* (i.e., nature or object) and if the identification between the two at any level is the fundamental mistake according to the system, then, obviously, the violation or denial of either of these may be taken as un-Sāṁkhyan in character. I am not urging that the term *Sāṁkhya* should be used in this sense, but only that if it be so used then something necessarily follows from such a usage. What is un-Sāṁkhyan would obviously depend upon what we understand by the word *Sāṁkhya*, and there is hardly anyone, as far as I know, who has not accepted the above two as essentially characterizing the school in Indian philosophy. It is, of course, true that according to some scholars, wherever the word *Sāṁkhya* has been used, it has not necessarily been used in that sense. Edgerton, for example, writes about its use in the Mahābhārata that "This word means based upon Sāṁkhya, which in 12,308.79 and 82 is used, not as a technical term of philosophy but as a word of every-day language, meaning 'reasoning, ratiocination'. . . It is the rationalizing, reflective, speculative, philosophical method."[4] However, as he admits, this is not a technical use of the term to designate a philosophical position, and it is only in the latter sense that we are concerned with it here.

The term *Sāṁkhya*, then, in its philosophical usage connotes a distinctive set of positions which, if agreed to by any writer on the subject, commits him to a denial of their contradictory opposites. Yet, a writer like Anima Sen Gupta seems to have no hesitation in describing a particular stage of Sāṁkhyan thought as theistic and monistic.[5] It does not seem to occur to her that a monistic Sāṁkhya is a contradiction in terms. If a thinker gives up the position of the ultimate ontological reality both of self and nature or *puruṣa* and *prakṛti*, then his thought cannot be characterized as

Sāṁkhyan in character. Even theistic Sāṁkhya can be accepted only in the sense in which *Īśvara* is accepted, say, in the *Yoga Sūtras*, that is, as a pre-eminent, ever-liberated soul, and not as a creater or God who is the source both of self and nature, *puruṣas* and *prakṛti*.

The point obviously is not merely a verbal one. It is not whether the word *Sāṁkhya* connotes this or that. A word, as everybody knows, may have any meaning attached to it. But if it is to designate a specific position in a particular context, then it should not be allowed to designate also the opposite position in the very same context. This would only defeat the purpose of thought itself. It may be said in defense of Anima Sen Gupta that she is only tracing the evolution of Sāṁkhyan thought, and that in the process of time a word can come to designate positions which are radically opposed to each other. But, firstly, this may just be being misled by the superficial use of the same word at different times in different works.[6] Secondly, even if a temporal continuity is granted, there is no point in calling the two by the same name when they connote radically opposed philosophical positions. It would only lead to confusion on the part of all who read or write on the subject. If early Sāṁkhya was monistic, as is alleged by some, then how was it different from Vedānta at that time? Equally, if it was theistic, how was it different from the devotional schools of those times? This point is important, as Sāṁkhya in the Indian tradition has never, as far as I know, been associated with the devotional way of religious seeking. To link it with theism, except in the accidental and adventitious way of the *Yoga Sūtras*, runs counter to the spirit of the school itself.

However, the issue is not confined to the so-called pre-*kārikā* Sāṁkhya alone. It spills over into the so-called classical Sāṁkhya itself. How are the *Kārikā* and the *Sūtras* to be interpreted; would not certain interpretations be un-Sāṁkhyan in character? These are the crucial questions which have to be faced and answered, especially in view of the fact that some interpreters have tried to read into them both theism and Vedāntism. The case of Vijñānabhikṣu is too well-known to be repeated here. But even with respect to the *Kārikā*, we are told that "A very recent commentary is the *Sāṁkhya-Taruvasantaḥ* by Muḍumba Narasiṁhasvāmin. The author has done with the *Kārikā* what Bhikṣu did in respect to the *Sūtras*. He believes that there is no radical divergence between the Sāṁkhya and the Vedānta."[7] The question, then, obviously is whether these interpretations are Sāṁkhyan in character or not. Is this repeated tendency to assimilate Sāṁkhya to something else, whether theistic or monistic, not a violation of the spirit of Sāṁkhya as a distinctive philosophical position?

Theism and monism may appear to be such forced interpretations on the *Kārikā* and the *Sūtras* as not to deserve any serious consideration on the part of any dedicated student of the subject. Classical Sāṁkhya is supposed by all to be atheistic and dualistic in character. A philosophical position which rejects the ultimate dualism of Self and Nature or Subject and Object does not deserve the name of Sāṁkhya at all.[8] But the issue is not confined to the rejection of just these two characteristics. There is a third one which, as far as I know, has never been the subject of discussion in the whole history of thought about this school of Indian philosophy. The issue I refer to concerns the condition of the soul or self in the state of liberation when it has achieved complete *kaivalya*, or release from the state of ignorance in this system. What exactly is the state of the *puruṣa* after it has achieved the state of true knowledge according to this system?

Before seeking an answer to this question, I may say that the concept of release or liberation in any particular system will be a function of what that system regards as bondage and the cause or causes to which it is due. As in most Indian philosophical systems, bondage is due to error, it will be the realization of what it regards as the true nature of reality which will give the soul release or liberation. One may, so to say, read off in an *a priori* manner the nature of the liberated consciousness if one knows what is held to be the fundamental error in a system. The differences in the different philosophical systems may, in fact, be characterized in terms of what they regard as fundamental ignorance or *adhyāsa*, as it is called in Sanskrit. If the systems are to be philosophically different, then what they hold to be the basic *adhyāsa* has also to be different.[9]

The fundamental *adhyāsa* in Sāṁkhya is, as everybody knows, the identification of the subject with the object or of the object with the subject. The classic statement of this is not found in a work ostensibly Sāṁkhyan, or written by a thinker even remotely thought by anybody to subscribe to Sāṁkhya philosophy. It is the *advaitic* Śaṁkara who opens his commentary on the *Brahma Sūtras* with a statement which, in my opinion, is the classic expression of Sāṁkhyan *adhyāsa*. He writes: "It is a matter not requiring any proof that the object and the subject whose respective spheres are the notion of the 'Thou' (the non-ego) and the 'ego', and which are opposed to each other as much as darkness and light are, cannot be identified."[10]

This quotation, even though from Śaṁkara, will, I hope, be taken as epitomizing the Sāṁkhyan position. The subject and the object cannot be and ought not to be identified. Their identification is the fundamental error and the dissolution of the error is the realization of the complete separation of the one from the other. When the subject realizes that it is not the object at any level whatsoever, it is released from all error and suffering and attains liberation or *mokṣa*. This realization of non-identity or complete distinction is itself the state of liberation, or at least ought to be so according to the Sāṁkhya. The statement 'I am not This' may be taken to characterize Sāṁkhyan liberation, provided we understand by 'I' the pure subject or *puruṣa* and by 'this' the pure object or *prakṛti*. Logically, then, the *puruṣa* in the state of liberation must be aware of *prakṛti* and of its complete separation from it in all its forms and at all its levels. The pure subject or *puruṣa* being of the character of consciousness, and consciousness being of the nature of witness (*sākṣin*), it must be aware of (*dṛṣṭā*) *prakṛti*, even in the state of liberation. The difference between bondage and liberation in Sāṁkhya cannot consist in the awareness or non-awareness of *prakṛti*, but in identification or non-identification with it.

With this background, if we ask ourselves what the position of the *Sāṁkhya-Kārikā* is on this question, we are led by different writers in different directions. Anima Sen Gupta writes: "The released *puruṣa* too perceives *prakṛti*, but is no longer deluded by her powers of creation."[11] As against this definite pronouncement, K. C. Bhattacharyya writes: "The knowing function also being of the same *buddhi* and not of the pure self tends to cease *absolutely*, the lapse of substantial *buddhi* being only a potentialisation into *prakṛti*. . . Thus the destiny of the knowing function of *viveka* is to end absolutely as function which means the termination of the illusion of embodiment on the one hand and of the content of knowledge on the other. The Self as *mukta* or in its essential nature is accordingly conceived to be contentless consciousness."[12] Obviously, if the *puruṣa* in its purity is a contentless consciousness, it cannot be aware of anything in the liberated state. But if it is so, how is it different from the *advaitic ātman* of Śaṁkara, which also is supposed to be a contentless consciousness? Bhattacharyya has not asked himself this question, but unless we ask this openly we may always be tempted unconsciously to give a non-Sāṁkhyan interpretation to a Sāṁkhyan position.

The whole issue, as far as Īśvarakṛṣṇa's *Sāṁkhya-Kārikā* is concerned, depends upon the interpretation we place on *kārikā* 68. *Kārika* 65 clearly states, "Thereby does the pure spirit, resting like a spectator, perceive Primal Nature which has ceased to be productive, and, because of the power of discriminative knowledge, has turned back from the seven forms (dispositions)."[13] Here the conscious awareness of *prakṛti* by the *puruṣa* after liberation is explicitly and unambiguously asserted. The same is indicated by the next *kārikā*, which states that, " 'she has been seen by me', (says) one (and is) indifferent; 'I have been seen', (says) the other (and desists from evolution); though there be conjunction of these, there is no prompting to (further) creation."[14] Both these statements are made clear in the next *kārikā*. *Kārikā* 67 makes this clear by stating, "virtue and the rest having ceased to function as causes, because of the attainment of perfect wisdom, (the spirit) remains invested with the body, because of the force of past impressions like the whirl of the (potter's) wheel (which persists for a while by virtue of the momentum imparted by a prior impulse)."[15] This is what is traditionally described as *jīvanmukti*, that is, liberation while being alive in the body. The previous two *kārikās*, then, may be taken to function only within the ambit of the later *kārikā* and may not be interpreted as making an absolute statement about the state of the liberated self in general, that is, whether embodied or disembodied. *Kārikā* 68, philosophically the last in the book, talks specifically of the self's separation from the body and the attainment of the state after that. It states: "Primal Nature, her object accomplished, ceasing to be active, (the spirit) on obtaining separation from the body, attains release (which is) both certain and final."[16]

The point is whether this release, which is gained after the separation from the body, contains an awareness of *prakṛti* or not. The term used in Sanskrit for the turning away of the Primal Nature after having accomplished its purpose is the same in both *kārikā* 65 and *kārikā* 68. The word used in *kārikā* 65 is '*vinivṛttam*,' while in *Kārikā* 68 it is '*vinivṛttau*.' Both are slightly different forms of the Sanskrit root *vṛt* compounded with the adverbial prefixed *vi-ni*. Not only this, the cause of the turning away is the same in both *kārikās*. It is the accomplishment of its purpose, which was the arousal of the discriminative knowledge in the *puruṣa* of its complete difference from *prakṛti*. The purpose is proclaimed by the *kārikā* in many of its verses.[17] As against this, the term for release which is used here is *kaivalya*. Literally, it means 'absolute aloneness,' which might be taken to imply the complete absence of even the awareness of any object whatsoever. Furthermore, if it is read in the light of *kārikā* 61, the conclusion that the self in the state of ultimate and absolute aloneness is not aware of *prakṛti* is strengthened. The *kārikā* states: "It is my belief that there is not any other being more bashful then Primal Nature, who because (of the realization) 'I have been seen *never again comes into the view of the spirit*.'"[18] Nothing could be more categorical than the italicized assertion here, and if we contrast it with the equally categorical assertion in *kārikā* 65 already quoted above, the conclusion is inescapable, that the opposed assertions relate to the liberation in the disembodied and the embodied state respectively.

This is the most reasonable interpretation of the *Kārikā* that I can think of. But it is not my task in this paper to argue which of the interpretations is really correct. K. C. Bhattacharyya has ascribed the knowing function to the *buddhi*, and thus according to him, even in *kārikā* 65 the *puruṣa* could not have become completely liberated as he is there still said to be able to perceive Primal Nature. One of the most recent commentators on the Sāṁkhya in the classical Indian tradition, Swāmī Hariharānanda Āraṇya, has characterized it as *vivekakhyāti*.[19] The same interpretation is supported in an indirect way by aphorism 55 of Book VI of the *Sāṁkhya-Sūtras*, which states that "Experience ceases at (discrimination of) Soul, (as being quite distinct from Nature); since it arises from its (Soul's) Desert. . ."[20] If experience ceases in an absolute sense, then obviously there can be no awareness of *prakṛti* at all.

However it be, the question that I wish to raise is, 'which of the two interpretations is more in accord with the spirit of Sāṁkhyan philosophy as a whole?' And since the question is asked this way, can there be any doubt about the answer? Can there be anyone who would fail to see that *kārikā* 65 describes the Sāṁkhyan position better than *kārikā* 68, if the latter be interpreted according to K. C. Bhattacharyya or Hariharānanda Āraṇya? And if so, what could be the possible reason for such an obvious judgment?

The reason is not hard to find. Sāṁkhya basically seems to characterize a style of philosophical thought which asserts the ultimate dualism of subject and object, and which maintains that the fundamental error consists in their confusion or identification in any form or at any level. If this is the heart of the Sāṁkhyan insight, then whatever goes against this will have to be considered un-Sāṁkhyan in character.

There may be the greatest possible variations on the theme, but if some variation tends to destroy the theme itself, then obviously it cannot be permitted to function within the style of that thought-system. To take a parallel example from the west, while it may be possible to have theistic or atheistic existentialism, it would be meaningless to have an existentialism which gives ontological and axiological primacy to essence over existence.

It is not that some thinkers may not actually show tendencies in that direction, but they will be tendencies that will be counter to the spirit of the system. In fact, a distinction between the thought of an individual thinker and the philosophical position represented by a school is the supreme desideratum if we want to do justice to philosophical thinking in India. Īśvarakṛṣṇa's *Sāṁkhya-Kārikā* may have un-Sāṁkhyan elements in it and yet be treated, not as the epitome of Sāṁkhyan thought in India, but as the work of an individual thinker. The schools should be treated as ideal types or morphological forms which are both intuited through their various presentations and which, to some extent, guide thought in its immanent development also.[21]

It should be noted in this context that the question, 'Which of these two interpretations is more in accord with the spirit of Sāṁkhyan philosophy as a whole?' is different from the question. 'which of these two interpretations is more in accord with the exact text of the *Sāṁkhya-Kārika* as we know it?' The second is a textual-historical question, while the first is primarily a philosophical one. The positivistically inclined may dispute the legitimacy of this distinction. They may ask, 'How can we know what Sāṁkhya is except by looking into the *Sāṁkhya-Kārikā*?' The obvious answer is to ask the counter-question, 'Does *Sāṁkhya-Kārikā* exhaust all that is or has been considered Sāṁkhya?' If it is conceded that there are other works purporting to propound Sāṁkhya philosophy, and that they do not all agree in each and every respect with what they consider to be the Sāṁkhyan doctrine, then how are we to choose among them? Shall we accept the most common elements in all of them and consider them alone as Sāṁkhyan? Shall we then close the possibility to any new Sāṁkhyan works ever being written in the future? Is it to be treated as a dead, closed system of thought with no possibility of any future development, change, or differentiation?

The question is not merely verbal, as many might think, and it is not confined by any means to Sāṁkhya alone. The issue can be raised with respect to each of the so-called schools of Indian philosophy and, in fact, extends to other areas of Indian thought and culture also.[22] On our answer to the question will depend the way we shall approach and interpret the millennia long tradition of Indian philosophy and culture. Also, the development of these traditions in a living manner will depend on how we conceive them—whether as something finished and final, fit only for the archives of the past, or as something vital and living, fertilizing the thought of the present and the future. It is time that the frozen moulds of the past are broken, and the living waters in them are freed to flow and make the thinking tradition in India bloom once more. All that Īśvarakṛṣṇa writes may not be Sāṁkhya. Or, for that matter, all that Śaṁkara writes may not be Advaita Vedānta. We have revered the past too long. Let new questions be asked, and may be the oracles will give a different answer, more relevant to the times we live in.

NOTES AND REFERENCES

1. The *kārikās* from 69 onwards explicitly make this claim. There is some controversy about the exact number of *kārikās* after the sixty-ninth in the original text. But this is irrelevant to what I am saying as *kārikā* 69, which is accepted by all, itself makes this claim, albeit implicitly.

2. See for some of the issues mentioned here 'Vedānta—Does. It Really Mean Anything?', and 'Three Myths About Indian Philosophy,' in this volume.
3. I personally think that these traditional classifications are philosophically misleading. But even if they are accepted, they ought not to be interpreted in such a way as to obliterate the distinctions between the one and the others.
4. Franklin Edgerton, *The Beginnings of Indian Philosophy* (London: George Allen & Unwin Ltd., 1965), pp. 35–36.
5. Anima Sen Gupta, *The Evolution of the Sāṁkhya School of Thought* (Patna: Patna University, 1959), p. 126.
6. As already pointed out, Edgerton believes that the word *Sāṁkhya* does not always occur as 'a technical term of philosophy' in the Mahābhārata. For a more radical opinion see. G. C. Pande, *Studies in the Origins of Buddhism* (Allahabad: Allahabad University Press, 1957), Chapter VIII.
7. S. S. Sūryanārāyaṇa Śāstrī, ed. and trans., *The Sāṁkhya-Kārikā* of Īśvarakrsna (Madras: University of Madras, 1948), p. xxiv.
8. This is obviously based on the presupposition that we want to preserve the traditional philosophical associations with the word and that we do not want it to connote a philosophical position designated by, say, *Advaita Vedānta.*
9. For a further elaboration of this idea and its specific application to Śāṁkara Vedānta, see 'Adhyāsa—A Non-Advaitic Beginning in Śāṁkara Vedānta,' in this volume.
10. *Brahmasūtrabhāṣya*, in Radhakrishnan and Charles A. Moore, (eds.), *A Source Book in Indian Philosophy* (Princeton: Princeton University Press, 1957), p. 509. The problem posed by this Sāṁkhyan *adhyāsa* in an *advaitic* work is discussed in the article referred to in the previous footnote.
11. *Op. cit.*, p. 49.
12. K. C. Bhattacharyya, *Studies in Philosophy*, Vol. I (Calcutta: Progressive Publishers, 1956), p. 192 (Italics mine.)
13. Śāstrī, The *Sāṁkhya-Kārikā* of Īśvarakṛṣṇa, p. 100.
14. *Ibid.*, p. 101.
15. *Ibid.*, p. 102.
16. *Ibid.*, p. 104.
17. *Ibid.*, see *kārikās* 21, 42, 56, 57, 58, 60, 63. There are, of course, some problems. *Kārikā* 62 flatly declares that the self is neither ever bound nor ever liberated. It is only the *prakṛti* which is so. However, the overwhelming evidence of the other *kārikās* points in another direction, especially *kārikā* 68, which philosophically closes the book by calling attention once again to the accomplishment of the object of Primal Nature by using the word *caritārthatvāt.*
18. *Op. cit.*, p. 95. (Italics mine.)
19. His work on Sāṁkhya and Yoga has been published in Bengali under the title *Pāntañjala-Yogadarśana* (Calcutta: Calcutta University, 1949).
20. The *Sāṁkhya Aphorisms of Kapila*, trans., James R. Ballantyne, Chowkhamba Sanskrit Studies, XXXIV (4th ed.; Varanasi: Chowkhamba Sanskrit Series Office, 1963), p. 451.
21. For a discussion of this point see 'Three Myths About Indian Philosophy' in this volume.
22. See in this connection 'Vedānta—Does it Really Mean Anything?' in this volume.

CHAPTER EIGHT

Adhyāsa—A Non-Advaitic Beginning in Śaṁkara Vedānta

Adhyāsa, the superimposition of one thing upon another which is essentially different from it, is a concept common to all schools of philosophy, Indian or western. If there is such a thing as error, then there is such a thing as *adhyāsa*, for it is merely another name for error, or rather, an analytically explicit description of what happens whenever any such thing as error occurs. *Adhyāsa*, then, is not special to Śaṁkara Vedānta. The only distinctive feature it has is the specific content of what it would regard fundamentally as *adhyāsa*, that is, error. *Adhyāsa*, in this sense, would be specific to each system, depending upon what it regards as the most basic error from which all the rest necessarily flows. The fundamental *adhyāsa*, or error, of one system would not, then, be the same as that of another system, since, in that case, the two systems would be identical.

Adhyāsa, therefore, is not one but many, even though there may be a formal similarity between them. Each is a superimposition of something upon something else, but what is superimposed on what is the real would be the source of differences among the different *adhyāsas*. For example, what would be an *adhyāsa*, for the Sāṁkhya would not be so for Śaṁkara Vedānta, if it is construed in strictly Advaitic terms. The reason, obviously, lies in the fact that, for the Sāṁkhya, the ultimate reality consists of two absolutely disparate entities, while, for Advaita Vedānta, reality is an absolute identity which, therefore, precludes the assertion of any difference whatsoever. The assertion of an ultimate difference is the central contention of the Sāṁkhya, while the absolute denial of all ultimate difference is the core of the Advaita assertion. This is important, for the Sāṁkhya will not remain Sāṁkhya if it admits the corrigibility of ultimate difference. Equally, the Advaita Vedānta will not be worth its name if it admits even the possibility of difference as an ultimate truth in its system.

The respective *adhyāsas* of the Sāṁkhya and the Advaita Vedānta can thus be deduced from their ultimate assertions. If it is true that the *puruṣa* (self or subject of all experience) and *prakṛti* (nature or the object of all experience) are the two ultimate realities, disparate and distinct, then their identification at any level will be the basic *adhyāsa*. If, on the other hand, only an ultimate and complete identity between the self and nature, or between the subject and object is the truth, then the assertion of any difference between them at any level is the basic *adhyāsa*. The former is the Sāṁkhya, and the latter, the Advaita Vedānta.

The *adhyāsa* of the Sāmkhya may be formulated, then, as 'I am this', where 'I' refers to the pure subject, self or *puruṣa*, and 'this' to nature, object or *prakṛti*. This basic identification is the heart of the error, according to the Sāṁkhya school. The paradigm formulation of the Advaita Vedānta, on the other hand, will be the exact opposite. Since ultimate difference is denied, the assertion of differences at any level is only a limited form of the primeval error. The *adhyāsa* of the Advaita Vedānta would be formulated as 'I am not this', where 'I' refers to the self, subject or *ātman* and 'this' to nature, object or *Brahman*.

This formulation of Advaitic *adhyāsa* seems logical and necessary enough. Yet, if we open Śaṁkara's commentary on the *Brahma-Sūtra*, the magnum opus of the Advaita Vedānta, we will be surprised to find that it is not so. The way in which Śaṁkara formulates the basic *adhyāsa* seems to be the exact opposite of what, logically, it ought to be. He writes, "It is a matter not requiring any proof that the object and the subject whose respective spheres are the notion of the 'Thou' (the non-ego) and the 'ego', and which are opposed to each other as much as darkness and light are, *cannot be identified*."[1] The trouble is with the word which has been translated as 'ego'. In Sanskrit, the term used by Śaṁkara is '*asmad*', which may safely be translated as 'the first person, or the I'. Gambhirananda has also translated the same passage: "It being an established fact that the object and the subject that are fit to be the contents of the concepts 'you' and 'we' (respectively), and are by nature as contradictory as light and darkness, cannot logically have any identity. . ."[2] The only substantial difference between the two translations consists in the translation of '*asmad*' as 'we' rather than 'ego'. But 'we' appears to be as wrong as 'ego', for what Śaṁkara seems to be talking about is not the empirical self, or the plurality of selves,[3] but the pure subject, which can never be known as an object at all.

It is quite clear that what Śaṁkara describes as the root form of all ignorance is the identification of the subject with the object in any of its forms and at any of its levels. This is plain and unmitigated Sāṁkhya doctrine, and even the wildest attempt at a reinterpretation cannot turn it into the Advaita Vedānta. For Advaita Vedānta, identification is the essence of the truth. In fact, it is the linguistic expression of the ultimate truth which spurns even the appearance of difference in the utterance of identity. The identity of *Ātman* and *Brahman*, the subject and the object, is the ultimate and distinctive contention of the Advaita Vedānta. Its opponents have criticized it on this score, and its supporters have claimed it as the supreme distinctive virtue of the system.

If identification is the heart of the Advaita Vedānta, then how can Śaṁkara define *adhyāsa* in its terms at the very beginning of his commentary on the *Brahma-Sūtra*? Either Śaṁkara is not an *advaitin*, as has been usually supposed, or our logical deduction of what an *advaitic adhyāsa* ought to be is totally wrong. Either of the alternatives seems difficult to accept. The deduction about *advaitic adhyāsa* seems logical enough, and, if Śaṁkara is not an *advaitin*, then who is?

The difficulty about the non-*advaitic* character of Śaṁkara's opening passage in the commentary on the *Brahma-Sutra* may be met in another way. It may be contended that on an absolutely non-dualistic position, there can be no *adhyāsa*, whether *advaitic* or non-*advaitic*. If there is nothing else besides the one reality, then what is there to be confused with what? Nothing can be superimposed upon another when there are no different things to be superimposed upon each other. There is no 'I' *as opposed to the 'thou'*, nor any 'thou' *as opposed to the 'I'*. How, then, can there be any *adhyāsa* between the two? If Śaṁkara, begins his commentary on the *Brahma-Sūtra* with a discussion of *adhyāsa*, it could only be from some other standpoint than that of Advaita, which is his fundamental philosophical position. The Advaita can have no *adhyāsa*; hence, if there is any talk of *adhyāsa* in any *advaitic* work, it can only be non-*advaitic* in character. Being *adhyāsa* and being *advaitic* are, in this view, a contradiction in terms.

This obviously does not meet the specific difficulty raised earlier about the character of *adhyāsa* with which Śaṁkara begins his main work on Advaita Vedānta. The difficulty was that the *adhyāsa* referred to is specifically Sāṁkhyan in character. The defense consists in pointing out that whatever *adhyāsa* Śāṁkara may talk about is bound to be non-advaitic in character. But this by no means proves or even explains why it has to be Sāṁkhyan in character. Śaṁkara, in fact, anticipates an objection which comes closely to the fundamental *advaitic* objection to all *adhyāsa*. He raises the objection: "... how is it possible that on the interior Self which itself is not an object there should be superimposed objects and their attributes? For everyone superimposes an object only on such other objects as are placed before him (i.e., in contact with his sense-organs), and you have said before that the interior Self which is entirely disconnected from the idea of the Thou (the non-ego) is never an object."[4] The point here is that *adhyāsa* can occur only between two objects. But in this context, Śaṁkara is emphasizing the term 'object' rather than the term 'two'. Had he emphasized the latter, he would have discovered the basic *advaitic* objection ot *adhyāsa* as described earlier.

The fundamentally untenable character of *adhyāsa*, however, need not be confined to the *advaitic* position alone. Error is untenable and unintelligible in any ontological perspective, whether monistic, dualistic, or pluralistic in character. The issue always formulates itself thus: how could error ever possibly arise in the heart of reality? In this respect, error is like evil. It is always with us, though we are fighting it all the time and though, in the last analysis, it ought never to have arisen. For the Sāṁkhya, as for the Advaita Vedānta, *adhyāsa* is unintelligible. The ultimate difficulty for the Sāṁkhya consists in its inability to give a satisfactory answer to the question as to how the confusing identification between *puruṣa* and *prakṛti* could ever arise. Similarly, for the Advaita Vedānta the question remains as to how there could be any *māyā* if *Brahman* alone is real. But this identity in the ultimately unresolved character of error does not, or at least, ought not to, destroy the specific content of error in each differing system of thought. Thus, even though error may be ultimately unintelligible in both the Sāṁkhya and the Advaita Vedānta, it does not follow that what they respectively conceive as error would also, in its specific content, be the same.

Advaitic error, then, cannot be the same as Sāṁkhyan error if the two systems of philosophy are to be considered as fundamentally distinct and different. It can hardly be doubted that the basic error, or *adhyāsa*, with which Śaṁkara starts is Sāṁkhyan in character. Thus, the paradox of the father of all Advaita philosophy in India beginning with a Sāṁkhyan *adhyāsa*, remains.

It is surprising that the paradox has been little noticed by any writer on Śaṁkara Vedānta. Since Śaṁkara starts with it, it has been taken to be the essence of the advaitic *adhyāsa*, and has been presented as such by every writer on the subject. Yet, once the issue is raised, it is quite clear that by no stretch of the imagination can it be regarded as such, and that the paradox of a Sāṁkhyan beginning and an *advaitic* ending needs to be resolved.

The resolution is not as difficult as may appear at first sight. Once we accept the fact that Śaṁkara has started with a Sāṁkhyan beginning and that he is an *advaitin*, the task is to retrace the steps which led from the one to the other. The task would have been impossible if there were no conceivable possibility of reaching the latter from the former. It would have been impossible if Śaṁkara had left no traces of the steps he took in his transition from the one to the other. But it was done so openly that, if it has remained unnoticed, it is only because no one seems to have felt the apparent incongruity between the *adhyāsa* with which *Śaṁkara* begins and the *advaitic* position with which he is so generally and so completely identified.

The step or steps are, in fact, spelled out by Śaṁkara himself. He writes, for example, "... the means of right knowledge cannot operate unless there be a knowing personality, and because the existence of the latter depends on the erroneous notion that the body, the senses, and so on, are identical with, or belong to the Self or the knowing person."[5] Here Śaṁkara is explicitly contending that there can be no knowledge, whether right or wrong, without the basic Sāṁkhyan *adhyāsa* with which he began as the fundamental error in the beginning of his work. Right knowledge, thus, is fundamentally as wrong as so-called 'wrong' knowledge. The distinction may be valid at the phenomenal level of pragmatic activity, but from the ultimate philosophical standpoint, both have to be treated as erroneous, because they equally rest on a fundamental error. There would, in fact, be no knowledge if there were no *adhyāsa*, that is, fundamental error.

Śaṁkara's argument is concerned, in this context, with the 'knowing personality' alone, but the limitation is purely adventitious. The explication made further in the course of the argument reveals quite clearly that what is being talked about is 'personality' in general, and not just the 'knowing personality.' It is 'personality' that "depends on the erroneous notion that the body, the senses, and so on, are identical with, or belong to the Self. . ."[6] Without assuming this identification, nothing can be known, felt, or willed. Thus, all human activities are rooted, according to Śaṁkara, in a basic error. Unless the self identifies itself with the intellect, mind, senses, and the body, nothing can ever be said, known, felt, or willed. While these activities continue, we may safely assume that we are in error. The moment the error ends, these activities will also end. What would remain is pure reality, indescribable by any of the terms that we know.

It may be argued that the steps we have traced lead to the notion of the indescribable real, and not to that of *advaita*, or non-dual reality. The two, however, are closely related. In fact, they are two faces of one and the same thing. The duality of truth and error, pleasure and pain, right and wrong, meaningful and meaningless, is endemic to the realm of knowledge, feeling, action, and articulation. These dualities define the very nature of these realms, and as these realms depend for their very being on a fundamental error, they will also completely vanish with the end of that error. The realm of the pure real is, then, the realm of the *advaita*, that is, the realm of non-duality *par excellence*. It should be remembered in this connection that the term '*advaita*' does not mean the assertion of a monistic view of reality, as has been generally supposed. It is not an answer to the question whether reality is one or many. It is the assertion that the real is the realm where the fourfold duality mentioned earlier does not apply. It is, thus, *advaita*, in the most literal and strict sense of the term.

The passage from a Sāṁkhyan beginning to an *advaitic* conclusion, is thus, clear. It should be remembered, however, that this was not the only route through which Śaṁkara could have reached his *advaitic* conclusion. He could have begun, for example, with pure advaitic *adhyāsa* and then drawn attention to the fact that, without differentiating oneself from the object, one could not say, know, feel, or will anything. Thus, the whole world of knowledge, feeling, action, and articulation would ultimately rest on a fundamental error. Only this time, the error would be *advaitic* rather than Sāṁkhyan. It was because all these processes presupposed the non-identification of the self with the not-self, that they rested on a fundamental error, and not because they involved the identification of the self with the not-self.

It may seem surprising as to how the same conclusion could be reached from two contradictory notions of *adhyāsa*. The reason for such an apparently anomalous situation, is simple. Every empirical activity of man requires both identification and differentiation. The identification is usually with the intellect, mind, senses, and body. The differentiation is between one object and another object, and between the whole world of objects and the so-called empirical ego, which is the result of identification. Thus, any philosophical system which regards all identification or all differentiation as fundamentally erroneous would necessarily lead to the relegation of the whole world of duality to the realm of unreality, or *māyā*. There need be no surprise at Śaṁkara's reaching an *advaitic* position from Sāṁkhyan premises. Nevertheless, it should be consciously realized that he took this route and not the other one, which perhaps would have been more logical for him. This is the only contention of this essay and it seems to be an indubitable one.

NOTES AND REFERENCES

1. S. Radhakrishnan and Charles A. Moore, (eds.), *A Source Book in Indian Philosophy*, (Princeton: Princeton University Press, 1957), p. 209 (Thibaut's translation. Italics mine.)
2. Swami Gambhirananda *Brahma-Sūtra-Bhāṣya of Śrī Śaṅkarācārya* (Calcutta: Advaita Ashrama, 1965), p. 1.
3. 'Ego' in Latin is supposed to mean 'I', but as the word is not italicized or printed as a Latin word in the translation, it is difficult to understand whether Thibaut is using it in the English or the Latin meaning. In any case, a more unambiguous term is available in English, and there is no reason why the translator should not have used it.
4. *A Source Book in Indian Philosophy*, pp. 509–10.
5. *Ibid.*, p. 510. (Italics mine).
6. *Ibid.*

CHAPTER NINE

VEDĀNTA—Does it Really Mean Anything?

Vedānta is, perhaps, the best known school of Indian philosophy. In India or abroad, among the laity or the educated, it is by far the most discussed and the most written about school of Indian philosophy. Even among the specialists of the subject, it is generally regarded as the most distinctive contribution of India to the philosophical thinking of the world. Indians have thought it worthy of propagation outside their country. Have we not had a Vivekananda and a Ram Tirtha going west to preach the message of Vedānta? And do we not have today the Ramakrishna Mission spreading the gospel of Vedānta everywhere in the world? From Deussen and Max Müller to Aldous Huxley and Christopher Isherwood, have not there been thinkers in the west who have regarded it as the finest flower of Indian thought? And has not the Indian tradition itself regarded it as the culmination of more than two millennia of serious philosophical speculation? Does not the first historian of Indian philosophy, Mādhavācārya, in his *Sarva-Darśana-Saṅgraha*, treat Vedānta as the final truth and synthesis of all the other systems of Indian philosophy?

That is overwhelming testimony. If one wants to add to it, one may reflect on the fact that the Upaniṣads, the primal source of all Vedāntic inspiration, form the earliest philosophical texts known to India. They are supposed to have exercised profound and overwhelming influence on the shaping of Indian philosophical thought, and we find that today they are as vital as ever. Vedānta is the only living school of Indian philosophy. The thought of many of the Indian thinkers of the present century has been described as neo-Vedāntist. The Vedāntic texts of the classical times form the bulk of philosophical writings in India. Nyāya is the only school which may be considered to be a rival in this field. But Nyāya became increasingly specialized, concentrating on logical problems, and lost some of its significance for philosophy in general. In this it reminds one of modern logic which too has developed increasingly as a proliferation of techniques divorced from the conceptual concerns of general philosophizing.

Vedānta, then, is the most dominant, alive and continuous tradition of Indian philosophizing that we know of. Yet, does it really mean anything at all? Does the term connote or signify anything philosophically significant? Or, is it only a word full of emotional significance, good for propagandistic purposes but, basically, signifying nothing.

These questions may appear strange and puzzling to the ordinary student of the subject. Even the specialist may feel that we are trying to raise dust where everything is clear. After all, the Radhakrishnans and Dasguptas, the Hiriyannas and the thousand and one Ānandas of the Ramakrishna Mission have already answered our questions. They could not possibly be wrong. Where, then, is the problem? What, then, is the question and why does it have to be asked at this time?

The wonder is natural enough. But philosophers should never cease to wonder, nor to raise questions even when they seem to question the very self-evident. Let us ask ourselves, 'Who is a Vedāntin?' and we would begin to see the point of the question we are asking. 'Who is a Vedāntin?' Is he a person who believes in the sole reality of *Brahman* and the complete non-residual identity of the self and the world with the *Brahman*? If so, Rāmānuja is not a Vedāntin. In case we wish to count him as one, we will have to change our definition. No, the self and the world are different from *Brahman*. Well, how different? What degree and quality of difference shall we allow ourselves to admit? Will the degree and quality of difference that will suffice to include Rāmānuja, suffice to include Madhva, Nimbārka, or Vallabha? And what, in that case, would happen to those who were counted as Vedāntins on the former, more limited, criterion? What, for example, happens to Śaṁkara if we choose a definition that will make Rāmānuja a Vedāntin? Does he remain one or does he not? Obviously, if the admission of the ultimate reality of difference in any form is compatible with being a Vedāntin, then Śaṁkara, on the basis of the traditional interpretation, could never be one. The same problem would obviously arise for Rāmānuja if Madhva is treated as a Vedāntin. In case the latter is counted as one, the former certainly could not be counted the same, for they hold very different philosophical positions. The story would repeat itself with every step, and we would have to face the difficult choice as to whom to call the real Vedāntin. Shall it be Śaṁkara, Rāmānuja, Madhva, Nimbārka or Vallabha? Or anyone whose ideas are different from theirs.

The question 'who is a Vedāntin?' then, is not easy to answer, since tradition holds so many to be Vedāntins whose philosophical positions are diametrically opposed to one another. If the term *Vedānta* were to connote a philosophical position, it is difficult to see how persons holding different and even opposed views concerning philosophical matters could be regarded as Vedāntin. *Vedānta*, then, could not be the name of a philosophical position or philosophical school as has generally been supposed. It could only designate something non-philosophical which could possibly be shared by persons who do not hold identical views with respect to philosophical matters. Only on the basis of some such presupposition as this, thinkers so different as Śaṁkara, Rāmānuja, Madhva, Nimbārka and Vallabha could possibly be regarded as Vedāntins.

The non-philosophical meaning of the term *Vedānta* is fairly well-known to the writers on Indian philosophy. Yet, they have failed to see its devastating implications, and to investigate it to the fullest extent possible. *Vedānta*, literally means 'the end of the Vedas', and this usually refers to the Upaniṣads which are supposed to be the last or concluding portion of the Vedas. By streching the meaning, it came to mean the philosophical position expounded in the Upaniṣads. Every Vedāntist, thus, is supposed to expound the philosophy of the Upaniṣads, and the differences between different Vedāntin may be understood as differences of interpretation with respect to what the Upaniṣads really propound concerning philosophical matters.

This, to a certain extent, seems close to truth. But it is only 'close' to it, though certainly close enough to give it the appearance of indubitable truth. The Upaniṣads are certainly the authoritative texts for Vedānta, but not the only texts which enjoy that position. Besides them, as is well known, there are the *Brahma-Sūtras* and the Gītā which are treated as authoritative by the thinkers of this school. The Upaniṣads, the *Brahma-Sūtra* and the Gītā form the classical triumvirate on which the philosophy known as Vedānta is supposed to rest. However, as there is no such thing as the Vedānta philosophy, what is meant is that the philosopher who contends that the philosophy he is propounding is the real philosophy of these three works is a Vedāntin. Vedānta, thus, is not distinguished by any particular set of philosophical beliefs, but by the contention that these are the beliefs of the three texts mentioned above.

The addition of the *Brahma-Sūtra* and the Gītā to the Upaniṣads as the authoritative texts for the Vedānta philosopher makes nonsense of the so-called literal meaning of the term *Vedānta*. The former two can, by no stretch of imagination, be conceived as belonging to the concluding portion of the Vedas. The *Brahma-Sūtras*, it may be argued, is a kind of summary of the Upaniṣads and thus may be treated as being identical with them. If, however, this were really the case, there would be little point in mentioning and treating it as a separate authoritative text. The *Brahma-Sūtras*, it should be remembered, are commented on and explicated alongside the Upaniṣads by a few of the great thinkers of this school. In their case, at least, it was not as if one who was commenting on the *Brahma-Sūtras* felt it irrelevant to comment on the Upaniṣads or vice versa. Rather he felt it necessary to comment simultaneously on both, as if they were two separate and coordinate authorities to be equally treated. The Gītā, for its part, is not even supposed to be a part of the Vedic corpus. It is explicitly referred to as a part of the Mahābhārāta, which is not held by anyone to belong to the concluding portion of the Vedas. It of course is true that the claim has been made for it that it contains the real essence of the Upaniṣads. But there can be little doubt about the spuriousness of the claim or the fact that it was made at a later date.

It has been argued that, in a sense, both the *Brahma-Sūtra* and the Gītā may be treated as attempts at synthesis of the various conflicting elements in the Vedas.[1] The first is an attempt to synthesize the apparently conflicting statements of the various Upaniṣads, while the second is an attempt to synthesize the conflicting claims of knowledge and action upheld in the various parts of the Vedas. The inclusion of these two apparently diverse texts as authoritative along with the Upanisads is thus supposed to become intelligible. The former two merely explicate the meaning of the Upaniṣads and render it in a coherent, intelligible form. There is, thus, no incongruence in holding them to be authoritative, and maintaining that Vedānta is the philosophy adumbrated in the concluding portion of the Vedas, that is, the Upaniṣads.

This theory, however attractive it may seem at first sight, faces certain difficulties. First, it concedes an important difference between the *Brahma-Sūtras* and the Gītā. The former is a synthesis only of the conflicting elements in Upaniṣadic thought. The latter, on the other hand, attempts to synthesize the conflict between the Upaniṣads and the non-upaniṣadic part of the Vedas, assuming, of course, that the Upaniṣads deal primarily with knowledge or *jñāna* and that the rest is concerned with ritualistic action or *karma* as the sole means to salvation. The Gītā, on the basis of this interpretation, could be relevant only for the person who held to the authoritative character of the whole of the Vedas including the Upaniṣads, and not for one who upheld that of the Upaniṣads alone. The Vedāntin is usually supposed to belong to the latter category, and thus could not possibly hold the Gītā to be an authoritative text for his own thinking. This, in fact, is true for pre-Śaṁkarite Vedāntins like Gauḍapāda and Bādarāyaṇa, who do not even mention the Gītā in their works.

Secondly, even the *Brahma-Sūtras*, on the basis of this theory, cannot have the authority which is usually ascribed to them in this system. They are only the first attempt at a coherent elucidation of the meaning of the Upaniṣads. But this would hardly give them any pre-eminent authority, as is usually done by the adherents of the system. It should, in theory, be completely irrelevant to comment on the *Brahma-Sūtras* if one has already adumbrated the meaning of the Upaniṣads by a direct commentary on them. But this is just not the case. Even the great Śaṁkara felt the necessity of commenting upon them both. Furthermore, according to this theory, it is the Upaniṣads that are the heart of Vedāntic reflection. But, among the great classical exponents of Vedānta, only Śaṁkara and Madhva have directed their attention to the Upaniṣads along with the *Brahma-Sūtras*. Rāmānuja, Nimbārka and Vallabha, have not bothered with them at all. However, they have all commented on the *Brahma-Sūtras*, thus giving it an importance over and above the Upaniṣads.

The problem of the exact number and nature of authoritative texts for Vedāntic thinkers has seldom been posited or discussed. It has been fashionable to repeat the names of the Upaniṣads, the *Brahma-Sūtra* and the Gītā in this connection. But if we ask ourselves whether all the so-called Vedāntic thinkers tried to establish the concordance of their views with these texts, we will be surprised. The answer is a distinct and definite 'No'. Not merely do the pre-Śaṁkarite Vedāntins ignore the Gītā, the post-Śaṁkarites ignore the Upaniṣads as well. Madhva is the only exception, but we have already mentioned him before.

The *Brahma-Sūtras* is the only text commented upon by all the great *ācāryas* of Vedānta, and thus may be considered as being the authoritative text of the system. However, there is one other text which has been commented upon and deemed authoritative by almost all the post-Śaṁkarite leaders of differing schools of Vedāntic thought. This is the *Śrīmad-Bhāgavata*. It has been commented upon by Rāmānuja, Madhva, Nimbārka, Vallabha and even Caitanya. Bhāskara is the only exception.

Thus, not only have the texts regarded as authoritative varied with the thinkers usually regarded as Vedāntins, there have also been positive additions to them. These additions had little to do with the tradition of thought enshrined in the Upaniṣads. Śaṁkara himself was the culprit in this respect, when he included the Gītā among the authoritative texts for his thought. The inclusion of the *Śrīmad-Bhāgavata* by post-Śaṁkarite masters completely destroys the myth of the exclusive and ultimate authority of the Upaniṣads for Vedāntic thought.[2]

The search for a non-philosophical content which may give some definite meaning to the term '*Vedānta*' seems to run into various difficulties. The usual attempt to equate it with the acceptance of the authority of the Upaniṣads, the *Brahma-Sūtras* and the Gītā is palpably false. The pre-Śaṁkarites ignore the Gītā and the post-Śaṁkarites add the *Śrīmad-Bhāgavata* to the list of the texts they regard as authoritative. The significance of the addition of this last text to the authoritative corpus has seldom been appreciated or understood by the writers on Indian philosophy. The *Śrīmad-Bhāgavata* is not a Vedic text, or even a continuation of the Vedas by any stretch of the imagination.[3] Yet, it is included and treated as authoritative alongside the *Brahma-Sūtras* by post-Śaṁkarite masters. If we add to these, the fact that they ignore the Upaniṣads, the conclusion that these thinkers were basically not interested in either expounding or developing the philosophy of the Upaniṣads seems to be clear.

The inclusion of the Gītā by Śaṁkara himself had opened the doors to this new interest and was, in fact, an open recognition of it. But Śaṁkara's heart still lay in the Upaniṣads, and his thought centered upon them. With his successors, this new interest emerges into the open and overcomes the centrality of Upaniṣadic thought. The open and unambiguous recognition of the *Śrīmad-Bhāgavata* proclaims the victory of devotion or Bhakti over philosophy. The Gītā, at least, had the semblance of philosophy. The *Śrīmad-Bhāgavata* cannot boast of that. The continued recognition of the *Brahma-Sūtras* is only a ritual verbal homage to an ancient past. The real centre of interest lies elsewhere.

Who, then, is a Vedāntin, and what is Vedānta? Shall we think of a Vedāntin as one who contends that what he is saying is in accordance with, or rather the real meaning of, either the Upaniṣads or the *Brahma-Sūtras* or the Gītā or the *Śrīmad-Bhāgavata* or some or all of these? This seems fair enough, for we are now not arguing that he believes in the authority of all of these, but only that he believes in the authority of at least one of them. This, it should be agreed, is reasonable enough. Here, at last, we have found the right answer. But have we?

First, it should be understood that in this view there is no such thing as a distinctively Vedāntin position different from others. One could, for example, be a Vedāntin and hold, say, the Cārvāka position. The only obligation that one would impose upon oneself would be to argue that this is the real meaning of at least one of the four texts mentioned above. The same will be true of Bauddha, Jaina, Sāṁkhya, Yoga, Nyāya, Vaiśeṣika and Mīmāṁsā as well.[4] One could be any one of these, and yet be a Vedāntin, if one were prepared to argue that the philosophical positions associated with these schools is the real position held by one or more of the above mentioned texts also.[5]

This obviously, is not a satisfactory position. If Vedānta is really such an arbitrary and nebulous thing that one can make it out to the whatever one wishes, then it is better that it be forgotten once and for all. But, is even this minimal, though meaningless, sense true? Does it represent the actual state of what has been traditionally called Vedānta in India? Has every thinker who is considered a Vedāntin tried to show the concordance of his thoughts with any of the texts mentioned above? What shall we say of Padmapāda, Prakāśātman, Sureś-vara, Prakāśānanada, Vācaspati Miśra or Madhusūdana Saras-vatī, or the innumerable others who regard themselves and are regarded by others as Vedāntins? It will be patently false to say that all of them have tried to argue the concordance of their philosophical thought with any or all of the traditional texts mentioned above. Even the minimum condition, therefore, does not hold.

There are thinkers who only argue their position, but do not undertake the further task of showing its identity with any of the four traditional texts which alone will make them Vedāntins. Yet, their thought may be the same as that of another who has undertaken this task as well. Nevertheless this identity in thought-content would not turn him into a Vedāntin, for we have already shown that it is not thought-content which determines whether one is to be called a Vedāntin or not.

The whole thing vanishes into thin air. The search for the meaning of Vedānta leads nowhere. The more we try to grasp its meaning and hold it, the more we find it slipping out of our hands. The most haloed term of Indian philosophical thought connotes nothing. It is an empty shell, mere verbiage, an absolute nothing. It needs to be banished from the realms of thought, if we are to be serious about thinking. Let us be serious. Let us banish it. But then shall we remain Indian and not love Nothing?

NOTES AND REFERENCES

1. Dr. G. C. Pande has contended for such a way of looking at the two texts in a conversation with the author. Dr. Pande held the Tagore Chair of Ancient History and Culture at the University of Rajasthan, Jaipur, India.
2. I am indebted for these facts to Dr. G. C. Pande, who has not hesitated to find for me information which may possibly be interpreted in a way which would conflict with his own theories.
3. If anyone chooses to do so, he does it at the risk of making the term 'Vedic' so universal as to degenerate into the meaningless.
4. It may be argued that these schools may also be defined, not in terms of the philosophical positions they hold, but in terms of the texts they regard as authoritative. This would, then, clearly demarcate them from the Vedāntins. But

the Buddhists and the Jains possess clearly defined authoritative philosophical texts, while the others have them only in a Pickwickian manner. On the whole issue of the myth of authority in Indian Philosophy, see in this volume *Three Myths about Indian Philosophy*. For other related myths, see *Three Conceptions of Indian Philosophy*, in this volume.

5. It may be objected that the Buddhists and the Jains will cease to be such if they accept the authority of any of the texts mentioned above. But, basically, there is no acceptance of any authority. One only argues that the position one holds oneself is also the real position of one of these texts. The Vedāntists themselves argue in the same way. Obviously, the authority of the texts could not be very authoritative if they could be interpreted in such diverse ways. See in this connection the articles mentioned above.

CHAPTER TEN

Yajña and the Doctrine of *Karma*—A Contradiction in Indian thought about Action

Yajña, by common consent, is considered to be the heart of the Vedas and the doctrine of *karma*, the most distinctively significant feature of Indian thought about action. Yet, it has seldom been seen that the two are essentially in conflict with each other. In fact, such a recent book as *Karma and Rebirth in Classical Indian Traditions*[1] fails to mention *yajña* in its index. Yet, the notion of *yajña* is important not only because it forms the essential core of Vedic thought, but also because it was later expanded by an analogous mode of thinking to cover activities which could not be regarded as *yajña* in the original Vedic usage of the term. The Gītā makes the *yajña* almost coterminus with creation.[2] And, though both in the Gītā and elsewhere many other things including the cosmos itself is seen as a *yajña*, the paradigmatic example continues to be the Vedic *yajñas*. Besides the varying rituals of the different *yajñas* and the diverse purposes for which they may be undertaken, one constant and essential element in all of them in the perspective of the doctrine of *karma*, is the relationship between the *yajamāna* and the *ṛtviks*, that is, the one for whom the *yajña* is being performed, and those who actually perform it. This is the basic distinction on which most of the Vedic, that is, the *Śrauta yajñas* are based.* Most of the *yajñas* are *actually* performed by persons who have been specially hired for the job, as they are specialists in the knowledge of ritual, which is essential for performing the *yajña*. Furthermore, the performance of *yajña* is a collective enterprise in which different groups of

* It is not clear whether the daily *agnihotra* is a Vedic *yajña* or not. It does not have the usual distinction of *yajamāna* and *ṛtvik* in it. But as most of the other *yajñas* do require such a distinction for their performance, our argument remains unaffected by it.

specialists coordinate their ritually prescribed activities to attain the desired result for the patron who has employed them.

The crucial features of the Vedic *yajña* from the viewpoint of the theory of action, therefore, are the following:

1. It is an action done by a group of persons *for* someone else who has engaged them for performing that action by paying the prescribed fee.
2. It is a *collective* action which can only be undertaken *jointly* by each person performing the part assigned to him in the total activity.
3. The action, though performed by many persons with each contributing separately to it, is still supposed to be *one* action.
4. The action, though done by many persons, is not regarded as *their* action, either singly or jointly, in the sense that the fruit of this action does not accrue to them.
5. The fruit of action acrues not to those who *actually* perform it, but to the one who has paid them to perform it.
6. The action is always undertaken for the achievement of a desired end, whether in this world or the next. In other words, it is a *sakāma karma*.

The distinction between the *yajamāna*, that is, the person for whom the sacrifice is performed, and the *rtviks*, that is, the priests who perform the sacrifice, is not clear-cut in the case of all the sacrifices. In the context of the *jyotiṣṭoma* sacrifice, for example, the *yajamāna* himself is technically regarded as a *ṛtvik*, in order to complete the total number of *ṛtviks* which is mentioned as seventeen in the *śruti* texts. The *Mīmāṁsā-Sūtra* 3.7.38 seeks to justify this on the basis of '*karmasāmānyāt*,' that is, the similarity of functions between the *ṛtviks* and the *yajamāna*. But if this were to be accepted, it would obliterate all distinction between the *yajamāna* and the *ṛtviks* not only in the context of the *jyotiṣṭoma*, but of all the other sacrifices.

Similar is the case with the *sattra* sacrifices, in which the distinction between the 'priests' and the 'sacrificers' does not obtain as "all the priests are from among the 'sacrificers' themselves (10.6.51–58)".[3] And, for this reason, 'there is no 'appointment' of Priests (Sū. 10.2.35, Bhā. trs. p. 1698); and the services of the priests at the *sattra* are not 'bought' or 'exchanged' for any promised 'fee' (10.2.35–38).[4] It is obvious from the above that normally a priest, that is, a *ṛtvik* is one whose services are 'bought' or hired for a promised fee. And this, in fact, is stated in the *Mīmāṁsā-Sūtra* 3.7.36, according to which a *ṛtvik* is one who is given the sacrificial fee as mentioned in the *dakṣiṇāvākya*. But if this were to be accepted, then the *yajamāna* could not be counted as a priest, for he has not been hired for the job by being given the sacrificial fee.

Yet, whatever the problems with respect to these specific sacrifices, by and large we may assume that there is a relevant distinction between the *yajamāna* and the *ṛtviks* in the context of the Vedic sacrifice, and that the latter are hired by the former for the performance of a sacrifice whose fruit he desires to obtain.

Prof. Staal in his well-known work on Vedic ritual, *Agni*, has tried to suggest that renunciation of the fruits of the sacrificial act is itself an integral part of the sacrificial act, and hence it would not be correct to consider it as motivated by the desire for the fruit for which the sacrifice was undertaken. He interprets *tyāga* as 'renunciation (of the fruits of the ritual acts)' and the *yajamāna's* statement when the officiating priest, on his behalf, makes the oblation into the fire to one of the gods, for example Agni, 'This is for Agni, not for me (*agnaye idaṃ na mama*),' taking *idaṃ* to refer to the fruit of the sacrifice itself.[5] It is not clear why *idaṃ* should be interpreted this way. It would be more natural to take it as refering to the *dravya*, 'the substance (used in oblations)', which is put into the fire accompanied by the saying of the *tyāga*-formula given earlier. To conflate the *tyāga* of the material into the sacrificial fire with the *karma-phala tyāga* of the Gītā,[6] and to interpret the former in the light of the latter, is to confuse two very different kinds of *tyāga* which have little in common. Had the two been even remotely similar, the author of the Gītā would not have castigated the Vedas in such harsh terms.[7]

Staal, of course, is aware of the contradiction his interpretation forces on the Vedic framework. In his own words. "at this point a contradiction begins to appear, which becomes increasingly explicit in the ritualistic philosophy of the Mīmāṁsā. The reason for performing a specific ritual is stated to be the desire for a particular fruit or effect. The stock example of the Mīmāṁsā is:

he who desires heaven shall sacrifice with the *agniṣṭoma* ritual (*agniṣṭomena svargakāmo yajeta*). But this fruit is renounced whenever the *yajamāna* utters his *tyāga* formula of renunciation. The effect, therefore, is not obtained."[8] Prof Staal has not even asked himself the simple question: 'how can one renounce what one has not got?' For surely, he does not want to maintain that the *yajamāna* has already got the fruit, i.e., heaven, which he is renouncing by uttering the formula.[9] In fact, had he taken seriously the discussion by Śabara in his *bhāṣya* on *ṣūtra* 11.1.1 and the others following it where the whole issue is discussed threadbare, he would not have made the statement or at least tried to give reasons why he wants to hold to the view in the teeth of over-whelming evidence to the contrary.

We may therefore accept that the *yajamāna* engages in most of the Vedic sacrifices, in order to attain some fruit, and that he usually employs some *ṛtviks*, i.e., priests, for the purpose. And, even if there are difficulties in determining who is a *ṛtvik*, there can be little doubt that the fruit of the activity of the Vedic *yajña* is supposed to accrue to the *yajamāna* who engages in it and hires others for that very purpose. Yet, this is exactly what is sought to be denied by the hard core of the doctrine of *karma*, which cannot but see the Vedic *yajña* as a paradigmatic example of a view of the universe which essentially sees it in immoral terms.

The hard core of the theory of the *yajña* is that one can reap the fruit of somebody else's action, while the hard core of the theory of *karma* denies the very possibility of such a situation ever arising in a universe that is essentially moral in nature. As both the strands lie at the very foundation of Indian thought about action, the contradiction between the two provides that tension which is evident to most students of the subject, and which has been documented to a certain extent in a recent book on the subject edited by Wendy O' Flaherty. The *Mīmāṁsā-Sūtras* themselves are aware of the problem, and, in a certain sense, treat the theory of *karma* in its hard core form as their *pūrvapakṣa*. In *sūtra* 3.7.18, the issue is raised whether all such sacrifices which are done for

* Surprisingly, Wendy O'Flaherty quotes Staal without giving any inkling to the reader that there is another side to the story—that, according to Staal himself, there is a contradiction in the situation. There could not be a more misleading quotation and, to cap it all, she does not even give the page number from which the quotation is exactly taken. See Wendy O'Flaherty, p. 12.

the sake of heaven should be 'performed entirely by the 'sacrificer' himself', or he need do only the Act of Dedication, that is, *utsarga*, and the rest may be done by himself or others, or only by others who have been hired for the purpose. The reason given for the first *pūrva-pakṣa*, that it is the sacrificer alone who should do everything is that "because, as a matter of fact, the result of an action accrues to a person only when he performs the act himself. . ."[10] The problem is raised again in the *Mīmāṁsa-Sūtras* 3.8.25, 3.8.26, 3.8.28 and 3.8.29. The issue in these *sūtras* relates to the question "whether the reward that is asked for accrues to the priest or to the sacrificer."[11] The issue is resolved in different ways in *Sūtras* 26, 28 and 29 respectively. *Sūtra* 3.8.28 resolves it in favour of the sacrificer as it is for his sake that the action is performed. *Sūtra* 3.8.28 argues, according to Śabara, that "in some cases, the result spoken of accrues to the priests—i.e., in those cases where the result in question is helpful in the performance. . ."[12] *Sūtra* 3.8.29 argues that in case "there is a direct assertion to that effect, the result is to be taken as accruing to the priests."[13]

It is obvious that Jaimini cannot accept the theory of *karma* as propounded in the tradition and formulated so explicitly in *sūtra* 3.7.18 by the opponent, if he has to save the practice of *yajña* as enjoined in the *Vedas*. A *yajña* is usually a complex affair lasting for days, or sometimes even weeks or years, and requires specialized knowledge of the ritual, that is, what is to be done, when and how, and with what objects, and by whom. It, therefore, cannot be done by any one person alone, to whom the fruit of that action may accrue, according to the theory of *karma* as formulated by the opponent of the Vedic *yajña*. There are, of course, many human goals which may only be achieved by collective human effort in which a large number of persons cooperate with their different specialized *karma*, and it is not clear how the principle of distribution of the fruit which is the result of such a collective effort would have to be formulated in accordance with the theory of *karma*. But, as far as the Vedic *yajña* is concerned, the situation is far different from this, as the problem there relates not to the formulation of the principle according to which the fruit is to be distributed amongst those who have collectively participated in the action, but of the accrual of fruit to a person who has done practically nothing except hiring others to perform the *yajña* for him. This, of course, happens all the time, but it is surprising that it should not have been seen as posing a problem for the theory of *karma* in the Indian tradition.

The theory of *karma*, it may be said, is itself not quite clear in its formulation. It has been argued recently that, at least in some of its formulations it permits or perhaps even requires such an interactional interpretation where the fruit of each person's action accrues to, or is shared by, others. The classic instance of this, even in the Vedic times, is supposed to be the *śrāddha* ceremony whereby the ritualistic offering given by the son is expected to help his deceased parents in their abode after death. The same will be true of the notion of pollution, particularly that variety of it which is *caused* by others through their voluntary or involuntary behaviour. Yet, however appropriate all these examples may be to show that certain kinds of action enjoined by the religious texts in the tradition lend themselves to an interpretation in which one person's action ostensibly affects another, it will not be quite correct to say that such an interpretation forms an integral part of the theory of *karma*, or that it is an alternative version of it. It is a fact that human beings appear to affect one another in substantial ways, and that they are supposed to be responsible for their actions, as they are considered to have initiated them. The task of a theory here, as in other fields, is to give a coherent and intelligible description of the relevant facts of human action. The theory construction with respect to the facts of human action, however, has another in-built demand. This is the demand not for intelligibility in general, but rather of 'moral intelligibility,' of intelligibility which may be acceptable to the moral conscience of man.

The theory of *karma* as elaborated in the Indian tradition, therefore, has to be seen not as a description of facts relating to human action, but as an attempt to render them intelligible in moral terms. This is the basic difference between the intelligibility of nature and the intelligibility of the human world. The former may be rendered intelligible by postulating the notion of causality in phenomena, but that alone would not render intelligible the world of men. The latter is constituted by human actions, and they are always characterized as 'good' or 'bad', 'right' or 'wrong', properties that can never be ascribed to natural events, except in a figurative or instrumental sense. The intelligibility of the human world, therefore, has to be a moral intelligibility and in a sense, all cultures and civilizations have tried to seek it in their own way. Religion, in the deepest sense, is a search for this intelligibility, though it is never just that. It would be the difference, then, that a culture displays in the solution of this general problem that would reveal its distinctiveness, if any, in this field.

The solution to the problem of the moral intelligibility of the human world in the Indian tradition takes a distinctive turn when from the intuitively self-evident proposition that the world will be a morally unintelligible world if I were to reap the fruit of somebody else's action, or if someone else were to reap the fruit of my actions, it draws the conclusion that in order that the world be morally intelligible, we must live in a 'morally monadic' world. In other words, if 'moral intelligibility' requires that each human being should reap *only* the fruit of his *own* actions, then no human being can *really* affect anyone else, however much the appearances may seem to justify the contrary. Nobody can *really* be the cause of my suffering or happiness, nor can I be the cause of suffering or happiness to anybody else. If I, or anyone else, seem to feel the opposite, that is an *illusion* which is to be rectified by cognitive reflection on the presuppositions involved in the notion of 'moral intelligibility' itself. In the same way that there are 'structural illusions' in the realm of the senses, so also, it is contended, there are 'structural illusions' in the moral realm also. The former are known to everybody; the latter, to nobody. Yet, the latter are as, if not more, important than the former, as they determine the very texture of human experience itself.

The foundational '*avidyā*' or ignorance in this perspective, then, would be to regard anything other than oneself as the cause of whatever happens to one, and the first step towards its rectification would be to realize its erroneous character, however well entrenched it may be in one's psyche or experience. But once the rectification is seen as necessary in order to render the world of human action 'morally intelligible,' it is also seen that I could not confine my existence to this life only, for the simple reason that if I do so, I would have to ascribe the advantages or disadvantages that my being born in a particular family with a particular psycho-physical constituion endows me with to chance or to other human beings. The only way I can avoid this is to postulate a past life of my own, which would provide the moral rationale of whatever happens to me from the moment of conception to such time when I become capable of moral reflection and voluntary action. Not only this, all the accidental features of my life are to be undestood in some such way if I wish to render the world morally intelligible.

It is, therefore, wrong to think that the hypothesis of a future life or rebirth is entailed by the theory of *karma* as it is understood in the Indian tradition. It is rather, only the postulation of a past life which is logically required by the theory. The future life is postulated only to complete the theory, as there seems no reason to think why if there was a past life, there should not be a future one also. Similarly, many of the actions one does in this life do not seem to produce any result that one would reasonably expect to get from them. And hence to explain the anomaly and correct it at a theoretical level, one has to postulate both a past and future life so that different facts may be somehow squared.

The demand for 'moral intelligibility' interpreted in a particular way, then, leads, not only to the treatment of the facts of birth and death as illusory, but also to 'moral monadism' which makes moral life in the usual sense impossible in principle. Normally, one cannot conceive of morality in a monadic universe, for morality implies an 'other-centric' consciousness where one can care for the other because one can affect the well-being of another, however marginal it may be. Once the ontological possibility of this is denied, morality in the usual sense becomes impossible and the fulfilment of the moral consciousness in man will have to take a different turn. The drama of morality, then, can only turn inwards, and be played with respect to one's own consciousness which is felt as being-what-it-ought-not-to-be. The fact of self-consciousness provides the possibility of the 'other' being located in one's own consciousness while the possibility of the 'is-ought' dichotomy is provided for by the feeling that the state of one's consciousness is not what it can be or ought-to-be. One not only alternates between states of consciousness which are pleasant or painful, depressing or happy, satisfying or dissatisfying, significant or insignificant, fulfilled or unfulfilled, but one also has fleeting glimpses of states of one's consciousness which one cannot but feel to be higher and deeper than what one normally experiences. The long Indian quest for a state of consciousness which is self-sufficient, self-fulfilled, self-effulgent, self-validating and unaffected and unruffled by anything else may be understood in some such terms as these.

This shifting of the moral focus to the arena of self-consciousness results in a Self-centric or *ātman*-centric perspective on action, where action is primarily conceived and judged in terms of not what it does to others, which, in any case, it cannot do in the theoretical perspective we are considering, but what it does to me, or rather to my state of consciousness, the two being identified in this perspective.[14] This may seem and, in fact, has seemed perverse to many people, particularly to those who treat the socio-political nature of man as his essential defining characteristic. The western tradition, following Aristotle, is the classic example of this[15], and most western thinkers find it hard to understand the predominantly amoral, or rather transmoral, nature of Indian thought. But the postulation of entities which are essentially unaffected by others is not as rare, or as idiosyncratic as most thinkers or writers on Indian thought about action tend to make it out to be. The attempt to eliminate all seeming interactions between particles as only apparent and illusory is not unknown to the history of science. In fact, it was one of the most respectable things to do at one time, and still remains the theoretical ideal of many scientists. As Pirgogine has argued, "Here we reach one of those dramatic moments in the history of science when the description of nature was nearly reduced to a static picture. Indeed, through a clever change of variables, *all interaction could be made to disappear*. It was believed that integrable systems, reducible to free particles, were the prototype of dynamic systems. Generations of physicists and mathematicians tried hard to find for each kind of system the 'right' variables that would *eliminate the interactions*."[16]

The elimination of seeming 'interactions' for theoretical reasons in the cognitive enterprise is intellectually respectable, and there is no reason why it should be looked at askance when attempted in non-western traditions for making the world 'morally intelligible'. Leibnitz's well-known notion of the monad is, perhaps, a transposition into the ontological realm of the notion of a 'free particle' in the physics of his times But Prigogine's view that this necessarily leads to a 'static' view of nature seems mistaken. What has actually happened is that the centre of dynamism has shifted from the 'external' to the 'internal' and is 'self-determined' rather than 'other-determined', as is usual in most views about nature. Leibnitz's monads are supposed to be centers of incessant activity, and so is the self in the perspective of the theory of *karma* as conceived in the Indian tradition. It is another matter that the valuational judgment of this activity is predominantly negative except perhaps in Kashmir Śaivism and certain forms of Vaiṣṇavism. But such a negative judgement is not essential to the theory itself, nor even to the way it has been usually construed in the Indian tradition.

Yet, whatever the turns and twists such a theory may take to explain away the seeming fact of interaction, the theory itself requires an explication not only of the notion of 'action,' but also of 'my action'. Can one conceive of 'action' in terms of just 'pure willing' or to use the Sanskrit term, as *saṁkalpamātra* without the resulting, or accompanying, bodily movements and their effect on the external world which has both living and non-living beings, including other human beings, in it? At a deeper level, the question is whether the notion of 'action' itself does not necessarily imply some 'other' which has to be changed by my action. This 'other' may, of course, be a physical situation or the state of beings other than myself, or my relationship to them, or their relationship to me. But if 'action' implies both a psycho-physical world of causality and some criteria of ascriptional identity on the one hand, and an interactive framework, on the other, then how can the demands of the 'moral intelligibility' of the universe, as interpreted and understood in the theory of *karma*, be fulfilled? This, is perhaps the basic question in the light of which the Indian thought about *karma* has to be articulated and understood.

That 'human action' has both a 'moral' and a 'causal' component has been known to thinkers in the western tradition, at least since Kant. But Kant posed the problem of morality in terms of 'freedom' and 'freedom' alone, without raising any question regarding the consequences of this 'free' action on oneself or others or both. The problem of reconciling the 'moral' and the 'causal', thus, has been primarily seen by him as an ontological, and not as a moral problem. By and large, this may be regarded as typical of the western tradition of thought in general. The Indian thinking, on the other hand, since its very inception in the Upaniṣadic and Śramaṇic times, seems to have seen the problem primarily in moral rather than ontological terms. Also, the problem is not posed in terms of the radical contradistinction between the realm of causality and the realm of freedom, but rather between 'natural causality' and 'moral causality', or causality as encountered in the realm of nature and the one encountered in the realm of 'moral action'. Freedom is, of course, presupposed by human action, but being 'action', it also implies consequences both in the human and the non-human world. The law of *karma* pertains to the realm of 'moral action', and tries to render the causality that reigns therein 'morally intelligible'.

'Moral action', thus, is seen as necessarily pre-supposing and involving 'causality' in the natural realm which, however, it subordinates to its own purposes. Yet, this causality also pertains to 'moral action' by virtue of the fact that in order to be 'action', it has to belong to the natural realm. It is, thus, the 'action' component of the 'moral action' which results in consequences for others, both in the human and the non-human world. An 'action', however, has consequences not only for others, but also for oneself. The theory of *karma* makes a radical difference between the two. The former, according to it, can have no moral component at all, as no one else can suffer the consequences of my action, if the world is to be 'morally intelligible'. On the contrary, in the context of the theory, only the latter may possibly have a moral dimension. It is only the moral consequences of my action which have to be suffered by me, according to the theory, and not any and every consequence of my action. I can and do suffer the non-moral consequences of others' actions, just as they can and do suffer the non-moral consequences of my action.

Interpreted in this way, the theory would have to provide criteria for distinguishing between moral and non-moral consequences of action. The one distinction which the theory itself entails is that the consequences of a moral action are those which may belong to oneself alone, and thus if we could find the sort of things that could belong *only* to oneself and to none other, that would provide one clue to the distinction. The 'experiencing' aspect of consciousness seems to be one such thing, as even if we accept the possibility of telepathic awareness of someone else's consciousness, the consciousness that is an object of such a direct awareness cannot but see it as the experience of someone else. In a sense, the situation is duplicated in introspective self-awareness, with the difference that one both oberves and undergoes the experience, a situation so well epitomized in the two birds of the Upaniṣad, one of whom savours the experience, while the other only witnesses it. The Sanskrit terms *bhoktā* and *dṛṣṭā* capture the distinction vividly, and it is the *bhoga* aspect of the *karma-phala* or the fruit of action which cannot but be undergone by the agent alone.[17]

The necessity of postulating the notion of 'agency' or *kartṛtva* for understanding the notion of *karma* has recently been questioned forcibly by Edwin Gerow in his article '*What is Karma (Kim Karmeti)? An Exercise in Philosophical Semantics*.'[18] However, the discussion is not only too general, but also too heavily centered on the grammatical tradition, to be of significant relevance to the theory of *karma* in the moral context with which we are primarily concerned. To say that '*karman* is *not* to be found associated with agents or willing'[19] is merely to say that the term can be, and is, used in such a wide sense so as to refer to any and every *vyāpāra*, including even such an event as the falling of a leaf[20] or the blowing of a breeze, etc. But in such contexts, it should be translated as 'event' or 'process', which has little to do with the notion of '*karma*', that is, action with which the doctrine of *karma* is primarily concerned. It is true that the notion of *kartṛtva*, as Gerow points out, has been under attack, specially in Advaita Vedānta, Sāṁkhya and Buddhism.[21] But, firstly, this obtains only at the ultimate ontological level and, secondly, this does not illuminate in any way either our or their understanding of the doctrine of *karma* which all of them also accept. That the doctrine of *karma* ultimately applies only to the phenomenal world is a truism for these systems, but so does everything else including all that can be talked about, known, felt or willed in the usual senses of these words. In fact, the whole *pramāṇa-prameya vyāpāra* itself belongs to the world of *avidyā* according to these schools, and yet, inconsistently enough, they argue against their opponents all the time. Even the author of the *Yoga Sūtras* after declaring *pramāṇa* as a *vṛtti*[22] whose *nirodha* is equated with *yoga*, cannot resist the temptation of arguing against other positions.[23] The problem of 'saving appearences' is there for all metaphysical constructions, and it is peculiarly so for 'moral action,' as it not only presupposes some freedom for the agent[24] and some objective ground for the distinction between right and wrong or good and bad, but also a world which behaves according to some predictability so that action may reasonably be undertaken.

The peculiar problem for the theory of *karma* as developed in the Indian tradition, however, is not the defence of these presuppositions, which are common to all theories of moral action, whether acknowledged or not, but the defence of that which is specific to it, namely, that the consequences of moral action can in no case accrue to anyone except the one who did it. It is surprising, therefore, that in his discussion of *karma*, Gerow nowhere mentions this crucial aspect of the issue, specially in the context of the specific Indian discussion of the subject. This is true not only for Gerow, but also Bhiḍe whose discussion of the subject Gerow has summarized so well in his paper. In fact, the latter on the very first page of his book on *The Karma Theory* mentions the feeding of Brahmins at Gayā or Prayāga for the sake of one's ancestors as an example of the widespread belief in the doctrine of *karma* in India today, without noticing that the example he has given contradicts *prima facie* the doctrine, as, according to it, nothing that I may do or not do can possibly affect anyone else, including my ancestors.[25]

The core problem of the Indian doctrine of *karma* has, thus, hardly been touched on either by Gerow or Bhide, though both of them have many interesting things to say about it in their respective articles. The paradox that 'moral monadism' which is a necessary consequence of the 'moral intelligibility' of the universe construed in a particular way makes morality in the usual sense impossible has hardly been noticed by anybody who has written on the subject. The issue is not between *pravṛtti* and *nivṛtti*, or between maximal and minimal transaction, or between the householder and the renouncer as many who have written on the subject contend. The issue actually relates to the notion of 'moral intelligibility' itself. Is it, or is it not, a necessary condition of 'moral intelligibility' that no one should suffer the consequences of anyone else's action? The Sanskrit terms for these necessary conditions which any viable theory of *karma* has to fulfil if it is to make moral sense of the universe are the impossibility of

कृतप्रणाश अकृताभ्यागम, which may be roughly understood as "non-perishability of what has been done, and non-receivability of what has not been done." But if these conditions are fulfilled, then moral action in the sense of action which is essentially concerned with the good of others rather than of oneself becomes, in an important sense, impossible. The only way out, as we have already suggested, is to interpret moral action as being essentially concerned with others, but only with respect to the *natural* consequences that my action may possibly have on them, and not with respect to the consequences which may accrue only to myself, according to the theory. But in that case, the distinction between the natural and the moral consequences would have to be clearly demarcated in order to reconcile the two contradictory demands being made on the theory.

The idea of *yajña* as elaborated and expanded since Vedic times emphasizes interdependence at both the human and the cosmic levels, and the fact that only through cultivating a spirit of mutual give and take one may attain prosperity, both here and in the hereafter, and thus maintain the worldly and the cosmic orders. But the idea of *karma* in this context as well as the one elaborated in the context of socio-political thought in India does not imply that one's actions, good or bad, cannot affect or rather ought not affect another. As Bhiḍe says, quoting the Vedic text इत्यत्र चैकस्य कर्मणः फलमन्यस्मिन् संक्रामयितुं शक्यमिति स्पष्टं लक्ष्यते[26] But if this is so, then it is in conflict with what is usually understood by the theory of *karma* in the Indian context. That this conflict has not been properly articulated, or solved in the classical thought on the subject is a fact that can hardly be denied. What is more surprising, however, is the fact that even contemporary writers on the subject have shown little awareness of it. The issue is not of an interactionist versus non-interactionist model supposedly typified by Marriott and Potter, respectively, as the editor of the volume on *Karma and Rebirth In Classical Indian Traditions*[27] would have us believe. The issue is how to meet the twin demands of moral intelligibility involving notions of justice, responsibility and accountability to oneself on the one hand, and the real exposedness to, and a genuine concern for others which is the *sine qua non* of the moral consciousness, on the other. The possible reconciliation of these two contradictory demands can, as noted earlier, be perhaps achieved through a distinction between natural causality and moral casuality which, in any case, is implied by the notion of voluntary action itself, though in that context it may have to be phrased differently. But as man himself seems to belong to two worlds, the world of nature and the world of free action where *saṁkalpa, ichhā, prayatna* seem to make a distinctive difference to the world, there should be little difficulty in recognizing the two types of causality.[28]

These two types, in a sense, are recognized in all cultures as they articulate the human condition itself. The distinctiveness of the Indian thought on the subject lies not only in construing the notion of 'moral intelligibility' in a particular way, but also of seeing that 'moral causality' is still causality and hence binds man, though in a different way. The theory of *mokṣa* is, therefore, elaborated to get rid of this bondage. But it introduces another dimension to the reflection on *karma* in the Indian tradition.

Yajña, karma and *mokṣa* provide the three major themes around which Indian thinking about human life seems to revolve. They pull it in opposite directions, as there is not only a tension but also inherent conflict between them. The theory of *yajña*, the theory of *karma* and the theory of *mokṣa* are elaborate constructions—each multiple in nature—built around these focal concerns of Indian thought.

One of the tasks before those who are interested in Indian thought and culture today is to articulate their adequacy and completeness in understanding human life in all its aspects and to see if it is possible to reconcile them, and if so, in what way. Beyond this, we have to extend and modify them in such a way as to incorporate into them our own insights relating to the human situation born of our knowledge of diverse cultures and civilizations. The theories, it should be remembered, claim a universality relevant to all human beings anywhere, anytime. We should not become prisoners of the Indologists' attitude which, by definition, restricts them to the Indian world-view only.

NOTES AND REFERENCES

1. Wendy Doniger O' Flaherty, (Ed). *Karma and Rebirth in the Classical Indian Traditions* (Delhi: Motilal Banarsidass, 1983).
2. *Śrīmad Bhagvad Gītā*, 3–10.

3. Ganganatha Jha, *Pūrva-Mīmāmsā in its Sources* (Varanasi: Benaras Hindu University, 1964), p 281.
4. *Ibid.*, p. 281.
5. Frits Staal in collaboration with C. V. Somayajipad and M. Itti Ravi Nambudri, *Agni: The Vedic Ritual of the Fire Altar* (Delhi: Motilal Banarsidas, 1984) p. 4–5.
6. *Ibid.*, p. 6.
7. See Gītā, 2.42–44.
8. Staal., p. 5.
9. There is a more serious contradiction pointed out by Staal later, but as it does not concern the issue of *yajña* being essentially a *sakāma karma*, we will not discuss it here.
10. Ganganatha Jha, p. 630, The Sanskrit original in the *Sabara-Bhāsya* reads, '*Yataḥ svayam prayuñjānasya phalam bhavati.*' p. 432.
14. A more detailed explication and elaboration of the *ātman*-centric perspective is attempted in the author's *Social Philosophy—Past and Future* (Simla: Indian Institute of Advanced Study, 1969).
15. The Confucian tradition of Chinese thought also seems to treat man as essentially a socio-political being without however giving rise to the type of socio-centrism which has been such a conspicuous feature of western thought. Perhaps, the difference might lie in Confucius's acceptance of heaven and his conceiving of man's relationship to it in terms of harmony. In any case, the reasons for the difference in the case of China need to be explored further by competent scholars in the field.
16. Ilya Prigogine and Isabella Strengers, *Order Out of Chaos* (London: Fontana Paperbacks, 1985), p. 72. (Italics mine).
17. There is a fashionable argument deriving from Wittgenstein which seeks to prove the impossibility of any such thing in principle, as all language is essentially 'public' in character. The protagonists of the argument forget not only that the 'private-public' dichotomy is in-built in the language, but also that there are theories of language which emphasize its unmanifest and transcendent aspects also.
18. *Indologica Taurinensia.* (Official Organ of the International Association of Sanskrit Studies), Vol. X, 1982 (Torino, Italy: Edizioni Jollygraphica).
19. Gerow. p. 99. (Italics author's).
20. Gerow's example, p. 95.
21. *Ibid.*, p. 112–13.
22. *Yoga-Sūtra*, 1.6.
23. *Ibid.*, 4.15–16.
24. The Buddhists do not believe in any agent, but they still have to postulate some sort of continuity to account for the law of *karma* which they accept as much as anyone else in the Indian tradition.
25. *The Karma Theory: its Origin, Nature, Proof and Implications* (Mysore: The University of Mysore, 1950). Prof. Gerow is to be thanked for bringing this important, but little known Sanskrit work, to the attention of the scholarly world.
26. Bhiḍe, p. 30.
27. Wendy O'Flaherty, *op. cit.*
28. It may be noted that this proposed reconciliation is different from the one suggested by Larson in his article "*Karma as a 'Sociology of Knowledge' or 'Social*

psychology of Process/Praxis' by postulating the distinction between *liṅga* and *bhāva* in the *Sāṅkhya* context. As *liṅga* itself is the result of past *bhāva*, the basic moral issue is not even faced in the way the problem is formulated. The whole discussion is vitiated by the acceptance of Marriott's formulation that transactionality/non-transactionality is the heart of the theory of *karma*. Mariott sees the whole thing in terms of caste interactions, as if interactions within caste or within family were no interactions at all. And what about the interactions between the king and the people or the one between states? Also, the concept of 'interaction' has been too much restricted to food and other such things as if other transactions between people were non-existent. The theory of *karma* is far wider than the restricted terms in which Marriott and others, following him, have framed it. For Larson's subtle, though tangential, discussion see Wendy O' Flaherty (ed.), pp. 311–316.

CHAPTER ELEVEN

The Myth of the *Puruṣārthas*

Any discussion of traditional Indian thought about man and society usually revolves around the notions designated by such terms as *varṇa, āśrama* and *puruṣārtha*. It is also generally assumed that the three are so intimately related to each other that each cannot be understood without the other. But even amongst these, the notion of *puruṣārtha* is perhaps more fundamental as it defines those ultimate goals of human life which give meaning and significance to it. The usual four-fold classification of the *puruṣārthas*, it is claimed, encompasses within it all the actual or possible goals that mankind may pursue for itself. Yet, is this truc, and do the terms designate in any clear manner the goals men pursue or ought to pursue?

The usual designation of the *puruṣārthas* is given as *dharma, artha, kāma* and *mokṣa*. There is, of course, the dispute as to whether originally there were only the first three *puruṣārthas* and that the fourth, i.e., *mokṣa*, was added later. But even if this is admitted, and there seems overwhelming evidence to support the contention, there still remains the question as to what is meant by these terms, and whether, if the Indian tradition is to be believed, they comprehend meaningfully all the goals that men pursue or ought to pursue in their lives.

If we forget *dharma*, which is regarded as the distinctive feature of human beings distinguishing them from animals, and concentrate only on *artha* and *kāma* for the present, we would discover that it is not very clear as to what is exactly meant by them. *Kāma*, in the widest sense, may be understood as desire and, by implication, anything that is or can be the object of desire. But then everything will come under the category of *kāma*, since obviously one can and does desire not only *artha* but even *dharma* and *mokṣa*. Such a use of the word *kāma* is not so unwarranted as may seem at first sight. There is the well-known saying in Sanskrit:

nāhaṁ kāmaye rājyaṁ, na svargaṁ, na cāpunarbhavam /
prāṇināṁ duḥkhataptānāṁ kāmaye duḥkhanāśanam //

Here *apunarbhavam*, that is, *mokṣa*, is expressly mentioned while *dharma* may be supposed to be indirectly implied in the last line. In order to avoid the difficulty, one may restrict the notion of *kāma* to certain forms of desire, or to certain objects of desire or both. Thus, it may be said that the term *kāma* refers only to those desires whose objects are sensuous in nature, or where desiring is done in such a way that it necessarily leads to bondage. But this would not only raise the question as to what is meant by bondage, but also whether *svarga*, which is supposed to be the object *par excellence* of Vedic sacrifices, is sensuous or non-sensuous in character. The Vedic injunction in this regard is unambiguous in its formulation. It clearly states '*svargakāmo yajeta*', that is, 'one who desires heaven should perform (the required) sacrifices'. Thus, it is clear that *svarga* is the object of *kāma* for the Vedic seers. Also, as the whole rationale of Vedic authority is supposed to rest on the distinction between *dṛṣṭa* and *adṛṣṭa phala, svarga* cannot but be treated as *adṛṣṭa* and heaven as non-sensuous in character, that is, as non-apprehensible by the senses. But if so, the restriction on *kāma*, as referring only to those desires whose objects are sensuous in character, would become invalid.

The Vedas, of course, also contain injunctions which promise *dṛṣṭa phala* only, and, as far as I know, no one has seriously argued that these parts should be treated as non-authoritative on this ground, or as having only lesser or secondary authority. There are, for example, sacrifices prescribed for those who desire to have a son or rainfall or other such worldly things, and the injunction for these has the same form as the injunction for those who desire *svarga*. The text says, for example: '*putrakāmaḥ putreṣṭyā yajeta, vṛṣṭikāmaḥ kārīryā yajeta*'. There is, thus, no essential difference between '*svargakāmaḥ*' and '*putrakāmaḥ*' or '*vṛṣṭikāmaḥ*', even though the latter are the sort of objects which are known to everybody while the former is accepted only on the authority of the Vedas. In fact, the Vedas are charged with containing false injunctions on the ground that these worldly objects of human desire are many a time not obtained in actual practice by the performance of the prescribed *yajñas*. *Nyāya-Sūtra* 2.1.58, in fact, raises it as an objection on behalf of the *pūrva-pakṣa*, and tries to reply to it in 2.1.59 by saying that the failure to get the desired result may be due to possible defects in the procedure adopted, the material used, the attitude of the sacrificer itself, or all of these together. The strategy adopted by the author of the *Nyāya-Sūtras*, if accepted, would make it impossible in principle to give a counter-example to any causal claim advanced by anybody. This is, of course, not the occasion to discuss the *Nyāya-Sūtras* but only to point out the fact that the so-called Vedic authority in that period was supposed to extend as much to the secular desires of man as to those which dealt with matters pertaining to life after death. Later, if Śaṁkara's evidence is to be believed, there would be an attempt to disentangle the two, and the Vedic authority confined only to matters which were regarded as strictly non-empirical in character. But if such a distinction were to be seriously insisted upon, a large part of the Vedas would have to be treated as redundant. Not only this, as what they promise in the empirical domain is also attainable through other means which have little to do with sacrifices, their importance for these purposes would only be marginal in character.

But whether *svarga* is treated as transcendentally sensuous or non-sensuous in character, there remains the problem of characterizing non-sensuous, non-transcendental objects of desire. How shall we characterize, for example, desire for knowledge or understanding? Shall we treat it as a *puruṣārtha* under the category of *kāma* or not? In the Sāṁkhyan framework, as everything, including *manas* and *buddhi*, is a part of *prakṛti*, there should be little difficulty in treating knowledge or understanding as coming under the category of *kāma* as *puruṣārtha*. But what about those who do not accept the Sāṁkhyan position? The Naiyāyikas, for example, treat *manas* as a distinct entity which is required to be postulated because of the fact that one does not have two perceptions at the same time, even though different senses are in contact with the same object at the same time. *Nyāya-Sūtra* 1.1.16 gives this as the reason for postulating *manas*. On the other hand, no specific reason has been given for postulating *buddhi* as a separate, independent *prameya* in 1.1.15. It only says that the terms *buddhi*, *upalabdhi* and *jñāna* are synonyms for each other. It would perhaps have been better if *buddhi* had been postulated to account for non-perceptual knowledge. Also, it is not clear what the role of *manas* is in non-perceptual knowledge or, for that matter, in the context of *karmendriyas* which, perhaps, may be regarded as relatively more important as far as the *puruṣārthas* are concerned. Of course, the *ātman* itself is supposed to be postulated as that which is required to account for *jñāna* besides *icchā, dveṣa, prayatna, sukha* and *duḥkha*, according to *Nyāya-Sūtra* 1.1.10. But then, what is the necessity of postulating *buddhi* as a separate *prameya*, if *ātman* is already postulated to understand *jñāna*?

Our task, obviously, is not to go into the details of Nyāya or to discuss its conceptual structure. What we want to point out is merely the fact that once we grant relative autonomy to the realm of the mind or intellect, then the desires pertaining thereto cannot be treated under *kāma* without transforming the nature of *kāma* itself. But once the term *kāma* is stretched to cover all ends of human seeking, there would remain no distinction between it and the other *puruṣārthas*. The difference between them could perhaps, then, be drawn on other grounds. *Artha*, for example, could mean instrumentalities for the satisfaction of what is desired, or even generalized instrumentalities such as power or wealth which could be used for the satisfaction of any and every desire. *Dharma* could mean the desire for social and political order without which no desire could be fulfilled. Or, alternatively, it could mean any ordering principle which would obviate or adjudicate the conflict between desires, whether of one and the same individual or of different individuals. *Mokṣa* could mean either the desire for freedom in all its senses, or the desire to be free of all desires— a second order desire which itself may take other forms also.

Perhaps, the idea of *niṣkāma karma* is such a second order desire with respect to all first order desires. It tries to suggest how desires 'ought' to be desired. But this 'ought', it should be noted, is essentially a conditional 'ought' as it is formulated in the context of the desire to be free from the consequences of one's actions. If one is prepared to accept the consequences of one's actions, the injunction to do *niṣkāma karma* will make no sense. It may be argued that consequences inevitably bind one, and that as no one desires bondage, the imperative for *niṣkāma karma* is essentially unconditional. However, it is not clear why all forms of bondage should be treated as intrinsically undesirable or why consequences should inevitably bind one—a point recognized in *bhakti* literature, where there is nothing wrong in being a servant of the Lord or even in being born again and again, if it is to be in his service, to do his work, or sing his praises.

Further, if *kāma* means desire, then *niṣkāma* should mean desirelessness, or a state where desire is absent. But not all desire necessarily leads to action, and if it is the action performed from desire, that is, *sakāma karma* which leads to bondage, then there is no reason to believe that desire or *kāma* by itself would lead to bondage. If desire is translated as *icchā*, then *karma* requires not merely *icchā* but also *prayatna* and *śarīra* with its *karmendriyas*. On the other hand, if *icchā* by itself is supposed to give rise to bondage, then *karma* would become redundant, unless it is argued that *karma* produces bondage of a different kind, or in addition to what has already been produced by *icchā*, *kāma* or desire.

This is not the place to discuss the whole notion of *niṣkāma karma* or the relation of *karma* to bondage or liberation. What we are interested in here is to understand the traditional notion of the *puruṣārthas*, and it is interesting to note in this connection that *karma* does not occur as a *puruṣārtha* at all. Perhaps, it is assumed as a generalized means of attaining all *puruṣārthas*. But, then, *karma* would become necessary for attaining not only *kāma*, *artha* and *dharma* but also *mokṣa*. This would be unacceptable to at least one major school of Indian philosophy, i.e., Advaita Vedānta, as according to it, *karma* is inevitably a sign of one's being in *avidyā* and hence in bondage. The Gītā, which emphasizes the inescapability of *karma* for all embodied beings, does not seem concerned with the ends which are sought to be achieved through action, but rather with the psychic attitude with which the action is undertaken as it is that which, according to it, is the cause of bondage and not action *per se*. But, then, *kāma* would denote not the end for which the action is undertaken, but the attitude with which it is done. The attitude, however, in such a case, cannot be treated as one of the *puruṣārthas* as it is not only not an end of human action, but is also naturally present in all human beings, and hence need not be striven for by any special effort on their part.

There is, of course, the problem as to how the word *puruṣārtha* itself is to be understood. Is it to be taken, for example, in a descriptive sense, that is, as describing what men actually pursue in their life? Or is it a prescriptive word which suggests what men ought to pursue in order to be worthy of being human? *Artha* and *kāma* as examples of *puruṣārthas* tend to suggest the former, while *dharma* and *mokṣa* lead to the latter interpretation. There does not seem much sense in saying one ought to pursue *artha* or *kāma*, as one naturally pursues them and needs no great exhortation to do so. And if one does not pursue them with great zeal or intensity, one is normally praised and not admonished for not pursuing them, particularly if one is pursuing some other ideal value, say, knowledge, social reform, political freedom, the end of exploitation and repression, or even such a thing as the creation of beautiful objects. I have used these examples consciously as it is difficult to subsume them in any straightforward manner under the categories of *dharma* or *mokṣa*, which are the only other *puruṣārthas* permitted to us by the traditional classification. Perhaps, the best way might be to construe it as being both descriptive and prescriptive, thus reflecting the human condition itself wherein the determination by norms and ideals, and the striving towards them is inbuilt into the condition itself. The Upaniṣadic terms *preyas* and *śreyas* describe well this amalgamation, though they do so by opposing them to each other, treating them as dichotomous opposites rather than as necessary components of the human situation.

However, to bring a prescriptive element into *kāma* and *artha* would not be to bring them under *dharma* or make them subservient to *mokṣa*, as in *tantra*, as has usually been understood, but rather to say that each human being has to pursue them for the utmost flowering and fulfilment of his being, and if he does not do so for any reason, it is a deficiency that ought to be rectified as soon as possible. This, however, does not only run counter to the dominant thrust of Indian thought in this field, but also runs against the difficulty that it is not clear what sort of ends are meant by the terms *kāma* and *artha* in the theory of the *puruṣārthas*.

Perhaps, the term *puruṣārtha* should be construed on the analogy of *padārtha* which plays such a crucial role in classical Indian thought about the nature of reality. But the so-called *padārthas*, which have been dealt with most thoroughly in the

Vaiśeṣika system of thought, themselves suffer from a basic ambiguity. It is not clear from the way things are stated in the *Vaiśeṣika-Sūtras*, or in the commentaries thereon, whether the enumerated *padārthas* are categories of language or thought or being. The term *pada* in *padārtha* would tend to incline one to the first alternative, but, as there is some talk of some of them being *buddhyāpekṣā*, one is inclined to the second alternative, at least as far as they are concerned. The third alternative is suggested by the way the first three *padārthas*, that is, *dravya, guṇa* and *karma* are treated in the text. The situation becomes further confused if we take *Vaiśeṣika-Sūtra* 8.2.3 into account which restricts *artha* to the first three *padārthas* only. But then what happens to the last three *padārthas*, that is, *sāmānya, viśeṣa* and *samavāya*? Are they *padārthas* or not? The usual way out is to treat them as *padārthas* in a *gauṇa* or secondary sense. But this would be to interpret *artha* in the sense of meaning, as it is only meaning which can be primary or secondary. But, then, *puruṣārtha* would mean that which gives meaning or significance to human life. However, in that case, *dharma* and *mokṣa* would lose that preeminence which normally is attributed to them.

There is another problem with the term *artha* as it occurs in the word *puruṣārtha*. *Artha* itself is a distinctive *puruṣārtha*, and hence could not mean the same as in the compound *puruṣārtha*. Normally, *artha* as a *puruṣārtha* is taken to mean wealth or power, or those generalized instrumentalities by which what is desired can be attained. But, in this sense, *dharma* itself would become a part of *artha* as it can be legitimately argued that without the maintenance of *dharma*, or what may be called the normative order, most people will not be able to fulfil their desires with any reasonable expectancy of success. The maintenance of social or political order would, then, be only a means for the satisfaction of *kāma* which would be the primary *puruṣārtha* of life. Further, as the distinction between means and ends is always relative, and changes with the way one perceives and orders what one seeks, the distinction between *artha* and *kāma* itself would become relative in character. As for *mokṣa*, it is usually supposed to transcend both *dharma* and *kāma* and thus occupies an anomalous position amongst the *puruṣārthas*, for it is never clear whether this transcendence should be understood as a negation or fulfilment of the other *puruṣarthas*. The Indian thought on this subject has never been able to make up its mind on either side, with the result that confusion has prevailed at the very heart of Indian theorization about the ultimate goal or goals whose seeking renders human existence meaningful. *Mokṣa*, however conceived, is a desire for release from desire itself, and hence negates the *artha* in the *puruṣārtha* in a radical manner. To use a metaphor from a different context of the use of *artha*, what is being asked for is a language in which there is no reference, except self-reference. Even this residuum is denied in Advaita Vedānta, which argues for the untenability of the very notion of *puruṣārtha* itself. The theory, which argues for the *nitya-siddha* nature of *mokṣa* against the one which treats it as *sādhana-siddha*, attests to this.

The essential ambivalence with respect to the relation between *mokṣa* and the other *puruṣārthas* is nowhere more evident than in the discussions on its relation to *dharma*, which is the most clear prescriptive or normative end. Is *dharma* necessary for attaining *mokṣa*? The usual answer is that it helps one in getting *svarga* but not *mokṣa*. *Dharma* as well as *adharma* are the causes of bondage and rebirth. For liberation, one has to go beyond both, that is, not only beyond *adharma* but *dharma* also. That is why the author of the Gītā has treated the Vedas as the realm of the three *guṇas*, that is, *sattva, rajas* and *tamas*, whose heart is *kāma* and whose injunctions, if followed, lead to *bhoga* and *aiśvarya*. *Mokṣa*, on the other hand, is beyond the three *guṇas*[1] and hence beyond the world which is constituted by them. But, then, it cannot exactly be called a *puruṣārtha* or, at least, a *puruṣārtha* in the same sense in which the other three are called *puruṣārthas*. Normally, only that should be designated as a *puruṣārtha* which can be realized, at least to some extent, by human effort. But all effort or activity is supposed to be due to the element of *rajas* which is sought to be transcended in *mokṣa*. Perhaps, that was one reason why Śaṁkara argued so insistently that *karma* cannot lead to *mokṣa*. In any case, the radical difference between *mokṣa* as a *puruṣārtha* and the other three *puruṣārthas* has not only to be recognized in any discussion on the subject, but also the radical incompatibility between them, at least in the direction to which their seeking would lead. The seeking for both *artha* and *kāma* leads one naturally out of oneself and seeks to establish a relationship with objects and persons, though primarily in instrumental terms. It is the pursuit of *dharma* which makes one's consciousness see the other, not as a means to one's own ends, but in terms of one's obligations towards it. Normally, such a sense of obligation arises only for other human beings or even all living beings, but it can be extended beyond these also. *Mokṣa*, however, is a transcendence of that other-centred consciousness from which the sense of obligation arises. In fact, the ontological roots of most conceptions of *mokṣa* in the Indian philosophical traditions either deny the ontological reality of the 'other' or relegate it axiologically to a peripheral position. The Advaita Vedānta radically denies the ultimate reality of the 'other', while the non-Advaitic schools primarily assert the relationship of the self to the Lord, and only secondarily the relation between one self and another. Basically, this relation is mediated through the relation of each to the Lord and is thus indirect in character. Sāṁkhya does assert the ontological plurality of selves, but they all are like Leibnitzian monads, having no interrelationship amongst themselves. The hard core Nyāya-Vaiśeṣika position denies the very possibility of any conscious relationship between selves in the state of *mokṣa*, as they are not supposed to be conscious in that state. Amongst the non-Vedic or even anti-Vedic traditions, the Jains seem to have more or less a Sāṁkhyan conception with little essential relationship between selves which have beome free. The Buddhists do not accept the notion of self, but they do accept a relationship between the realized and the unrealized persons, and articulate it in their notion of *kàruṇā* or *mahākaruṇā*. Parallel to this is the notion of the *Bodhisattva* who feels his obligation to the suffering humanity to such an extent that he is prepared to forego entering the state of *nirvāṇa* in order to help them. But even though this is a great advance in the articulation of the relationship between those who have attained liberation and those who have not, it is still an asymmetrical relationship. It is the suffering humanity that needs the *Bodhisattva*; the *Bodhisattva* has no need of it. The seemingly similar notion of *avatāra* in Hindu thought is even more asymmetrical, as it is a relationship between God and man. It is only in certain schools of *bhakti* that the relation becomes a little more symmetrical, as God is supposed to need men almost as much as men need God. But the relation between men, as we have pointed out earlier, becomes basically contingent as it is only as *bhaktas*, that is, as devotees of the Lord, that they can have any real relation with one another.

Tantric thought, on the other hand, does seem to conceive of a necessary relationship with the 'other' without which one cannot be oneself. But then, this 'other' is confined to a member or members of the other sex only, and the relationship is restricted primarily to the sphere of sex. In the Tantric perspective, men need only women, and presumably, women need only men for self-realization. However, if one reads the texts, it all seems a male affair—at least, at first sight. In fact, if one considers such a ritual as the *kumārī pūjā*, or the worship of the virgin, it is difficult to see how she is involved as a *sādhikā* or seeker in the process. Rather, the whole thing shows a callous disregard for the feelings of the female, and the traumatic effect that such a ceremony may have on her for life.

The self-centric and male-centric character of large parts of Hindu *sādhanā* need to be explored in greater depth and with greater detachment than has been done until now. One of the possible reasons for this may, perhaps, be the identification of the feminine principle itself with *prakṛti* and *māyā*, which are conceived as non-self or even antagonistic to self, and as the main cause for the non-realization by the self of its own nature. The roots of the self-centredness of Indian thought, on the other hand, may be said to lie in its ontological, ethical and psychological analyses of the human situation which gradually came to be accepted as unquestioned truth by a large part of the culture over a period of time. The analysis is epitomized in the famous statement of Yājñavalkya, the outstanding philosopher of the Upaniṣadic period, in the *Bṛhadāraṇyaka Upaniṣad* that nothing is desired for itself, but is desired only because it is dear to the self.[2] The illusion referred to here is the illusion that any object whatsoever can be dear for itself, the truth being that it is dear only because it subserves the interest of the self. The self in this context is, of course, supposed to be the Self with a capital 'S' and not the little ego or the self with a small 's' which is associated with *ahaṅkāra, manas* and *buddhi* which are supposed to constitute the *antaḥkaraṇa* in some shools of traditional philosophical thought in India, and with which the self is usually identified. But such an identification, however inevitable or natural it may seem, is the root of that foundational ignorance which is the cause of all suffering, according to these thinkers. It hardly matters whether the self, so conceived, is with a capital or a small 's' as the centre of all concern, striving, and attention remains something that is not the other but oneself. There is, of course, no 'other' in Advaita Vedānta, but that does not mean that the 'other' is treated as one's own self with a capital 'S', but rather as someone who ought to treat the 'others' as one does oneself, that is, as absolute ontological nullities.

The statement of Yājñavalkya, it should be noted, does not hesitate to use the word '*preyas*' in the context of the *ātman*, that is, the self with a capital 'S', and hence does not seem to subscribe to that radical distinction between *śreyas* and *preyas* which is usually made in this context. Rather, it points to a continuity in the concern with *preyas* which, it is contended, cannot be given up in principle as it is the very nature of Being as consciousness to seek it, for it is what it essentially is. The only problem is the illusion with which it is also primordially endowed, that it can achieve it through something other than itself. The difference between *kāma* and *mokṣa*, on this understanding, would then consist in the fact that the former is necessarily the result of the illusion that the happiness of the self can be achieved through anything other than itself, while the latter is the giving up of the illusion. But giving up the illusion does not necessarily mean that one is happy or fulfilled or blissful; it only means that one is not dependent on anything else for the achievement of such a state. It may be argued that if it depends completely upon oneself, then what could possibly stand in the way of its non-achievement? Perhaps, it could be the attitude of the self to itself. The famous words '*ekohaṃ, bahu syām*' suggest some such dissatisfaction at the root of creation itself. The concept of *līlā* does not get away from this difficulty as the impulse to play requires as much a dissatisfaction with the previous state as anything else. But if non-dependence on anything else, or even the total absence of all 'other', does not ensure that there shall be no dissatisfaction with the state of one's own being in the sense that one does not want a change in it, then the way is opened for the perception that it is not the 'other' which is the cause of one's bondage, but the attitude that one has to the 'other', or perhaps the stance that one takes towards the state of one's own consciousness. This could perhaps provide the clue to the ideal of *niṣkāma karma* adumberated by the author of the Gītā.

The return to the ideal of *niṣkama karma* does not, however, tell us how to pursue *kāma* or *artha* or even *dharma* in a *niṣkāma* way. The author of the Bhagvad-Gītā, it should not be forgotten, is also the author of the Kāma-Gītā, if the identity of the two is admitted. The Kāma-Gītā is propounded by Vāsudeva in the *Āśvamedhikaparva* of the Mahābhārata and consists of *Ślokas* 11-17 in Canto 13 of the 14th *Parva*. The short Gītā concludes not only by making fun of all those who try to destroy *kāma* by stationing themselves in *mokṣa*, but also declares itelf to be '*sanātana*', *i.e.*, eternal and '*avadhya*', i.e., indestructible—terms that remind us of the characteristics of Brahman itself.[3]

It may also be noted that the term used in the Kāma-Gītā for the state of those who are supposed to be steadfast in *mokṣa* is *mokṣarati*, a term that resonates with what *kāma* stands for in its central meaning in the Indian tradition, that is, sex.

It is, of course, true, as Charles Malamoud has argued, that there is always a wider and a narrower meaning of each of these terms, and that the discussion of the *puruṣārthas* continuously slides between the two. According to him, in "the sliding from the narrow to the wide meaning, it is always possible to make *dharma*, *artha* or *kāma* into the + 1 that encompasses the two other terms in the list, and the *mokṣa* to boot."[4] It is not clear, however, whether the statement is supposed to apply to the fourth *puruṣārtha*, that is, *mokṣa* also. *Prima facie*, the term *mokṣa* does not seem to have a wide or a narrow meaning; it simply has a fairly determinate, specific meaning, even though it may be conceived of differently in different systems of philosophy, or even of spiritual *sādhanā*. Also, in the usual interpretation, it cannot encompass the other *puruṣārthas*, specially *artha* and *kāma*, as not only does it transcend them, but, also negates them. Their functioning as active *puruṣārthas* in the life of any human being may be taken as a positive sign of the fact that not only has *mokṣa* not yet been achieved, but that it is not even being striven for.

The deeper problem, however, relates to the notions of narrow and wider meanings of the three *puruṣārthas*. Professor Malamoud has tried to give the narrow and the wider meanings of each of the three *puruṣārthas*, but it is difficult to agree with his formulations. *Dharma*, for example, in its narrow meaning is, for him, "the system of observances taught by the Veda and the texts stemming from it."[5] To the unwary reader, this may seem very specific and definite, but it is nothing of the kind. The texts are so many and prescribe so may conflicting things that to talk of a 'system of observances' is to hide the difficulty, or even the impossibility of determining what one's *dharma* is. If *dharma* in the narrow sense were as clear or as unproblematic as Malamoud seems to make it, the Mahābhārata would not have been written. The determination of what *dharma* means is the central enquiry of that great epic, and it is difficult to say whether any definite answer has been given at the end. Perhaps, the massage is that no such simple answer can be given. On the other hand, it is difficcult to see how *dharma* in the wider sense as "the order of the world and of society" or as "the point of view allowing perception of the whole as a system organized into a hierarchy,"[6] can even be treated as a *puruṣārtha* in the sense that it is something to be achieved or realized by one's actions. An 'order of the world and of society' can obviously not be a *puruṣārtha*, though the achieving of the vision of such an order may perhaps count as one. However, it should be remembered that the achievement of such a vision is the cessation of all activity so as to see things *sub specie aternitatis á la* Spinoza, or as revealed in the *viśva rūpa* or cosmic vision presented in the eleventh Canto of the Bhagvad Gītā is to see that everything is what it is, and could not be otherwise. One may, of course, try to order one's own actions in accordance with the vision or to say 'Thy will be done' or '*kariṣye vacanam tava*' as Arjuna does in the Gītā, but that would be to admit that the cosmic order permits an essential indeterminancy of a certain sort, that is, whether one would act in accordance with the vision or not. Or, rather, as most of the time one does not have the vision, and does not know what the so-called cosmic order is, one has to live and act in the context of this essential and almost inalienable ignorance.

Dharma and *mokṣa*, as *puruṣārthas*, have difficulties of a different order in the context of their so-called wide or narrow senses than *artha* or *kāma*. But the latter two are not exempt from difficulties, even though they may be of a different order. Malamoud contents himself by saying that "*artha* is a most elastic notion",[7] and seems to think that this absolves him from the responsibility of giving its narrow and wider meanings which he had promised to do earlier. The examples given by him later from the *Arthaśāstra* on page 46 are themselves not very clear regarding the point that is being made, unless they are taken as illustrative of the elasticity or even the ambiguity of the concept. The *Arthaśāstra*, it may be remembered, is concerned with the *puruṣārtha* of a king, but as everybody cannot be a king, what is described therein cannot be regarded as a *puruṣārtha*, if *puruṣārtha* is to mean that which is and can be an end for every human being by virtue of the fact that he is a human being. *Artha* in the sense of wealth may be a *puruṣārtha* for everybody, but in the sense of political power it can hardly be regarded as such. But there are no *śāstras* to tell how to pursue *artha* as a *puruṣārtha* in the sense of wealth, unless all the diverse methods of cheating the state described in the *Arthaśāstra* are treated as such.

Kāma as a *puruṣārtha*, on the other hand, has perhaps no such problems as to whether in the wider sense of desire, or narrower sense of sexual desire it can be a *puruṣārtha* for everybody. The *Kāma-Sūtra*, which is a text ostensibly devoted to *kāma* as a *puruṣārtha*, gives both the wider and the narrower meanings in *Sūtras* 1.2.11 and 1.2.12. The first defines *kāma* as the fitting relationship betwen each sense and its object which, when in perfect harmony, give pleasure to the self conjoined with the mind.[8] The second emphasizes the preeminence of the sense of touch and the supervening pleasure derived from it that is supposed to be the *kāma par excellence*.[9] But it seems that the second definition does not carry forward the insight of the first definition. *Kāma* in the narrow sense, the sense in which the *Kāma-Sūtra* is concerned with it, may be treated as the paradigmatic case in which not only all the senses find simultaneous fulfilment from their appropriate objects, but where the subject is also simultaneously the object, the enjoyer who is also the enjoyed. Malmoud, however, is not using the wider or narrower senses of *kāma* in the sense of the author of the *Kāma-Sūtras*, but of Bhoja the author of *Śṛṅgāra-Prakāśa*. Bhoja's attempt to universalize the concept of *śṛṅgāra* is certainly interesting, but it is not clear how it illumines the notion of *puruṣārtha*. On the contrary, it renders it still more confusing, for it is difficult to see how *rasa* can be a *puruṣārtha*; for if it is to be treated as one, it would not only have to be a *puruṣārtha* alongside other *puruṣārthas*, but also be multiple in character.

But however one may conceive of the wider or the narrower senses of the *puruṣārthas*, it hardly helps in solving the problems pointed out earlier, nor does it illumine the problem of the interrelationships between them. Professor K. J. Shah, in one of the most thoughtful articles on the subject, has suggested that the *puruṣārthas* as goals of human life should be treated as interactional in character, and not as hierarchical. He argues:

> We must realize that artha will not be a *puruṣārtha* unless it is in accord with *kāma*, *dharma* and *mokṣa*; *kāma* in turn will not be *kāma*, unless it is in accord with *dharma* and *mokṣa*; and *dharma* will not be *dharma*, unless it too is in accord with *mokṣa*. Equally *mokṣa* will not be *mokṣa* without the content of *dharma*; *dharma* will not be *dharma* without the content of *kāma* and *artha*. The four goals, therefore, constitute one single goal, though in the lives of individuals the elements may get varying emphasis for various reasons.[10]

But if there is only one single goal, then what is it, and what are its relations to these four goals? Shah is a careful thinker, but, if one reads carefully what he has written, one would find diverse and conflicting pulls in it. One is, for example, surprised to find *artha* omitted when he is talking of *kāma*, and both *artha* and *kāma* omitted when he is talking of *dharma*. Is the omission deliberate or accidental? What has *mokṣa* to do with *kāma* and *artha*? Why does it have to relate to them only through the medium of *dharma*? Are *artha* and *kāma* only contents, *dharma* both form and content, and *mokṣa* only pure form, according to Shah? There may be satisfactory answers to these questions, but unless they are given, merely saying that there is only 'one single goal' will not suffice.

The relationship between the *puruṣārthas*, and the hierarchy between them, have been the subject of discussion and debate even in classical times. One of the best known of these discussions is in the Mahābhārata, where Yudhiṣṭhira asks all his four brothers as well as Vidura as to which of the *puruṣārthas* among *dharma*, *artha* and *kāma* is the highest, the lowest and intermediate in importance.[11] Arjuna extols *artha* in the sense of production of wealth through agriculture, trade and diverse forms of crafts as the highest of the *puruṣārthas*. Bhīma, on the other hand, extols *kāma* as the essence of both *dharma* and *artha*, while Nakula and Sahadeva try to support Arjuna's position with some modifications. Vidura tries to give an extensional definition of *dharma*, and describes what it consists of. Yudhiṣṭhira, at the end, talks of the transcendence of *artha*, *dharma* and *kāma* in *mokṣa*, though he is candid enough to admit that he knows nothing about it. He ends by making a statement which sheds little light on the issue and, in fact, has a fatalistic flavour about it. All in all, it is a poor show on the part of the heroes of the great epic on this profound theme which is of such importance to fundamental reflection on human life. The situation appears even more disquieting if we remember that the reflection is taking place after the Great War in which Arjuna had been given the discourse on the Gītā by Krishna, and after Yudhiṣṭhira had to face moral problems of the most difficult kind. It is not a little ironic that the one who comes nearest to talking about *niṣkāma karma*, which is supposed to be the central message of the Gītā, is not Arjuna but Yudhiṣṭhira.

However, even if we leave aside the Mahābhārata discussion regarding the interrelationship and the hierarchy between the *puruṣārthas* as unilluminating, the usual traditional answer in terms of the supremacy of *dharma* is not helpful either. And this is for the simple reason that it is not clear what *dharma* is. The four sources usually given by Manu and others for finding what *dharma* is are of little help, as not only are they in conflict with each other, but there are deep conflicting divisions within each of them. The so-called revealed texts are no less conflicting than the tradition embodied in custom, or the behaviour of people generally known as good, or one's own inner conscience. The question as to whether they should be treated in a descending or ascending order of importance is irrelevant, as none of them by themselves, or even all of them together, can help in settling any difficult problem of *dharma* except in an *ad hoc* or pragmatic manner.

The oft-repeated traditional theory of the *puruṣārthas*, thus, is of little help in understanding the diversity and complexity of human seeking which makes human life so meaningful and worthwhile in diverse ways. The *kāma*-centric and *artha*-centric theories of Freud and Marx are as mistaken as the *dharma*-centric thought of sociologists and anthropologists who try to understand man in terms of the roles that he plays, and society in terms of the norms of those roles and their interactive relationships. For all these theories, the independent seeking of any value which is different from these is an illusion, except in an instrumental sense. The ultimately suicidal character of all such theories is self-evident, as they do not provide for any independent value to the life of the intellect which they themselves embody. Fortunately for the Indian theory of *puruṣārthas*, it has postulated the ideal of *mokṣa* which is tangential to all the other *puruṣārthas*. But it too has no place for the independent life of reason as a separate value, or for that matter for any other life which is not concerned primarily with *artha*, *dharma*, *kāma* and *mokṣa*. This is a grave deficiency, and points to the necessity of building a new theory of the *puruṣārthas* which would take into account the diverse seekings of man, and do justice to them.

NOTES AND REFERENCES

1. Bhagavad Gītā, II 46.
2. *Bṛhadāraṇyaka Upaniṣad* 2.4.5: *na vā are sarvasya kāmāya sarvaṁ priyaṁ bhavatyātmanastu kāmāya sarvaṁ priyaṁ bhavati/*
3. *yo māṁ prayatate hantuṁ mokṣamāsthāya paṇḍitaḥ/tasya mokṣaratisthasya nṛtyāmi ca hasāmi ca/avadhyaḥ sarvabhūtānāmahamekaḥ sanātanaḥ*—Mahābhārata 14, 13–17.
4. Charles Malamoud, 'On the Rhetoric and Semantics of *Puruṣārtha*' in T. N. Madan (ed.), *Way of Life: King, Householder, Renouncer: Essays in Honour of Louis Dumont*, (New Delhi: Vikas Publishing House, New Delhi, 1982), p. 44.
5. Malamoud, p, 44
6. *Ibid.*, p. 44.
7. *Ibid.*, p. 44.
8. *śrotratvakcakṣurjihvāghrāṇānāmātmasaṁyuktena manasādhiṣṭhitānāṁ sveṣu sveṣu viṣayeṣvānukūlyataḥ pravṛttiḥ kāmaḥ*—1/11
9. *sparśaviśeṣaviṣaviṣayāttvasyābhimānikasukhānuviddhā phalavatyarthapratītiḥ prādhānyātkāmaḥ*—1/12
10. T. N. Madan, Op. cit., p. 55–73.
11. The Mahābhārata, Śāntiparva, adhyāya, 161.

self-evident, as they do not provide for any independent value to the life of the intellect which they themselves embody. Fortunately for the Indian theory of *puruṣārthas*, it has postulated the ideal of *mokṣa* which is tangential to all the other *puruṣārthas*. But it too has no place for the independent life of reason as a separate value, or for that matter for any other life which is not concerned primarily with *artha*, *dharma*, *kāma* and *mokṣa*. This is a grave deficiency, and points to the necessity of building a new theory of the *puruṣārthas* which would take into account the diverse seekings of man, and do justice to them.

NOTES AND REFERENCES

1. Bhagavad Gītā, II. 46.
2. *Bṛhadāraṇyaka Upaniṣad* [illegible]
3. [illegible] —Mahābhārata 14. 13–17.
4. Charles Malamoud, 'On the Rhetoric and Semantics of *Puruṣārtha*' in T. N. Madan (ed.), *Way of Life: King, Householder, Renouncer: Essays in Honour of Louis Dumont*, (Vikas Publishing House, New Delhi, 1982), p. 34.
5. Malamoud, p. 34.
6. *Ibid.*, p. 35.
7. *Ibid.*, p. 34.
8. [illegible] —1/11.
9. [illegible] —11/12.
10. T. N. Madan, *Op. cit.*, p. 35–43.
11. The Mahābhārata, Śāntiparva, adhyāya 161.

Index